JavaScript® For Kids

FOR DUMMIES®

A Wiley Brand

by Chris Minnick and Eva Holland

FOR DUMMIES®
A Wiley Brand

JavaScript® For Kids For Dummies®

Published by: **John Wiley & Sons, Inc.,** 111 River Street, Hoboken, NJ 07030-5774, www.wiley.com

Copyright © 2015 by John Wiley & Sons, Inc., Hoboken, New Jersey

Published simultaneously in Canada

For general information on our other products and services, please contact our Customer Care Department within the U.S. at 877-762-2974, outside the U.S. at 317-572-3993, or fax 317-572-4002. For technical support, please visit www.wiley.com/techsupport.

Wiley publishes in a variety of print and electronic formats and by print-on-demand. Some material included with standard print versions of this book may not be included in e-books or in print-on-demand. If this book refers to media such as a CD or DVD that is not included in the version you purchased, you may download this material at http://booksupport.wiley.com. For more information about Wiley products, visit www.wiley.com.

Library of Congress Control Number: 2015945282

ISBN 978-1-119-11986-9 (pbk); ISBN 978-1-119-11989-0 (ebk); ISBN 978-1-119-11988-3

Manufactured in the United States of America

10 9 8 7 6 5 4 3 2 1

Contents at a Glance

Introduction 1

Part I: What Is JavaScript? Alert! JavaScript Is Awesome! 5

Chapter 1: Programming the Web..7
Chapter 2: Understanding Syntax 22
Chapter 3: Giving and Receiving Data 33
Chapter 4: Fiddling with Web Applications 51

Part II: Animating the Web................................... 69

Chapter 5: JavaScript and HTML..71
Chapter 6: JavaScript and CSS...89
Chapter 7: Building an Animated Robot..104

Part III: Getting Operations................................ 123

Chapter 8: Building Your Dream Car with Operands 125
Chapter 9: Putting It Together with Operators 136
Chapter 10: Creating Your Own JavaScript Word Game.....................153

Part IV: Arrays and Functions............................ 171

Chapter 11: Creating and Changing Arrays....................................173
Chapter 12: Making It Functional 190
Chapter 13: Creating a Wish List Program 206

Part V: Freedom of Choice 231

Chapter 14: Making Decisions with the If...Else Statement 233
Chapter 15: Doing Different Things with Switch 252
Chapter 16: Choose Your Own Adventure.....................................267

Part VI: Loops 293

Chapter 17: What's This Loop For?.................................295
Chapter 18: Using While Loops 309
Chapter 19: Building a Lemonade Stand 326

Index 355

Table of Contents

Introduction... 1

    About This Book 1
    Foolish Assumptions.. 3
    Icons Used In This Book 3
    Beyond the Book 4
    Where to Go from Here... 4

Part I: What Is JavaScript? Alert! JavaScript Is Awesome! 5

Chapter 1: Programming the Web 7

    What Is Programming?.. 8
    Talking to Computers... 9
    Choosing a Language 11
    What Is JavaScript? 12
    Get Your Browser Ready 15
    Opening the Web Developer Tools 16
    Introducing the JavaScript Console 18
    Running Your First JavaScript Commands............................. 19
    Having Fun with Math 21

Chapter 2: Understanding Syntax 22

    Saying Precisely What You Mean 23
    Making a Statement 24
    Following the Rules 25

Chapter 3: Giving and Receiving Data 33

    Mastering Variables 34
    Understanding Data Types... 38
    Prompting the User for Input 42
    Responding to Input 44
    Combining Input and Output 48

Chapter 4: Fiddling with Web Applications. 51

    Introducing JSFiddle.. 52
    Creating a JSFiddle Account... 63
    Sharing Your Fiddle... 65
    Saving Your App 67

Part II: Animating the Web 69

Chapter 5: JavaScript and HTML 71
Writing HTML...72
Knowing Your HTML Elements...78
Adding Attributes to Elements 81
Changing HTML with JavaScript...83

Chapter 6: JavaScript and CSS....................... 89
Meet Douglas the JavaScript Robot 90
CSS Basics...90
CSS Properties Give You Style 93
Customize Your Own JavaScript Robot!.....................................103

Chapter 7: Building an Animated Robot 104
Changing CSS with JavaScript...105
Make Douglas Dance! 109

Part III: Getting Operations................................. 123

Chapter 8: Building Your Dream Car with Operands ... 125
Knowing Your Operands 126
Working with Objects..130
Configuring Your Dream Car 132

Chapter 9: Putting It Together with Operators........ 136
Introducing the Super-Calculator 137
Super-Calculator Tricks 150

Chapter 10: Creating Your Own JavaScript
Word Game... 153
Creating a Variable Story...154
Creating the Word Replacement Game..154

Part IV: Arrays and Functions............................. 171

Chapter 11: Creating and Changing Arrays........... 173
What Are Arrays?...174
Creating and Accessing Arrays..175
Changing Array Element Values 176
Working with Array Methods..177
Learning the Ways of Arrays..178

Chapter 12: Making It Functional **190**

Understanding Functions 191
Knowing What Functions Are Made Of...193
Building Function Junction..196

Chapter 13: Creating a Wish List Program **206**

Introducing the Wish List Program 207
Forking the Code...208
Writing the HTML 210
Writing the JavaScript Code...212

Part V: Freedom of Choice.................................. 231

**Chapter 14: Making Decisions with the
If...Else Statement** **233**

Boolean Logic..234
Introducing if...else Statements 236
Combining Comparisons with Logical Operators 238
Freshening Up the JavaScript Pizzeria..240

Chapter 15: Doing Different Things with Switch **252**

Writing a Switch..253
Building the Activity-of-the-Day Calendar 255

Chapter 16: Choose Your Own Adventure **267**

Planning the Story 268
Playing the Game..269
Forking the Code...271
Tiptoeing through the HTML and CSS 272
Writing the Martian Rescue! JavaScript..276

Part VI: Loops.. 293

Chapter 17: What's This Loop For? **295**

Introducing the for Loop 296
Random Weather Forecasting...299

Chapter 18: Using While Loops **309**

Writing a while Loop...310
Coding the Lunch Game..312
Moving to Your Own Website 318

Chapter 19: Building a Lemonade Stand **326**
Playing the Game 327
A Lesson in Business 329
Building the Game 334
Improving the Lemonade Game 352

Index **355**

Introduction

JavaScript For Kids For Dummies is an introduction to the basics of JavaScript coding. In each chapter, we walk you step-by-step through creating JavaScript programs for the web. Designed for kids of all ages, with no coding experience, we strive to introduce this technical topic in a fun, engaging, and interactive way.

JavaScript is the most widely used programming language in the world today. That's why we think you've made a great decision by beginning your journey into the world of coding by picking up this book.

JavaScript is fun and easy to learn! With some determination and imagination, you'll be on your way to creating your very own JavaScript programs in no time!

Just as the only way to Carnegie Hall is to practice, practice, practice, the only way to become a better programmer is to code, code, code!

About This Book

We seek to "de-code" the language of JavaScript for you and give you an understanding of the concepts. With the ability to move at your own pace, *JavaScript For Kids For Dummies* will get you up to speed. In this book, you learn how to create fun games and programs. We even show you how to customize and build your own versions of the games that you can post to the web and share with your friends!

Whether you know a little JavaScript or you've never seen it before, this book shows you how to write JavaScript the right way.

Topics covered in this book include the following:

- The basic structures of JavaScript programs

- JavaScript expressions and operators

- Structuring your programs with functions

- Writing loops

- Working with JavaScript, HTML5, and CSS3

- Making choices with `if...else` statements

Learning JavaScript isn't only about learning how to write the language. It's also about accessing the tools and the community that has been built around the language. JavaScript programmers have refined the tools and techniques used to write JavaScript over the language's long and exciting history. Throughout this book, we mention important techniques and tools for testing, documenting, and writing better code!

To make this book easier to read, you'll want to keep in mind a few tips. First, all JavaScript code and all HTML and CSS markup appears in monospaced type like this:

```
document.write("Hi!");
```

The margins on a book page don't have the same room as your monitor likely does, so long lines of HTML, CSS, and JavaScript may break across multiple lines. Remember that your computer sees such lines as single lines of HTML, CSS, or JavaScript. We indicate that everything should be on one line by breaking it at a punctuation character or space and then indenting any overage, like so:

```
document.getElementById("thisIsAnElementInTheDocument").
                addEventListener("click",doSomething,false);
```

HTML and CSS don't care very much about whether you use uppercase or lowercase letters or a combination of the two. But, JavaScript cares a lot! In order to make sure that you get the correct results from the code examples in the book, always stick to the same capitalizations that we use.

Foolish Assumptions

You don't need to be a "programming ninja" or a "hacker" to understand programming. You don't need to understand how the guts of your computer work. You don't even need to know how to count in binary.

However, we do need to make a couple of assumptions about you. We assume that you can turn your computer on, that you know how to use a mouse *and* a keyboard, and that you have a working Internet connection and web browser. If you already know something about how to make web pages (it doesn't take much!), you'll have a jumpstart on the material.

The other things you need to know to write and run JavaScript code are details we cover in this book, and the one thing you'll find to be true is that programming requires attention to details.

Icons Used In This Book

Here's a list of the icons we use in this book to flag text and information that's especially noteworthy.

This icon highlights technical details that you may or may not find interesting. Feel free to skip this information, but if you're the techie type, you might enjoy reading it.

This icon highlights helpful tips that show you easy ways or shortcuts that will save you time or effort.

Whenever you see this icon, pay close attention. You won't want to forget the information you're about to read — or, in some cases, we'll remind you about something that you've already learned that you may have forgotten.

Be careful. This icon warns you of pitfalls to avoid.

Beyond the Book

We've put together a lot of extra content that you won't find in this book. Go online to find the following:

- **Cheat Sheet:** An online Cheat Sheet is available at www.dummies.com/cheatsheet/javascriptforkids. Here, you find information on converting CSS property names to JavaScript; a list of common web browser events that JavaScript can respond to; and a list of words that can't be used as JavaScript variables, functions, methods, loop labels, or object names.

- **Web Extras:** Online articles covering additional topics are available at www.dummies.com/extras/javascript forkids. In these articles, we cover things like HTML5 form input tricks, how to name JavaScript variables, JavaScript troubleshooting tips, and more.

Where to Go from Here

Coding with JavaScript is fun, and when you get a little knowledge under your belt, the world of interactive web applications is your oyster! So buckle up! We hope you enjoy the book and our occasional pearls of wisdom.

If you want to show us changes and improvements you make to our games, or programs you come up with on your own, you can do so on Facebook (www.facebook.com/watzthisco), Twitter (www.twitter.com/watzthisco), or via email at info@watzthis.com. We're excited to see what you come up with!

Part I

What Is JavaScript? Alert! JavaScript Is Awesome!

In this part . . .

■ Programming the Web.............................. 7

■ Understanding Syntax 22

■ Giving and Receiving Data............................ 33

■ Fiddling with Web Applications........................ 51

For Dummies can help you get started with lots of subjects. Visit www.dummies.com to learn more and do more with *For Dummies!*

Programming the Web

JavaScript is a powerful language that's easy to learn! In this chapter, we explain the basics of programming, tell you what JavaScript is, and get you started with writing your first JavaScript commands.

One of the most important parts of starting any new project is to make sure you have your workshop stocked with all the correct tools. In this chapter, you install and configure all the programs you need and start experimenting with some real JavaScript programs!

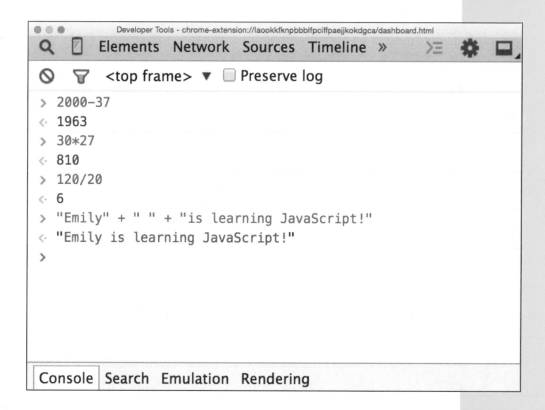

What Is Programming?

A *computer program* is a series of instructions that can be understood and followed by a computer. *Computer programming*, also known as *coding*, is what we call it when we write these instructions. Computers can't do things on their own. They need a computer program to tell them what to do. Computer programmers write code to make computers do all sort of things.

Another name for a computer program is *software*.

The women who invented programming

Electronic computers as we know them were first invented in the 1930s. But it was the middle of the 1800s when the first computer program — a set of instructions designed to be carried out by a machine — was written.

The author of the first computer program — and, therefore, the world's first computer programmer — was a woman named Ada Lovelace. A mathematician in England, she was the first person to envision computers that could do much more than just crunch numbers. She foresaw computers being able to do all the things we use computers for today: including working with words, displaying pictures, and playing music. Her unique insights earned her the nickname "The Enchantress of Numbers."

Compilers are programs for converting programming languages into machine language. The first compiler was created by Grace Murray Hopper in 1944. This invention led to computer programs that could run on different types of computers, and eventually to JavaScript. Hopper is also credited with being the inventor of the term *debugging* for fixing problems in computer programs. The term was inspired by the removal of an actual moth from an early computer. Hopper became known as "The Queen of Software" or "Amazing Grace" for her contributions to modern computing.

Computer programs help people to do many thousands of things, including the following:

- ✓ Playing music and videos

- ✓ Performing scientific experiments

- ✓ Designing cars

- ✓ Inventing medicines

- ✓ Playing games

- ✓ Controlling robots

- ✓ Guiding satellites and spaceships

- ✓ Creating magazines

- ✓ Teaching people new skills

Can you think of more examples of things that computers can do?

Talking to Computers

At the heart of every computer is a central processing unit (CPU). This CPU is made up of millions of tiny, very fast switches (called *transistors*) that can be either on or off. The position of each of these switches at any time determines what the computer will do.

Software written by programmers tells these switches when to turn on or off and in what combination by using *binary codes*. Binary codes use zeros and ones to form letters, numbers, and symbols that can be put together in order to perform tasks.

Every single thing that a computer does is the result of a different combination of many zeros and ones. For example, to represent a lowercase letter *a,* computers use the following binary code:

```
0110 0001
```

Each zero or one in a binary number is called a *bit,* and a combination of eight bits is called a *byte.* When you hear the words *kilobyte, megabyte,* and *gigabyte* used to tell how big a file is, what it's talking about is the number of eight-bit binary codes it takes to store the file.

Table 1-1 lists the most commonly used storage sizes.

Table 1-1	How Many Bytes Is That?	
Name	**Number of Bytes**	**What It Can Store**
Kilobyte (KB)	1,024	Two to three paragraphs of text
Megabyte (MB)	1,048,576	800 pages of text
Gigabyte (GB)	1,073,741,824	250 songs (as MP3s)
Terabyte (TB)	1,099,511,627,776	350,000 digital pictures
Petabyte (PB)	1,125,899,906,842,624	41,943 Blu-ray discs

A typical small computer program might contain anywhere from a couple kilobytes to a couple megabytes of instructions, images, and other data. Because it's unlikely that you have enough time in your busy day to type out thousands, or even millions, of ones and zeros, if you want to tell a computer what to do, you need a translator who speaks both human languages and computer (or *machine*) language. Computer programming languages are this translator.

Every computer program is written using a computer programming language. Programming languages allow you to write complex series of instructions that can be translated (also known as *compiled*) into machine language. Through compilation, these instructions are eventually turned into binary codes that a computer can understand.

Choosing a Language

People have created hundreds of different computer programming languages. You might ask yourself why there are so many programming languages, if they all essentially do the same thing: translate human language into machine language. That's an excellent question!

There are a few main reasons why there are so many different programming languages. New programming languages are written to allow programmers to

✔ Write programs in new and better ways than were previously available.

✔ Write programs for new or specialized types of computers.

✔ Create new kinds of software.

Examples of computer programming languages include the following:

✔ C

✔ Java

✔ JavaScript

✔ Logo

✔ Objective C

✔ Perl

✔ Python

✔ Ruby

✔ Scratch

✔ Swift

✔ Visual Basic

Our short list of programming languages only scratches the surface. For a more complete list of programming languages, visit http://en.wikipedia.org/wiki/List_of_programming_ languages.

With so many programming languages to choose from, how do you know which one to use? In many cases, the answer is determined by what you want to do with the languages. For example, if you want to program apps for the iPhone, you have three choices: Objective C, JavaScript, or Swift. If you want to program games to run on Mac or Windows, you have more choices, including C, Java, or JavaScript. If you want to make an interactive website, you need to use JavaScript.

Are you seeing a pattern here? JavaScript is everywhere.

What Is JavaScript?

In the early days of the web, every web page consisted of nothing but plain text in different sizes with links between pages. There were no web forms, there certainly wasn't any animation, and there weren't even different styles of text or pictures!

We're not complaining! When the web was new, it was exciting to click from page to page and discover new things. Even more exciting was how easy the web made it for anyone to be able to publish anything at all and have the potential for anyone else on the Internet to read it.

But when people got a taste of what the web could do, they wanted more features! Graphics, text colors, forms, and many other features were introduced very quickly.

Of all the things that were invented in the earliest days of the web, the thing that has had the biggest impact over the longest time was JavaScript.

JavaScript was created in order to make it possible for web browsers to be interactive. Interactive web pages can range from simple forms that provide feedback when you make a mistake, to 3D games that run in your web browser. Whenever you visit a website and see something moving, or you see data appearing and changing on the page, or you see interactive maps or browser-based games, chances are, it's JavaScript at work.

To see some examples of websites that are made possible by JavaScript, open up your web browser and visit the following sites:

✏ **ShinyText (`http://cabbi.bo/ShinyText`):** ShinyText is an experimental website that uses JavaScript to display a word. You can adjust different properties of the word, such as Reflection Power and Repulsion Power to see what effect these changes have on how the letters in the word react when you move them around with your mouse. Figure 1-1 shows ShinyText in action.

Even if you don't understand how it works (we sure don't!), ShinyText is fun to play with, and it's a great example of what's possible with JavaScript.

Figure 1-1: ShinyText uses JavaScript to produce a 3D physics simulation.

✔ **Interactive Sock Puppet (`www.mediosyproyectos.com/ puppetic`):** Interactive Sock Puppet is another 3D animation. This time, you can control the movements and facial expressions of a JavaScript puppet. Figure 1-2 shows the Interactive Sock Puppet looking quite happy.

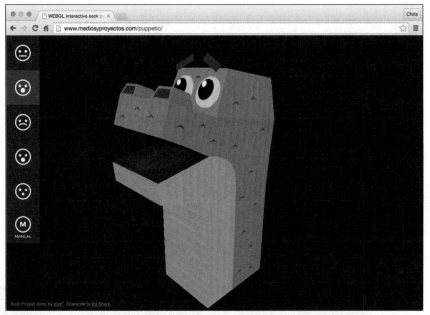

Figure 1-2: Interactive Sock Puppet lets you control a JavaScript dinosaur sock puppet.

✔ **Facebook (`www.facebook.com`):** Facebook uses a lot of JavaScript (see Figure 1-3). When you see a smooth animation or video playback, or when a list of posts updates by itself, that's JavaScript at work!

Some of these examples use some very advanced features of web browsers. We recommend that you use the latest version of Google Chrome to view these. The examples may not work in older web browsers.

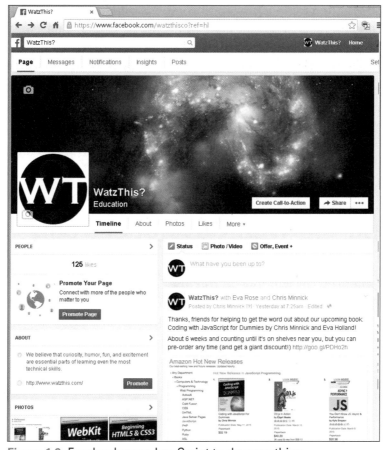

Figure 1-3: Facebook uses JavaScript to do everything.

Get Your Browser Ready

The one essential tool that you need for working with JavaScript is a web browser. You have many different web browsers to choose from, and nearly all of them will do a great job running JavaScript. Odds are, you already have a web browser on your computer.

The most widely used web browsers today are Firefox, Safari, Chrome, Internet Explorer, and Opera. For this book, we'll be using Chrome. Google Chrome is currently the most popular web browser. It has a number of great tools for working with JavaScript.

If you don't already have Chrome installed, you'll need to download and install it. You can install Chrome by opening any web browser and going to `www.google.com/chrome/browser/desktop`. Follow the instructions found on that page to install Chrome on your computer. When you have Chrome installed, start it up.

In the next section, we show you the Chrome Developer Tools, which help website designers and JavaScript programmers to see exactly what's going on inside the browser so they can write better web pages and programs.

Opening the Web Developer Tools

After you have Chrome installed and launched, look at the top of the browser window. In the upper-right corner, you see three lines. This is the icon for the Chrome menu. If you expand the Chrome menu, you see a list of options similar to those shown in Figure 1-4.

Figure 1-4: The Chrome menu.

If you scroll down to the bottom of this menu and select More Tools, a new menu of options appears, as shown in Figure 1-5. These secret tools are the JavaScript coder's best friends.

Figure 1-5: The More Tools menu.

Select Developer Tools from the More Tools menu. A new panel opens at the bottom of your browser window that looks like Figure 1-6.

The Developer Tools give you all the information you need for finding out how any web page works, for testing and improving your own web pages and JavaScript programs, and much more.

Notice that the there's a menu at the top of the Developer Tools with different options, including Elements, Network, Sources, Timeline, Profiles, Resources, Audits, and Console. If you click each of these, you'll see a different set of options and data in the Developer Tools panel.

We describe the different components of the Developer Tools as they become necessary throughout this book, but for now, the most important part of the Developer Tools is the one labeled Console. Click the Console tab now.

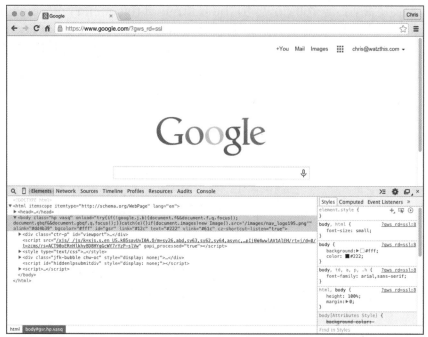

Figure 1-6: The Developer Tools.

Introducing the JavaScript Console

The Developer Tools Console, also known as the JavaScript Console, shown in Figure 1-7, gives you information about the JavaScript that's currently running in the browser window.

If there are errors in the JavaScript code of a web page, you see information about the errors in the console. This is a very helpful tool and one of the main features of the JavaScript Console.

Another very cool capability of the console is that you can type JavaScript into the console panel and it will run. In the next section, you learn why this is useful and how to do it.

The JavaScript Console is a useful tool for JavaScript programmers, but it also has the potential to be misused. If someone you don't know or trust asks you to paste code into the JavaScript Console, make sure you understand what that code does first.

Figure 1-7: The JavaScript Console.

Running Your First JavaScript Commands

Now it's time to start experimenting with some real JavaScript code! If you don't already have it open, open the JavaScript Console by selecting it from the Other Tools menu under the Chrome menu, or by clicking the Console tab in the Developer Tools.

Follow these steps to run your first JavaScript commands:

1. Click inside the JavaScript console, near the >, to start inserting code.

2. Type **1 + 1** and then press Return (Mac) or Enter (Windows).

    The browser gives you the answer on the next line.

Notice that when the answer is returned to you, it has an arrow on the left side of it that points to the left. This arrow indicates that the value came from JavaScript rather than from your input. Any value that comes from JavaScript is called a *return value*. Every command that you run in JavaScript produces some sort of return value.

Simple math is one thing, but JavaScript can do much, much more. Let's try out some other commands and see just how quickly we can get some answers around here.

Before we get started, let's clean up the console and remove any previous commands, errors, and return values in there. To clear the console, look at the upper-left corner and click the circle with the line through it. Everything inside the console will be erased, and now you've got a clean slate.

Click your mouse next to the > and try out the following JavaScript commands. Make sure to press Return (Mac) or Enter (Windows) after each one to see the results.

JavaScript Command	Description
`2000 - 37`	This is a simple math problem, but this time we're using the minus sign to subtract the number on the right from the number on the left.
`30 * 27`	The asterisk (*) is how you tell JavaScript to multiply numbers.
`120 / 20`	The forward slash (/) tells JavaScript to divide the number on the left by the number on the right.
`"Your name" + " " + "is learning JavaScript!"`	Yes, you can add words together with JavaScript! When you run a command that adds words together, it's called *concatenation*. The result will be that the words are combined into a single word. Notice that the words in the above JavaScript command are inside quotes. These quotes are very important. We tell you exactly why they're important in Chapter 2.
`Your name + + is learning JavaScript!`	When you don't use quotes, JavaScript doesn't like that one bit. It returns an error message containing the keyword `SyntaxError`. A syntax error means that you've written something that isn't valid JavaScript. Any time you see a syntax error, it means that you've goofed. Take a close look at your code and look for typos, missing punctuation, or missing quotes.

Having Fun with Math

Now it's your turn to try out some math problems on your own! Clear out your commands and the return values and errors from the previous section and experiment with the console.

Here are some ideas to get you started:

- Multiply together two decimal numbers.

- Run multiple commands in one line (for example, `1 + 1 * 4 / 8`).

- Type a number without any symbols at all and then run it.

- Add a word (remember to use quotes!) to a number (without quotes).

- Add a number (without quotes) to a word (with quotes).

- Combine your first name with the last name of your celebrity crush. Remember to add a space between the first and last name! For example, `"Eva" + " " + "Harry Styles"`.

- Try to produce extremely large return values.

- Try to produce extremely small return values.

- Try to do an impossible math problem, such as dividing a number by zero.

- Try multiplying a number by a word (in quotes). For example, `343 * "hi!"`. The result of this will be NaN, which stands for "not a number."

CHAPTER 2

Understanding Syntax

Just as spoken languages have rules (called *grammar*), computer programming languages have rules (called *syntax*). When you understand the basic rules of speaking JavaScript, it actually looks similar to English.

If you thought that your teacher correcting you when you say "ain't" was strict, wait until you see how strict JavaScript is! It won't even listen to a thing you say if you make certain kinds of syntax errors.

In this chapter, you learn the basics of JavaScript syntax and how to avoid being scolded by the syntax police!

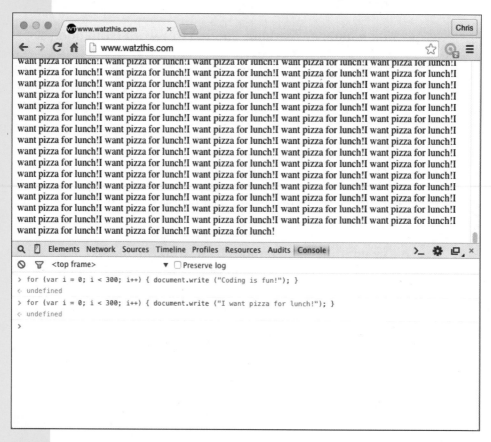

Saying Precisely What You Mean

In order to be compiled correctly into machine language instructions, programs need to be written very precisely.

Chapter 1 explains what a program is and how programs are translated into machine language using the process called *compilation.*

As a programmer, your job is to think about the big picture of what you want the program to do, and then break it down into bite-size steps that can be accomplished by the computer without errors. For example, if you wanted to ask a robot to go downstairs and get you a sandwich, you might start your instructions like this:

1. Rotate head toward stairs.

2. Use visual sensors to look for obstacles.

3. If an obstacle is found, determine what it is.

4. If the obstacle is a cat, try to lure the cat away from the top of the stairs by:

   - Throwing a toy down the hall

   - Speaking the cat's name

   - Gently nudging the cat with your hand until it walks away

5. If there is no obstacle, rotate left foot in the direction of the stairs.

6. Place left foot in front of right foot.

7. Look for an obstacle.

8. Determine whether you're at the top of the stairs.

9. If you're not at the top of the stairs, rotate right foot in the direction of the stairs.

10. Place right foot in front of left foot.

11. Repeat steps 1 through 10 until you're at the top of the stairs.

You've written 11 instructions already and the robot hasn't even started walking down the stairs, much less making a sandwich!

A real computer program to tell a robot to go downstairs and make a sandwich would need to contain far more detailed instructions than the ones shown here. At each step along the way, each motor would need to be told precisely how long to turn on, and each possible condition and obstacle would need to be described and dealt with in detail.

All these instructions need to be written as individual JavaScript commands, or *statements*.

You can find out more about how to control robots with JavaScript by visiting `http://nodebots.io`!

Making a Statement

In English, we talk in sentences. In JavaScript, a single instruction to the computer is called a *statement*. Like a sentence, statements are made up of different parts and have certain rules that they must follow in order to be understood.

Listing 2-1 shows an example of a statement.

Listing 2-1   **A JavaScript Statement**

```
alert("Coding is fun!");
```

This statement causes a web browser to open up a popup alert window with the sentence "Coding is fun!" If you type this statement into the JavaScript Console in Chrome, you'll see something like what's shown in Figure 2-1.

Figure 2-1: The output of a JavaScript alert statement.

Notice that the statement in Listing 2-1 contains a keyword, some symbols (parentheses and quotes), and some text (`Coding is fun!`), and it ends with a semicolon.

Just as an infinite number of sentences can be written using English, an infinite number of statements can be written with JavaScript.

The word `alert` is an example of a JavaScript keyword. Many JavaScript statements begin with keywords, but not all of them do.

 The semicolon is what separates one statement from another, just as a period separates one sentence from another. Every statement should end with a semicolon.

Following the Rules

 JavaScript has several rules that must be obeyed if you want your computer to understand you. The first two rules are:

✔ Spelling counts.

✔ Spacing doesn't count.

Let's take a look at each of these rules in more detail. We'll write a new message printer program to serve as an example. Listing 2-2 is a JavaScript program that prints out the words "Coding is fun!" 300 times.

Listing 2-2 A Program to Print a Message 300 Times

```
for (var i = 0; i < 300; i++) { document.write ("Coding is
              fun!"); }
```

Follow these steps to test this program:

1. Open the Chrome web browser.

2. Open the JavaScript Console from the More Tools menu under the Chrome menu.

   You can also use the keyboard combination to open the JavaScript Console. Press ⌘+Option+J (Mac) or Ctrl+Shift+J (Windows).

3. Type the program in Listing 2-2 onto one line in the JavaScript Console and press Return (Mac) or Enter (Windows).

   If you entered everything correctly, you'll see the message appear in your browser window 300 times, as shown in Figure 2-2.

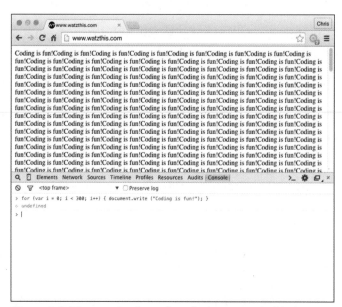

Figure 2-2: The result of running the program in Listing 2-2.

This "Coding is fun!" program uses a technique called a `for` loop in order to do something many times with only a little bit of code. We talk more about `for` loops in Chapters 17 and 18.

Take a close look at the code in Listing 2-2. Notice that the text that gets written to the browser window is enclosed in quotes. The quotes indicate that this text is to be treated as words, rather than as JavaScript code.

Using text in strings

In programming, we call a piece of text inside of quotes a *string*. You can remember this name by thinking of text inside quotes like a piece of string with letters, numbers, and symbols tied to it. These letters stay in the same order and each one takes up a certain amount of space on the string.

For example, try typing the code from Listing 2-2 into your JavaScript console again, but change `Coding is fun!` to another message, such as what you want for lunch or dinner.

Figure 2-3 shows the output of the program from Listing 2-2 when the message is changed to "I want pizza for lunch!"

Any character you can type can be put into a string. However, there's one important exception that you need to remember: If you want to use quotation marks inside a string, you have to tell JavaScript that the quotation marks are part of the string, rather than the end of the string.

The way to put quotation marks inside a string is by using a back-slash (\) before the quotation marks. Using the backslash in a string tells JavaScript that the next character is something special and doesn't mean what it normally would mean. When you add a backslash before a quotation mark in a string, it's called *escaping* the quotation mark.

For example, if you want to change the string to:

```
Joe said, "Hi!"
```

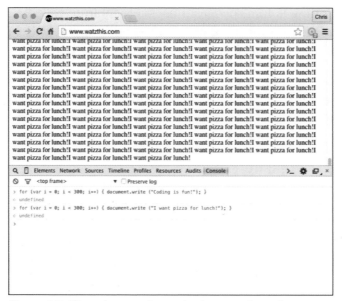

Figure 2-3: Changing a string only changes the string.

You would need to write the string as:

```
"Joe said, \"Hi!\""
```

Listing 2-3 shows our message printer program with escaped quotation marks in the message.

Listing 2-3 Escaping Quotation Marks

```
for (var i = 0; i < 300; i++) { document.write ("Joe said,
        \"Hi!\""); }
```

You might be asking yourself now, "If the backslash is used to tell JavaScript that the next character is special, how do I print out a backslash?" Great question! The answer is just to use two backslashes (\\) for each backslash that you need to print out.

As with most things in JavaScript, there is another way to use quotes inside a string: by surrounding the string with different quotes. JavaScript doesn't care whether you use single quotes (') or double quotes (") to mark text as a string, as long as you use the same type of quotes at the beginning and end of the string.

If you surround your string with single quotes, you can use all the double quotes that you want inside the string, without escaping them. But single quotes must be escaped.

If you surround your string with double quotes, you can use all the single quotes you want inside the string, but double quotes must be escaped.

Listing 2-4 shows the message printer program with the string in single quotes and double quotes inside the string.

Listing 2-4   **Double Quotes within Single Quotes**

```
for (var i = 0; i < 300; i++) { document.write (' Joe
         said, "Hi!" '); }
```

Using text in code

Unlike in strings, the contents and spelling of text outside of quotes matters a lot. When text isn't surrounded by quotes (single or double) in JavaScript, it's considered part of the code of the JavaScript program.

JavaScript code is very picky about spelling and capitalization. In JavaScript code, the following words are completely different:

```
FOR
for
For
```

Only the one in the middle means anything special to JavaScript. If you try to use the other two in the message printer program, you'll get an error, as shown in Figure 2-4.

The special meaning of `for` is explained in Chapter 17.

JavaScript is also very picky about spelling. Many times, when we're coding and something just isn't working right, the problem turns out to be that we accidentally left out a letter or mixed up the order of two letters.

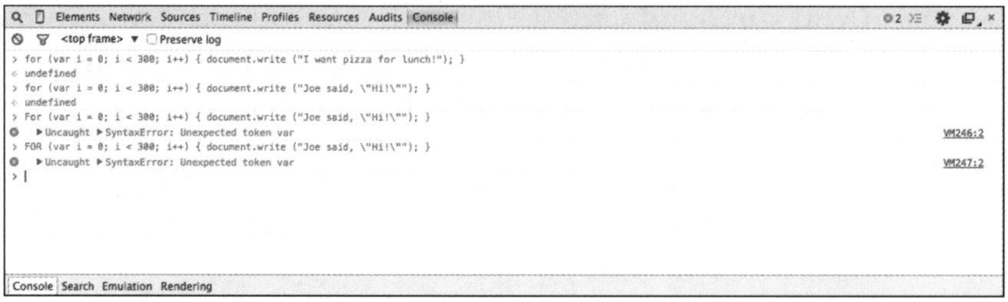

Figure 2-4: Capitalizing a JavaScript keyword wrong produces errors.

Just as typos in writing often go unnoticed, these types of errors can be very difficult to track down, so get into the habit early on of typing slowly and carefully and you'll save yourself a lot of time in the long run!

Paying attention to white space

White space is all the spaces, tabs, and line breaks in your program. JavaScript ignores white space between words and between words and symbols in code. For example, in our message printer program, we could make the whole thing easier for people to read by spacing it out over multiple lines, as shown in Listing 2-5.

Listing 2-5   White Space Makes Programs Easier to Read

```
for (var i = 0; i < 300; i++) {
    document.write ("Coding is fun!");
}
```

Listing 2-5 shows the way that we would recommend spacing out this program.

Notice that we've inserted line breaks after the opening curly bracket ({) and before the ending curly bracket (}). Curly brackets are used for grouping pieces of code (also called *statements*) together into what's called a *block*. In this program, they mark the part of the program that should be repeated 300 times — namely, printing out a message.

Curly brackets are a good spot to put some white space to help you read the code more easily. Another great spot to put a line break is after each semicolon (;). In JavaScript, the semicolon is used to mark the end of a statement, much as a period is used to mark the end of a sentence in English.

If you try to run the program split over three lines in the JavaScript Console in Chrome, you'll get an error message when you press Return (Mac) or Enter (Windows) after the first line. This is because the console tries to run your code every time you press Return or Enter, and the first line (ending with {) isn't a complete JavaScript statement. To enter this code into the console with line breaks, hold down the Shift key while pressing Return or Enter after each of the first two lines.

Notice that the statement between the curly brackets is indented. The indentation helps people reading the code to see that this statement is happening inside another statement — namely, the for statement that creates the loop.

We recommend using either two spaces or four spaces to indent statements. Some people use tabs to indent statements. Which one you use is up to you. Once you decide, however, stick with it. If you use two spaces to indent code inside of a block, you shouldn't sometimes use four spaces or a tab. Neatness counts!

Making comments

JavaScript comments are a way that you can put text into a program that isn't a string or a statement. This may not sound so great, but the thing that makes comments so important and useful is precisely that they don't cause JavaScript to do anything at all.

Programmers use comments within their code for several reasons:

- ✔ To tell their future selves, and anyone else who works on the program in the future, why they wrote something in the particular way they did

- ✔ To describe how the code they wrote works

✓ To leave themselves a note telling what they still need to do, or to list improvements that they intend to make at a later date

✓ To prevent JavaScript statements from running

JavaScript has two different kinds of comments: single-line and multi-line.

✓ **Single-line comments:** Single-line comments cause everything following them on the same line to be a comment. To create a single-line comment, use two slashes (//) back to back. For example, in Listing 2-6, the first three lines are single-line comments and the fourth line contains a statement that will be executed, followed by a comment.

✓ **Multi-line comments:** Multi-line comments are comments that can be more than one line long. To create a multi-line comment, start with /* and end the comment with the exact reverse, */. Listing 2-7 shows an example of a multi-line comment.

Listing 2-6   Single-Line Comments

```
// The following code won't run.
// alert("Watch out!");
// The next statement will run.
alert("Have a nice day!"); // pops up a nice message
```

Listing 2-7   A Multi-Line Comment

```
/*

    AlertMe, by Chris Minnick and Eva Holland

    A program to alert users that they are
    using a JavaScript program called AlertMe,
    which was written by Chris Minnick and Eva
        Holland.

*/
```

Giving and Receiving Data

Programs come in many different sizes and have many different purposes. Here are three things all programs have in common:

- A way to receive information from the user

- A way to give information back to the user

- A way to store and work with information in between giving and receiving

Information, or data, that a program receives from a user is called *input*. What the program gives back to the user is called *output*. In the time between when a program receives input and produces output, it needs some way to store and work with the various types of data that has been inputted, so it can produce output.

The question of whether it's better to give or receive isn't important! It's all good. In this chapter, you learn how JavaScript can help you to get, receive, and just plain have data!

Dear Eva,

We are pleased to inform you that your song, 'Can't Stop Coding!,' has been voted the Best Song of All Time by the awarding committee.

Sincerely,
The Grammy Awards

Mastering Variables

In the real world, when you want to store something, give something away (as a gift, for example), move something, or organize something, you often put it in a box.

JavaScript doesn't care about heart-shaped boxes of chocolates or shoeboxes with the latest sneakers. What JavaScript loves is data. To store and move around data, JavaScript uses a special kind of box called a *variable*. A variable is a box you can assign a name to. This name will represent all the data contained in that box, or variable.

Variables make it possible for the same program to work with different input to produce different output.

Creating variables

Creating a variable in JavaScript is pretty simple. To create a variable, you use the `var` keyword, followed by the name of the variable, and then a semicolon, like this:

```
var book;
```

As a programmer, you have a lot of flexibility when naming your variables. You can be very creative in naming your variables, but you don't want to get too crazy. Most important, your variable names should accurately describe the data that you store inside them.

Each of the following variable declarations creates a variable with a good and descriptive name. By looking at them, you can probably guess what the data stored inside them looks like.

```
var myFirstName;
var favoriteFood;
var birthday;
var timeOfDay;
```

Notice how we separate words in variable names by using capital letters for every word after the first one. Variable names can't contain spaces, so programmers have created several other ways to separate words. This particular style is called *camelCase*. Can you guess why it has that name?

After looking at these examples, what would you name variables for storing the following pieces of data?

✔ Your pet's name

✔ Your favorite school subject

✔ The age of your best friend

✔ Your street address

In addition to the rule that variable names must not contain spaces, there are several other rules that you must follow:

✔ Variable names must begin with a letter, an underscore (_), or a dollar sign ($).

✔ Variable names can only contain letters, numbers, underscores, or dollar signs.

✔ Variable names are case sensitive.

✔ Certain words may not be used as variable names, because they have other meanings within JavaScript. These so-called *reserved words* are as follows:

break	case	class	catch
const	continue	debugger	default
delete	do	else	export
extends	finally	for	function
if	import	in	instanceof
let	new	return	super
switch	this	throw	try
typeof	var	void	while
with	yield		

Storing data in variables

After you've created a variable, you can store any sort of data inside it. When the data is in there, you can recall it at any time. Let's try it out!

1. Open the JavaScript Console in Chrome.

2. Create a new variable named book by typing the following and then pressing Return (Mac) or Enter (Windows):

```
var book;
```

You've created your container, or variable, and named it "book."

When you press Return or Enter, the JavaScript Console displays the word undefined. This is exactly what you want to happen. JavaScript is just telling you that your code ran correctly and that it doesn't have anything to tell you.

It may seem funny that JavaScript tells you that it has nothing to tell you. But, trust us, it's way better that it says something, even if it's just undefined than if it were to give you the cold shoulder and say nothing at all.

3. Put a value into your new variable by typing the following code.

```
book = "JavaScript For Kids For Dummies";
```

You've now put data inside your variable, where it will be stored.

When you press Return or Enter, JavaScript responds with the name of the book.

You only need to type **var** when you first create and name your variable. When you want to change the data inside your variable, you only need to use the variable's name.

4. Now, temporarily forget the name of this book. Got it? Now, imagine that you need to recall the name of this book so that you can tell your friend about it! To recall the data, or value, in a variable, you can just type the name of the variable in the console. So, type the following:

   ```
   book
   ```

   The console recalls the string that was assigned to the book variable and prints it out, as shown in Figure 3-1.

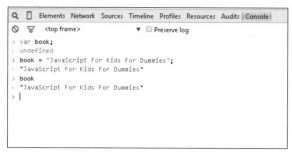

```
Q    Elements  Network  Sources  Timeline  Profiles  Resources  Audits | Console
       <top frame>                    ▼  Preserve log
> var book;
  undefined
> book = "JavaScript For Kids For Dummies";
  "JavaScript For Kids For Dummies"
> book
  "JavaScript For Kids For Dummies"
> |
```

Figure 3-1: Printing out the value assigned to a variable.

Notice that we didn't use a semicolon (;) when typing — we just used a variable name in the JavaScript Console. The name of a variable isn't a full JavaScript statement, so it doesn't require a semicolon. We're just asking JavaScript for the value of the variable, just as if we had asked it 1 + 1.

5. Now try changing the value of the book variable by typing the following statement into the JavaScript Console:

   ```
   book = "The Call of the Wild";
   ```

6. Type **book** into the JavaScript Console to retrieve its new value.

   The console prints out "The Call of the Wild" (or whatever you entered as the new value of book.

In addition to text, variables can also hold several other different types of data. In the next section, we show you each of the basic (also known as *primitive*) data types that JavaScript understands.

The data inside a variable can also be called the *value* of a variable.

Understanding Data Types

JavaScript variables have just one job — to hold and store data — and they do this job quite well. Using and creating variables are easy. There are many different types of data in the world, such as numbers, letters, and dates. JavaScript makes some important distinctions between these and other different kinds of data that you, as a coder, need to be aware of.

Data types are how a program knows whether 03-20-2017 is a date (March 20, 2017) or a math problem (subtract 20 from 3 and then subtract 2017 from the result).

JavaScript recognizes three basic data types: string, number, and Boolean.

The string data type

The string data type holds text. We explain the basics of how strings work in Chapter 2, but there are a few other cool tricks that you can do with strings besides just storing and printing them.

One cool string trick is to count how many characters the string is made up of. The way you do that is to use .length after the string, or after a variable holding the string.

For example, to find out the length of the string held inside the book variable you create in the previous section, type **book.length** into the console. The console responds right away with a number, as shown in Figure 3-2.

```
Q  🗋  Elements  Network  Sources  Timeline  Profiles  »      >_  ⚙  🗔, ×
⊘  ▽  <top frame>              ▼ ☐ Preserve log
> book = "JavaScript For Kids For Dummies";
< "JavaScript For Kids For Dummies"
> book
< "JavaScript For Kids For Dummies"
> book = "The Call of the Wild";
< "The Call of the Wild"
> book
< "The Call of the Wild"
> book.length
< 20
> |
```

Figure 3-2: Getting the length of a string.

Every string, even an empty string, has a length. The length of an empty string, of course, is 0. Because it's something that describes a string, we call length a *property* of a string.

You see the word *property* used a lot when people talk about JavaScript. A property is something that describes or is a part of something. For example, a car's color is a property of the car, a person's name is a property of the person, and a string's length is a property of the string.

In addition to finding out the length of a string stored in a variable, you can also just attach the length property to a string in quotes to find out its length:

```
"I am a string.".length
```

Count the letters in this sentence. There are 10 — 11 if you count the period at the end of the sentence. But when you enter this command into the JavaScript console, you get 14. Do you know why?

The spaces in a string count just as much as the letters, punctuation, symbols, and numbers in the string. To use the analogy we make in Chapter 2, it's all just knots on the string (14 of them to be precise) to JavaScript.

In addition to properties, strings also have things that they can do, or that can be done to them. In programming, we call these things that can be done with or to something its *methods*.

The most commonly used string method is `indexOf`. The job of `indexOf` is to look at your string, find a certain character or group of characters inside it, and tell you what position they're at. In the following statement, we look for the position of the word *am* in a string:

```
"I am a string.".indexOf("am");
```

When you run this statement in the console, the result is 2. Try retyping the command, but this time look for the capital *I*.

```
"I am a string.".indexOf("I");
```

The result is 0.

This brings us to a very important concept in JavaScript called zero-based numbering. Unlike people, who have ten fingers and generally start counting at the number one, JavaScript starts counting at zero. So, in the previous example, when JavaScript wants to tell you that `I` is the first character in the string, it says that `I` is at position 0.

If JavaScript were on a sports team, it would proudly wear a shirt that read "We're number 0!"

The number data type

Another type of data that JavaScript understands is the number data type. Numbers can be positive or negative, as well as whole numbers or decimal numbers. Numbers are stored in variables without using quotation marks.

The range of possible numbers that can be used in JavaScript goes from very, very small to very, very large. We won't bore you with a bunch of zeros right now, but the biggest number that you can use in JavaScript is far greater than the number of stars in the universe. It's even bigger than the number of *atoms* in the universe! JavaScript can do any math problem or counting problem that you would want it to do.

One thing to watch out for, however, is what happens when you try to combine two different data types, such as strings and numbers.

JavaScript generally tries to be pretty clever. If you open the console and type "**10**" + **10**, JavaScript will assume that you meant for both pieces of data to be strings, and will put them together and give you the result 1010.

On the other hand, if you type **10** * "**10**", JavaScript will assume that you meant for the string "10" to actually be the number 10, and it will give you the result 100. JavaScript does this because it knows there is no way to multiply two strings together.

The Boolean data type

The Boolean data type can store one of two possible values: true or false.

Boolean values are the result when you do comparisons in JavaScript, which we cover in more detail in Part V of this book. If you ask JavaScript something like: "Is 3 equal to 30?," it will respond with a Boolean value of false.

The Boolean data type is named after the mathematician George Boole, so it's always capitalized.

Let's do a few experiments with Booleans. Open the JavaScript Console and try typing each of the following statements, pressing Return or Enter after each one to see the result. Note that we've used a single-line comment after each statement to explain what it means. You don't need to type these comments into the console, but you can if you want.

```
1 < 10 // Is 1 less than 10?
100 > 2000 // Is 100 greater than 2000?
2 === 2 // Is 2 exactly equal to 2?
false === false // Is false exactly equal to false?
40 >= 40 // Is 40 greater than or equal to 40?
```

```
Boolean (0) // What is the Boolean value of 0?
Boolean (false) // What is the Boolean value of false?
"apples" === "oranges" // Is "apples" exactly equal to
              "oranges"?
"apples" === "apples" // Is "apples" exactly equal to
              "apples"?
```

In addition to the statements you would expect to be false, JavaScript also considers the following values to be false:

0	null	undefined
"" (an empty string)	false	

Prompting the User for Input

Now that you know how variables can hold different types of data, let's explore the process of getting data from a user and storing it inside your variables.

One way to ask a user for data is by using the `prompt` command. To try out the prompt command, open the JavaScript console and type the following:

```
prompt("What is your name?");
```

After you press Return or Enter, a pop-up window appears in your browser window with a text field, as shown in Figure 3-3.

After you enter your name and click OK, the pop-up window disappears, and the value that you entered in the pop-up displays in the console, as shown in Figure 3-4.

That's all well and good if all you want to do is capture data and immediately repeat it back like a parrot. But what if you want to do something with the user-entered data? To do that, you need to store it in a variable.

Figure 3-3: Prompting the user for input.

Figure 3-4: Displaying your name.

Storing user input

To store user-entered data in a variable, you create a new variable and then follow it with =. You then follow it with the prompt statement.

```
var username = prompt("What is your name?");
```

It's important to note that a single equal sign (=) in JavaScript is called the *assignment operator*. Its job is to put the value on the right into the variable on the left. We talk more about operators in Chapter 9.

When you press Return or Enter, a pop-up window appears in your browser, just as before.

When you enter your name in the pop-up window and click OK, the JavaScript Console prints out undefined, indicating that the statement is finished and there's nothing else for it to do.

To see the value you just entered, you can type the variable name into the console. JavaScript responds with the value of the variable, as shown in Figure 3-5.

Figure 3-5: Getting the value of a variable from a prompt.

Responding to Input

Now that you know how to get data from the user, and how to store that data, let's take a look at two of the ways that you can use JavaScript to respond to the user.

Using alert()

The alert() command pops up a notification box in the user's browser containing whatever data is between the parentheses.

If you want to display an alert with a simple string message, you can do so by enclosing a message within quotes between the (and) after `alert`. For example, type the following statement into your JavaScript Console:

```
alert("Good job!");
```

When you press Return or Enter, the browser displays an alert message containing the message "Good job!"

You display numbers in alerts by putting numbers without quotes between the parentheses. For example, try this statement:

```
alert(300);
```

The alert pop-up displays the number 300. You can even do math inside an alert. For example, try this one:

```
alert(37*37);
```

The alert displays the result of multiplying 37 and 37.

If you put a word between the parentheses in the `alert` statement without quotes, JavaScript treats the word as a variable. Try running the following two statements:

```
var myNameIs = "your name";
alert(myNameIs);
```

The browser pops up a window containing your name.

By combining different data types into one alert statement, you can start to do some really interesting and useful things. For example, try typing each of the following statements into the JavaScript Console, one at a time:

```
var firstName = "your name";
var yourScore = 30;
alert("Hi, " + firstName + ". Your current score is: " +
        yourScore);
```

As you can see, by using `alert()`, you can create all sorts of fun and interesting pop-ups to entertain and inform the user, such as the alert in Figure 3-6.

Figure 3-6: Creating interesting pop-ups.

The special life of objects

Objects are a special data type in JavaScript, like numbers and strings. However, objects are flexible and can store data about anything using properties and methods.

You can picture JavaScript objects as being like objects in the real world. For example, in the real world, you can have a yellow truck. In JavaScript, this yellow truck object would have a color property of yellow and we would write it like this:

```
truck.color="yellow";
```

The truck would also have a method called `drive`, and we would write that like this:

```
truck.drive();
```

Using document.write()

In JavaScript, a web page is called a *document.* When you change something on the current web page using JavaScript, you do so by telling JavaScript to change the document object.

One way to make changes to the current web page is by using the `write` method.

A method is something that can be done or that something can do.

Every document (or web page) has a `write` method that causes whatever you put between the parentheses after the method name to be inserted into the web page. You can use `document.` `write()` in the same ways that you used `alert()`. For example, open a new, blank browser window and try out the following statements in your JavaScript Console:

```
document.write("Hi, Mom!");
document.write(333 + 100);
```

Notice that statements after the first one are added right after the first statement, without a line break or space. You can add space after or before writing text with `document.write` by using the characters `<br>`. For example:

```
document.write("How are you?<br>");
document.write("I'm great! Thanks!<br>");
document.write("That's awesome!");
```

You can clear out the current contents of the browser window by typing **chrome://newtab** into the browser address bar or by opening a new browser tab.

The result of entering these three lines into the JavaScript Console is shown in Figure 3-7.

`<br>` is an HTML tag. We talk much more about HTML in Chapter 5.

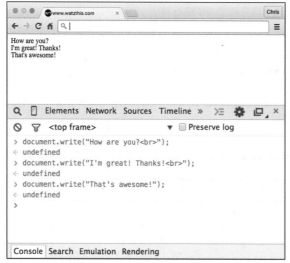

Figure 3-7: Three lines of text in a browser.

Combining Input and Output

Now, let's combine input and output to display customized output, based on input from a user. This is really the heart of what JavaScript can do for web pages!

Follow these steps in the JavaScript Console to create a letter to yourself in your web browser. Make sure to press Return or Enter after the end of each statement (after each semicolon).

1. Type the following to create a variable containing your first name.

   ```
   var toName = "your name";
   ```

2. Type the following to create a variable containing the person the letter is from:

   ```
   var fromName = "The Grammy Awards";
   ```

   You can change The Grammy Awards to anyone you'd like to get a letter from.

3. Type the contents of your letter into a variable.

   Use <br> to insert line breaks and don't press Return or Enter until after you type the semicolon.

   Here's the letter we came up with:

   ```
   var letterBody = "We are pleased to inform you that your song,
               'Can\'t Stop Coding!,' has been voted the Best Song
               of All Time by the awarding committee.";
   ```

4. Write `document.write()` statements to output each of the three parts of your letter.

   For example:

   ```
   document.write("Dear " + toName + ",<br><br>");
   document.write(letterBody + "<br><br>");
   document.write("Sincerely,<br>");
   document.write(fromName);
   ```

   When your letter is done, it should resemble ours, shown in Figure 3-8.

Figure 3-8: A fully customized letter displayed in the browser.

Fiddling with Web Applications

In Chapter 1, we explain and demonstrate the JavaScript Console. In Chapters 2 and 3, we show you how to put multiple statements together to form a program. In this chapter, we kick things up a notch and introduce you to our favorite JavaScript playground: JSFiddle. Instead of swings and slides, you'll be playing with JavaScript statements, HTML tags, and CSS styles.

JSFiddle lets you write and experiment with JavaScript code from within your web browser. You can use it to try out code, get feedback on your code, share your code, and even work on programs with your friends! You'll learn how to use JSFiddle to view, modify, save, and share JavaScript web applications, too.

You may be wondering what we mean by *web application.* A web application (or *web app*) is software that runs in a browser and is usually powered by JavaScript. Google Earth, for example, is a popular web app you may be familiar with. It can look up and show you nearly any place on Earth in high-resolution photos. Google Earth is also a *website* because you can access it using a web address, or URL. Do you think JSFiddle is a web app, a website, or both? It's actually both. In fact, every web application is a website. Not all websites are web applications, however.

In this chapter, you use JSFiddle to experiment with some animations. In the end, you have a JavaScript bubble machine that you can customize as much as you want! It's called JSFiddle because you can use it to "fiddle" with JavaScript. So, let the fiddling begin!

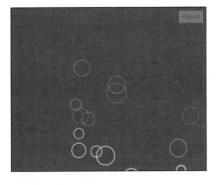

Introducing JSFiddle

To get started with JSFiddle, open your web browser and type **http://jsfiddle.net** into the address bar. You'll see the JSFiddle website, shown in Figure 4-1.

JSFiddle's user interface window consists of three panes where you can enter different types of code including HTML, CSS, and JavaScript. You see the results of what you type inside these boxes in the Result pane. The toolbar on the left lets you configure additional options, and the top toolbar has buttons for running, saving, and cleaning up your code.

You can resize any of the panes in JSFiddle by clicking and dragging the border that separates them.

For now, we're mostly concerned with the JavaScript pane. The JavaScript pane works in much the same way as the JavaScript Console. With JSFiddle, the code you enter won't execute until you tell it to run.

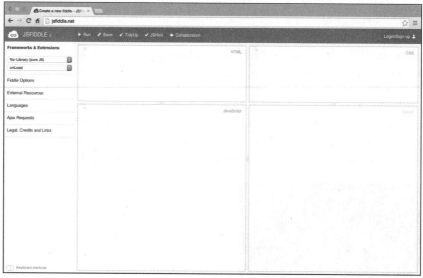

Figure 4-1: JSFiddle's clean and compartmentalized user interface.

Follow these steps to run your first JSFiddle program:

1. Click inside the JavaScript pane.

2. Type the following JavaScript statement:

```
alert("Hi, everyone!");
```

3. Click the Run button on the top toolbar.

   A pop-up window containing the message "Hi, everyone!" appears.

4. Close the pop-up window by clicking OK.

There's nothing surprising in the behavior of that simple JavaScript program. If you've read the first three chapters of this book, you're already familiar with how the alert statement works.

Running JavaScript isn't the only great thing JSFiddle can do. With JSFiddle, you can also use the HTML and CSS panes to run code that works together with your JavaScript code! In the next few sections, we cover each of these panes in more detail and demonstrate their use. But first, we give a quick demonstration of what JSFiddle is capable of.

Viewing our fiddles

We're going to let you in on a secret. Every program in this book is available for you to view, run, copy, and play around with at http://jsfiddle.net/user/forkids/fiddles. That's right! We've done your homework! We've formatted it nicely for you and tested it out.

This is our own JSFiddle public dashboard. The public dashboard is where any JSFiddle user can share programs (known as "fiddles" in JSFiddle) with the world.

Although we've typed up every project for you already, it's important that you go through each step of every project for yourself so that you really understand. To get the most out of this book, feel free to copy, modify, completely change, and rewrite our code to see what it does and make it your own! Keep on fiddlin'!

Playing with fiddles

Before you get too carried away with viewing all the cool projects from other parts and chapters, take a look at some programs that aren't part of this book. JSFiddle lets anyone create an account and share their programs in a public dashboard — and many excellent and very experienced JavaScript programmers do!

When programmers share their programs on JSFiddle, they agree that anyone who wants to can make a copy of their work, change it, and republish it. However, it's always polite to give the original author credit when you borrow code. We've made copies of each of the programs below so that we can be sure that they'll be the same when you view them. If you want to find out who the original author of a program is, open Fiddle Options from the left navigation bar.

Follow these steps to view and run some of the programs in our list of amazing JSFiddle demos:

1. Go to our public dashboard at `http://jsfiddle.net/ user/forkids/fiddles`.

   You see a list of all the examples and projects from the entire book.

   You may need to use the page navigation at the bottom of the list to see additional pages of results.

2. Find a demo that sounds interesting to you and open it.

   When the program opens, it will automatically start running.

If you find a program that you like, try figuring out how it works! Change some values to see what happens.

Anything that you do to a program in JSFiddle won't overwrite the original. You can try changing things all you want, and no harm will come of it. The worst that can happen is that the program won't run.

Fiddling with CSS

The CSS pane in JSFiddle is located in the upper-right corner. Besides working with JavaScript in JSFiddle, we can also fiddle with the Cascading Style Sheets (CSS) in our web application. CSS allows you to change how elements such as text and graphics appear. If you want to change the color of the text on your page, you use CSS.

We cover CSS in much more detail in Chapter 6. For now, follow these steps to try out changes to one of our programs:

1. Go to `http://jsfiddle.net/forkids/vaj023L5`.

   You see the Bubbles demo, shown in Figure 4-2.

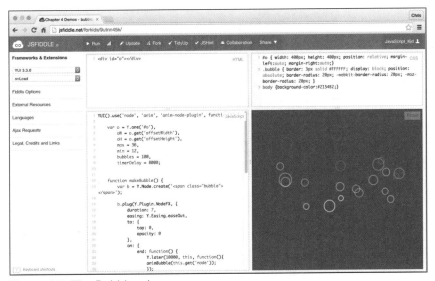

Figure 4-2: The Bubbles demo.

2. Take a closer look at each of the four main areas of the screen.

   Three of them have some code, and the fourth is displaying the bubble animation. Can you figure out just by reading the code what any of this might do?

3. Look at the CSS pane (in the upper right).

   You see three lines of code.

4. Find the code that reads `border: 3px solid #FFFFFF;` and change it to `border: 8px solid #FFFFFF;`.

5. Click the Run button in the top toolbar to start the animation over.

   You'll notice that the walls of the bubbles have gotten much thicker, as shown in Figure 4-3.

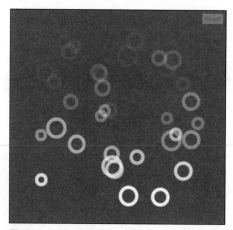

Figure 4-3: The bubble walls have gotten thick!

Based on the change that you just made and the effect that it had on the output of the program, what do you think the part of the statement that says `solid` does? To find out, try the following steps:

1. In the CSS pane, change the first value after `border:` to a smaller number (such as 2 or 3) and click Run.

   The walls of the circles get thin again.

2. Change the second value after `border:` to one of the following words:

- dotted

- dashed

- double

- groove

- ridge

- inset

- outset

3. Click Run to see what it does.

This value tells the browser what the style of the border should be. Figure 4-4 shows the bubbles with the border style set to dotted.

Now take a look at the third value after `border:`, which is currently set to #FFFFFF. This string of characters represents the border color property of the bubbles.

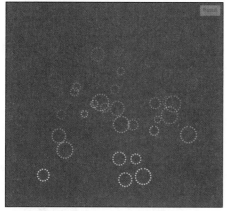

Figure 4-4: Bubbles with a dotted bubble style.

Color in CSS is usually written using a special code called *hexadecimal notation,* which uses three sets of values ranging from 00 to FF to tell the browser how much red, green, and blue to put in.

We cover CSS colors in detail in Chapter 6. You can also use many of the standard color names that you know. A list of the most common color names that web browsers understand is shown in Table 4-1.

Table 4-1	Standard HTML Color Names	
Color Name	Hexadecimal Value	Color Swatch
Aqua	#00FFFF	
Black	#000000	
Blue	#0000FF	
Fuchsia	#FF00FF	
Gray	#808080	
Green	#008000	
Lime	#00FF00	

Color Name	Hexadecimal Value	Color Swatch
Maroon	#800000	
Navy	#000080	
Olive	#808000	
Orange	#FFA500	
Purple	#800080	
Red	#FF0000	
Silver	#C0C0C0	
Teal	#008080	
White	#FFFFFF	
Yellow	#FFFF00	

Follow these steps to change the color of the bubbles:

1. Choose a color name or its hexadecimal code from Table 4-1.

2. Replace the color value (#FFFFFF) in the CSS pane with your new value.

3. Click Run.

   Your new color appears in the Result pane.

Fiddling with HTML

Now take a look at the HTML pane, in the upper-left corner. Compared to the CSS and JavaScript panes, this one doesn't have much going on in it at all!

HTML, which we cover in Chapter 5, creates structure for web pages and containers for JavaScript programs to do their things in. In the case of the Bubbles demo, the HTML just makes a place on the page for the bubbles to go into.

But you can do much more with HTML! To make some changes to the HTML for the Bubbles demo, try the following:

1. Put your cursor after `</div>` and type the following:

   ```
   <h1>I love bubbles!</h1>
   ```

   Your HTML pane should now have the following HTML code:

   ```
   <div id="o"></div><h1>I love bubbles!</h1>
   ```

   HTML code is actually called HTML *markup* for reasons that we explain in Chapter 5.

2. Press Run to see your changes in the Result pane.

   The bubbles now have a special message below them, as shown in Figure 4-5.

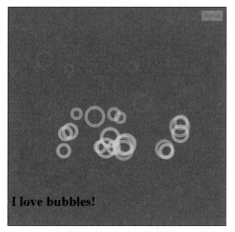

Figure 4-5: Colorful bubbles, now with a special message.

In HTML, <h1> and </h1> are known as tags. Tags around text tell the browser that the text represents something special. In this case, <h1> represents a first-level header, the largest and most important header on the page.

Another very useful HTML tag is the <p> tag, which marks paragraphs. To insert a <p> tag, follow these steps:

1. After the </h1> tag, press Return (Mac) or Enter (Windows) to move to the next line.

2. Type **<p>** and then type anything at all that you want to say. When you're done, end the paragraph by typing **</p>**.

3. Click Run to see your changes in the Result pane.

Fiddling with JavaScript

The JavaScript pane, in the lower-left part of the JSFiddle interface, is where the really interesting things happen.

1. In the JavaScript pane, find the line that reads max = 36 and change it to max = 80.

2. Click Run.

   Many of the bubbles, but not all of them, are now larger than
   they were before.

Based on the behavior of the bubbles when you changed the value
of max, do you have a guess as to what will happen if you change
the line that reads min = 12? Try it out and see if you're right!

If you guessed that max controls the maximum bubble size and
min controls the minimum bubble size, you're absolutely correct. Figure 4-6 shows the Result pane with max set to 80 and
min set to 20.

Figure 4-6: Changing the values of min
and max changes the size of the bubbles.

The next two lines in the JavaScript pane are bubbles = 100
and timerDelay = 8000. You can change these values using
the steps you've used several times now:

1. Change the value.

2. Click Run to see the results of the change.

Try changing both of these values to see what happens. By
playing around with these values (or maybe just by guessing),
you'll discover that the value of bubbles tells how many bubbles

should be created and `timerDelay` has something to do with the speed of the bubbles.

Can you figure out exactly what the `bubbles` and `timerDelay` values do by experimenting with them? ***Hint:*** The value of `timerDelay` is a number of milliseconds (or thousandths of a second). So, 8,000 milliseconds equals 8 seconds. Change the value to `10000`, click Run, and then time the action on the screen. Then change the value to `1000`, click Run, and time it again.

If you guessed that `bubbles` controls how many bubbles will be created and `timerDelay` controls how quickly those bubbles appear, you're correct!

Creating a JSFiddle Account

Creating a JSFiddle account isn't required in order to proceed with the book, but it will make viewing and sharing your work later on easier.

Follow these steps to create a JSFiddle account:

1. Click the Fork button in the top menu.

   When you create your own version of a program that's based on someone else's code, it's called *forking* their code.

2. Select the URL of your program in the browser address bar and copy it, or just write it down somewhere so you can use it after you create an account.

3. Click the Login/Sign Up link in the upper-right corner of the screen.

   The Log In page appears, as shown in Figure 4-7.

4. Click the Sign Up link under the login form.

   The Create an Account page appears.

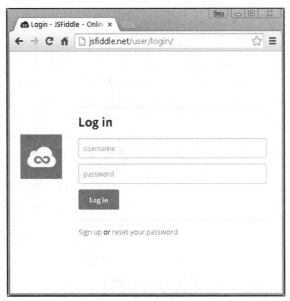

Figure 4-7: The JSFiddle Log In page.

5. Fill out the Create an Account form and click Create an Account.

   The Edit Your Profile page appears, as shown in Figure 4-8. If you like, you can make changes here and save them, but that isn't required.

6. Click the Editor link at the top of the screen.

   The main JSFiddle screen appears with your new username in the upper-right corner of the screen.

7. Paste or type the URL that you saved in Step 2 into the browser address bar and press Return or Enter.

   You're brought back to your version of the Bubbles demo.

8. Click Fork again to bring your version of the program into your new JSFiddle account.

   Notice that the URL in the browser address bar now contains your JSFiddle username!

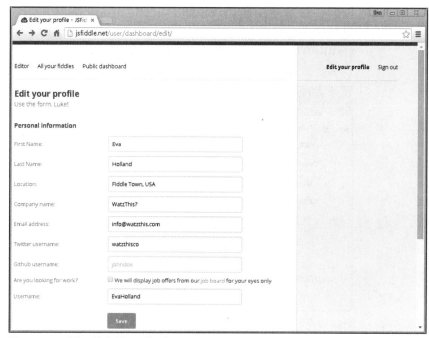

Figure 4-8: The Edit Your Profile page.

Sharing Your Fiddle

Now that you've created your own personalized version of the Bubbles demo, it's time to show your friends!

1. Click the Share button in the top toolbar.

   You'll see the option to copy the address for your Bubbles demo, to view the program in full-screen mode, and to share your program on Facebook or Twitter.

If you want to share your programs on Facebook or Twitter, remember to tag us (@watzthisco on Twitter or `www.facebook.com/watzthisco`), and we'll check out your creations!

2. Highlight the full-screen URL in the Share menu, as shown in Figure 4-9, and copy it by pressing ⌘+C (Mac) or Ctrl+C (Windows) or by choosing Edit⇨Copy in your browser.

Figure 4-9: Highlighting the full-screen URL.

3. Open a new browser window tab (by pressing ⌘+T [Mac] or Ctrl+T [Windows]) and paste the full-screen address into the address bar.

   The bubbles display onscreen without the code panes.

If the Bubbles demo doesn't work for you in full-screen mode, try changing the `https` in the browser address bar to `http` and press Return or Enter.

If you want to return to the original Bubbles program, you can do so by going back to our public dashboard at `https://jsfiddle.net/user/forkids/fiddles`.

But what if you want to have your own dashboard where you can create and save your own collection of JSFiddle programs? Read on!

Saving Your App

Now that you have your own account, you can create your own public dashboard.

To create your own public dashboard on JSFiddle follow these steps:

1. With your latest version of the Bubbles app on your screen, click Fiddle Options in the left navigation bar.

   The Fiddle Options menu opens.

2. Type a name for your Bubbles program.

   This can be anything you like, but we recommend including the word *bubbles* in the name so that you remember what it is later!

3. Click Update in the top toolbar.

4. Click Set as Base in the top toolbar.

   JSFiddle creates a new version of your program each time you save it. The Set as Base button makes the currently displayed version of your program the version that displays when someone links to your program from your public dashboard.

5. Click your username in the upper-right corner of the screen and select Public Dashboard.

   Your public dashboard appears, complete with your version of the Bubbles program listed. Your dashboard should resemble Figure 4-10.

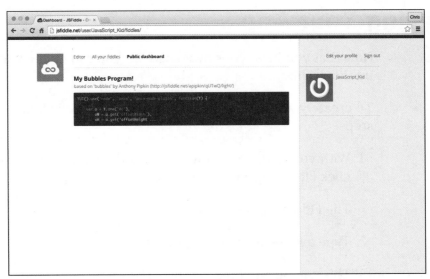

Figure 4-10: Your very own public dashboard on JSFiddle!

Part II
Animating the Web

In this part . . .

JavaScript and HTML 71

JavaScript and CSS 89

Building an Animated Robot 104

JavaScript and HTML

JavaScript and the web go together like cheese and pizza: You could have one without the other, but why?

JavaScript gives web pages the ability to change dynamically in response to user input. To get the most out of the integration between JavaScript and the web, you need to know a little bit about how web pages are built.

In this chapter, we explore the language of the web, HTML, and we show you how to use JavaScript to work with and change the HTML inside of web pages.

Result

Eva

I'm learning to build dynamic web pages with JavaScript and HTML!

Things I Like

Here are some of the things I like to do:

- Write
- Dance
- Travel

Change Your List

Writing HTML

HTML stands for Hypertext Markup Language. That's a fancy way of saying that HTML is a language that's used to create links (hypertext). HTML is so much more than simply a language for creating links, though.

HTML forms the skeleton that the text, pictures, and JavaScript in web pages attaches to.

Seeing what text looks like without HTML

Markup languages, such as HTML, were invented in order to give documents (such as letters, books, or essays) structure that a computer can understand and do things with.

Listing 5-1 shows a simple list that a person can understand with no problem.

Listing 5-1   A List

```
Things I Need
carrots
celery
spinach
```

As a person, you see this list and immediately understand it. But to a computer, this list has some issues. For example, a computer has no way of knowing that Things I Need is a title rather than an item on the list. Figure 5-1 is what it looks like when you view Listing 5-1 with a web browser.

To make this text document understandable to a web browser, we need to use HTML to "mark it up."

Using HTML: It's all about the tags

HTML is made up of tags. The tags on clothes give you information about what the clothes are made of and how to wash them. Similarly, tags in HTML give you information about the content of a web page.

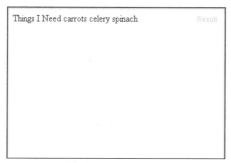

Things I Need carrots celery spinach   Result

Figure 5-1: Listing 5-1 rendered as HTML in JSFiddle.

Tags are made up of keywords inside of angle brackets (< and >) and then come in two basic types: the beginning tag and the ending tag. Here's an example of a beginning tag:

```
<p>
```

The p tag, is how you mark up text in a document as a paragraph.

Most beginning tags also have matching ending tags. The only difference between a beginning tag and an ending tag is that an ending tag has a / before the name of the tag. For example, here's the ending p tag:

```
</p>
```

To use tags, just put the thing that you want to mark up (such as text, images, or even other tags) between the beginning and ending tags. For example, here's how you would mark up a paragraph of text in HTML.

```
<p>This is a paragraph of text. A paragraph has space
before and after it in order to separate it from the
other paragraphs of text in a document.</p>
```

When you have a beginning tag, an ending tag, and content between them, we call the whole thing an *HTML element*.

HTML has a bunch of tags that you can use to label different parts of a document. Examples of tags include <p> for paragraph, <img> for image, <audio> for audio clips, <video> for video clips, `<header>` for the top of a web page, and `<footer>` for the bottom of a web page.

Listing 5-2 shows the list from Listing 5-1 marked up as an HTML document, made up of tags and text.

Listing 5-2   A Simple HTML Document

```
<html>
  <head>
    <title>My Grocery List</title>
  </head>
  <body>
    <h1>Things I Need</h1>
      <ol>
        <li>carrots</li>
        <li>celery</li>
        <li>spinach</li>
      </ol>
  </body>
</html>
```

Figure 5-2 shows what the web page in Listing 5-2 looks like when you view it with a web browser. That's much better, right?

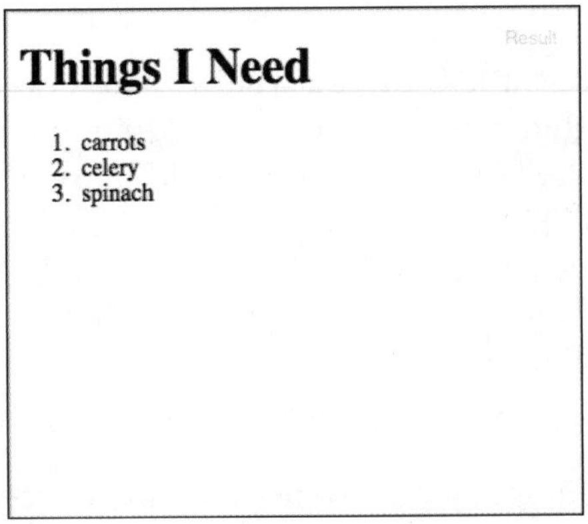

Figure 5-2: Listing 5-2 rendered as HTML in JSFiddle.

Notice that HTML tags don't actually appear in the web browser. Instead, they modify how the web browser displays text, images, and more.

Looking at the basic structure of a web page

Creating web pages is pretty easy once you know a few things about how they're built. The first thing to know is that most web pages share a very similar basic structure, and they all must abide by just a few basic rules.

The first rule of creating HTML documents is that tags need to be opened and closed in the right order. One way to remember the order in which tags are opened and closed is FILO, which stands for First In, Last Out.

Notice that the web page in Listing 5-2 starts with the <html> tag and ends with the </html> tag. This is how every web page should start and end. All the other tags in a web page are "inside" the html tags, and they're closed according to FILO.

For example, the <head> element is inside of <html>. Therefore, the closing head tag must come before the closing html tag. The <ol> tag (which stands for ordered list) comes after the <body> tag, so <ol> is inside of <body> and the </ol> tag must come before the </body> tag.

Another rule of creating HTML documents is that web pages always have a head element and a body element.

✔ **The head element:** The head element is like the brain of your web pages. JavaScript code often goes into the head element, but it doesn't display in the web browser window.

In Listing 5-2, we have only a title element in the head. The title is what displays at the top of the browser window or in your browser's tab when you're on a web page. The contents of the title element are also typically what shows up as a link in search results.

✔ **The body element:** The body element is where everything that you want to display in the web browser goes.

In Listing 5-2, we have several elements in the body. Let's take a look at each of these:

● **The h1 element:** The h1 element can be used to identify the most important header on your web pages. Headers typically identify sections of documents or web pages. For example, if this chapter were a web page, the first h1 element would come right after the chapter introduction and would read "Writing HTML."

● **The ol element:** Following the h1 element, we have an ol element. ol stands for ordered list. An ordered list is a list of items that are numbered or lettered in a particular order. HTML also lets you make unordered lists, by using the ul (for unordered list) tag.

● **The li element:** Following the ol element, we have an li element. Inside of either an ol or ul element, you can use any number of li elements (li stands for list item) to create the individual list items in your list.

Creating your first web page

Follow these steps to make your own list in JSFiddle.

1. Open your web browser and browse to http://jsfiddle. net.

2. Drag and drop the pane borders to make the HTML pane in JSFiddle as large as you like.

   We're only going to be working with the HTML pane for now, so make sure you're comfortable and have plenty of space.

3. Type the following basic HTML template into the HTML pane.

```
<html>
  <head>
    <title>HTML Template</title>
  </head>
  <body>
    <h1>A basic HTML template</h1>
  </body>
</html>
```

As soon as you type <html>, you get a warning message from JSFiddle, as shown in Figure 5-3, telling you that <html> is already included in the output. What's going on here is that the basic HTML template is so basic that JSFiddle will just help you out by putting it in there for you. Thanks, JSFiddle!

```
 1  <html>                                           HTML
 2      <head>
 3          <title>HTML Template</title>
 4      </head>
 5      <body>
 6          <h1>a basic HTML template</h1>
 7      </body>
 8  </html>
 9
10
```
No need for the **HTML** tag, it's already in the output.

No need for the **HEAD** tag, it's already in the output.

Figure 5-3: JSFiddle shows a warning.

4. Because the basic template is already there, go ahead and delete everything from the HTML window except for what's between <body> and </body> (the h1 element).

Always keep in mind that the <html>, <head>, and <body> elements should be part of every web page, even if you don't need to type them yourself when you're working in JSFiddle.

5. Click Run.

The text between the `<h1>` and `</h1>` tags will display in the Output pane, formatted as a first-level heading, as shown in Figure 5-4.

A basic HTML template

Result

Figure 5-4: Running a basic HTML template in JSFiddle.

Knowing Your HTML Elements

HTML has quite a few elements. Because this is a JavaScript book, we don't have room to talk about each of the elements here. But we'll cover just enough of them to allow you to build some awesome web pages. For the rest, you can go online to read more.

There are some really good books on HTML, such as *Beginning HTML5 and CSS3 For Dummies,* by Ed Tittel and Chris Minnick (Wiley). You can also find a complete list of every HTML element online. Our favorite free online resource is at `https://developer.mozilla.org/en-US/docs/Web/HTML/Element`.

Table 5-2 lists the most commonly used HTML elements, along with descriptions of what they're for.

Table 5-2	The Most Common HTML Elements	
Element	**Name**	**Description**
`<h1>` through `<h6>`	Headings (levels 1 through 6)	A section heading.
`<p>`	Paragraph	A paragraph.
`<em>`	Emphasis	Adds emphasis to a word or words. Typically displayed as italics in web browsers.

Element	Name	Description
`<strong>`	Strong	Represents strong importance. Typically displayed as bold text in web browsers.
`<a>`	Anchor	A link.
`<ul>`	Unordered list	A bulleted list.
`<ol>`	Ordered list	A numbered list.
`<li>`	List item	An item within an ordered or unordered list.
`<img>`	Image	An image.
`<hr>`	Horizontal rule	A horizontal line on the page.
`<div>`	Division	A way to separate a document into different parts.

Let's have some fun with your new elements. We're going to write a fun web page all about you!

Go back to JSFiddle and follow these steps:

1. Delete everything from the HTML pane and click Run.

   The Output pane should now be blank.

2. Create a first-level header for your page, using the h1 element, and put your name into it.

3. Put a horizontal rule below the first-level header.

4. Add a p element and type a favorite quote, a sentence about yourself, or the following text between the start and end tags:

   ```
   I'm learning to build dynamic web pages with JavaScript and
           HTML!
   ```

5. Put the em element around the sentence (inside of the p element) you typed in the previous step.

6. Click Run.

If you're following along closely, your code should look something like this:

```
<h1>Eva</h1>
<hr>
<p><em> I'm learning to build dynamic web pages with JavaScript
        and HTML!</em></p>
```

The output should now look something like Figure 5-5 (but with your own information, of course!).

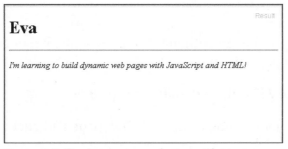

Figure 5-5: The beginnings of a beautiful home page.

7. Create another horizontal rule, followed by a new paragraph.

8. Create a level-2 heading (using the h2 element) and put the words "Things I Like" inside of it.

9. Create a new paragraph and put the following text into it:

```
Here are some of the things I like to do:
```

10. Now, create an unordered list with three blank list items.

Here's the code for that:

```
<ul>
  <li></li>
  <li></li>
  <li></li>
</ul>
```

11. Put something that you like to do into each of the list item elements.

Listing 5-3 shows what our sample code looks like now.

Listing 5-3   **The Updated Home Page**

```
<h1>Eva</h1>
  <hr>
  <p><em>I'm learning to build dynamic web pages with JavaScript
          and HTML!</em></p>
  <hr>
  <h2>Things I Like</h2>
  <p>Here are some of the things I like to do:</p>
  <ul>
    <li>Write</li>
    <li>Dance</li>
    <li>Travel</li>
  </ul>
```

Click Run to preview your web page in the output pane. It should now look like Figure 5-6.

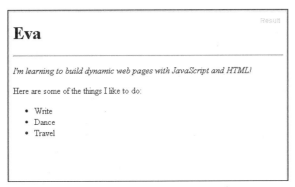

Figure 5-6: The home page, with a list of things.

Adding Attributes to Elements

HTML elements are pretty powerful just by themselves, and they can make web browsers do some pretty fancy things with your content. However, HTML has another trick up its sleeve that makes HTML even better: HTML attributes!

HTML attributes are a way to give web browsers more information about elements. Attributes are added to elements using what's called a *name/value pair.* For example, the img element uses attributes to tell what image should be displayed, and what should be displayed instead of the image if the file isn't found:

```
<img src="picture.jpg" alt="Here's a picture of me">
```

In this example, src and alt are attributes.

Each element in HTML has a list of attributes that can be added to it. Some attributes, such as src and alt, change the way an element behaves or what it does. Other attributes, such as the id attribute, just provide the browser with more information about the element.

The id attribute uniquely identifies a single element in your document. You may have any number of li elements, for example, but if you give each li element an id attribute, you can tell them all apart . . . and so can JavaScript!

We'll be making use of the id attribute quite a bit in upcoming programs.

Let's add some id attributes to the HTML in your home page now.

1. Add an id attribute to the h1 to identify it as containing your name.

   ```
   <h1 id="myName">
   ```

2. Find the p element between the two hr elements, and modify the starting tag to add an id of aboutMe, like this:

   ```
   <p id="aboutMe">
   ```

3. Add a unique id attribute to each of the list items, like this:

   ```
   <li id="firstThing"></li>
   <li id="secondThing"></li>
   <li id="thirdThing"></li>
   ```

When you're finished adding `id` attributes, your web page should look something like Listing 5-4.

Listing 5-4   The Updated Home Page with `id` Attributes Added

```
<h1 id="myName">Eva</h1>
<hr>
<p id="aboutMe"><em>I'm learning to build dynamic web
          pages with JavaScript and HTML!</em></p>
<hr>
<h2>Things I Like</h2>
<p>Here are some of the things I like to do:</p>
<ul>
  <li id="firstThing">Write</li>
  <li id="secondThing">Dance</li>
  <li id="thirdThing">Travel</li>
</ul>
```

Click Run to preview the web page in JSFiddle. You should notice . . . nothing. The page looks exactly the same with the `id` attributes as it does without them. Yes, we know, it's not that exciting. But wait until you see what JavaScript can do with `id` attributes!

Changing HTML with JavaScript

By using JavaScript, you can change any part of an HTML document in response to input from the person browsing the page. We show you exactly how to do that in this section.

But before we get started, let's take a look at a couple concepts that we use in this section. The first is a method called `getElementById`.

As discussed in Chapter 3, a method is an action that's done to or by an object in a JavaScript program.

Fetching elements with `getElementById`

`getElementById` is probably the easiest and most commonly used way for JavaScript programmers to work directly with HTML. Its purpose is to locate an individual element in a document so that you can change it, delete it, or add something to it.

Another word for locating an element is *selecting* an element.

To use `getElementById`, first make sure that the element you want to select has an `id` attribute. Then just use the following formula to locate that element:

```
document.getElementById("id-value")
```

For example, to select an element with an `id` value of `myName`, you can use this code:

```
document.getElementById("myName")
```

Getting what's inside an element with `innerHTML`

When you have an element, the next logical thing to do is to make a change to it.

`innerHTML` is a property of every element. It tells you what's between the starting and ending tags of the element, and it also lets you set the contents of the element.

A property describes an aspect of an object. It's something that an object *has* as opposed to something that an object *does*.

For example, let's say you have an element like the following:

```
<p id="myParagraph">This is <em>my</em> paragraph.</p>
```

You can select the paragraph and then change the value of its innerHTML with the following command:

```
document.getElementById("myParagraph").innerHTML = "This
              is <em>your</em> paragraph!";
```

Trying it out: Changing a list

Now that you know a little about getElementById and innerHTML, let's take a look again at our HTML home page.

You'll add a button and JavaScript code to your home page to let you change your list of favorite things with the click of a button.

1. Add a button below the list with the following HTML:

```
<button id="changeList" type="button">
  Change Your List
</button>
```

The button element causes the browser to create a button in your browser window with the label of the button set to the text between the starting and ending tags.

2. Create three new variables in the JavaScript pane.

```
var item1;
var item2;
var item3;
```

These three variables will be used to hold the values input by the user before they get written to the web page.

3. Make JavaScript pay attention to clicks on the button by adding this to the JavaScript pane in JSFiddle:

```
document.getElementById("changeList").onclick = newList;
```

We use a method called `getElementById` to locate the element in the document that has an `id` attribute set to `changeList`. As you know, this is the `id` value of the button.

When JavaScript has found the button, we use the `onclick` event handler to tell it to watch for clicks on that button. An event handler is exactly what it sounds like. It tells JavaScript how to handle different types of events that happen in the browser. In this case, mouse clicks.

If the event handler detects a click on the button, we tell it to run the function that we've called `newList`. A function is like a program within a program. We talk much more about functions in Chapter 12. For now, all you need to know is that functions don't run until you tell them to by "calling" them.

4. Type these lines to ask the user for new list items:

```
function newList(){
   item1 = prompt("Enter a new first thing: ");
   item2 = prompt("Enter a new second thing: ");
   item3 = prompt("Enter a new third thing: ");
   updateList();
}
```

The first line of this block of code is what makes it a function. It tells JavaScript not to run the code between { and } until the function is called (using its name, `newList`).

Inside the function, we gather three new list items from the user, using the prompt command.

Finally, we tell JavaScript to run the function called `updateList`, which we'll write in the next step.

5. Tell JavaScript to update the three list items.

```
function updateList() {
   document.getElementById("firstThing").innerHTML = item1;
   document.getElementById("secondThing").innerHTML = item2;
   document.getElementById("thirdThing").innerHTML = item3;
}
```

The updateList function finds each of the list items using their id attribute values. It then uses a method called innerHTML to change the value that's between the starting and ending tags of the list item to the values that the user entered into the prompt.

After the updateList function gets run, the values of the three list items should change to the new values entered by the user.

When you're finished, your code in the JavaScript pane should match Listing 5-5. Check it very carefully before moving on to make sure you don't have any syntax errors.

Listing 5-5   The Final JavaScript for the HTML Homepage App

```
var item1;
var item2;
var item3;

document.getElementById("changeList").onclick = newList;

function newList() {
    item1 = prompt("Enter a new first thing: ");
    item2 = prompt("Enter a new second thing: ");
    item3 = prompt("Enter a new third thing: ");
    updateList();
}

function updateList() {
    document.getElementById("firstThing").innerHTML =
            item1;
    document.getElementById("secondThing").innerHTML =
            item2;
    document.getElementById("thirdThing").innerHTML =
            item3;
}
```

6. Click Run to try out your new program.

If you did everything correctly, you should now be able to click the button, enter new text into each of the three prompt windows, and then see the new items instead of the three original list items, as shown in Figure 5-7.

Result

Eva

I'm learning to build dynamic web pages with JavaScript and HTML!

Things I Like

Here are some of the things I like to do:

- Swimming
- Singing
- Parties

Change Your List

Figure 5-7: The final, changeable, list program.

JavaScript and CSS

We've all got our own individual style. One person might sport a tuxedo and another might feel most at home in white jeans and a white T-shirt. Styles come and go, and what looks great today might look silly tomorrow.

Changing clothes and our personal styles gives us the freedom to change the way we look. The things that make people themselves, however, don't change when they change clothes.

In the same way, it's possible to change the way a web page looks without changing the content and structure of the web page.

The language used to change a web page's style is called Cascading Style Sheets (CSS). In this chapter, we show you what CSS is and how you can use it to give your web applications style.

CSS dresses up your web page by adding colors, borders, backgrounds, and varying sizes to elements. CSS can change where elements are positioned on your screen, and it can even control special effects such as animation!

Meet Douglas the JavaScript Robot

In this project, you modify and add styles to an HTML robot named Douglas. We just got Douglas delivered from the robot factory this morning. His JavaScript skills are outstanding, he doesn't need much maintenance (just a new variable to play with every now and then), and he tells good jokes!

The only problem is, his looks are a bit boring! Sure, he's got some nice blue eyes, and his "I <3 JS!" T-shirt is pretty cool. But he just doesn't look like the fun and goofy robot that we know Douglas to be. So, let's give him a unique style all his own!

To get started, open your web browser and log into the public dashboard at `http://jsfiddle.net/user/forkids/fiddles`. Then follow these steps:

1. Find the fiddle called Chapter 6: Robot Style – Start and click the title to open it.

   You can also go directly to the Robot app by going to `http://jsfiddle.net/forkids/m9nfspxp`.

   You see a screen with HTML in the HTML panel and some CSS in the CSS panel.

2. Click Fork in the top menu to make a copy of the fiddle in your own JSFiddle account.

Now you're ready to start giving Douglas some style!

CSS Basics

Take a look at the first three lines in the JavaScript Robot CSS pane.

```
body {
  font-family: Arial;
}
```

These three lines form a *CSS rule*. A CSS rule consists of two main components:

- ✒ **Selector:** The selector indicates what element or elements the CSS rule applies to. In this example, the selector is body.

- ✒ **Declaration block:** The declaration block contains one or more CSS declarations, which indicate how to style the selected element or elements. In this example, we have just one declaration, font-family: Arial;.

CSS selectors

The selector is the part of the CSS rule that comes before the {. CSS selectors tell the web browser what HTML elements a style should apply to.

When you select an element to apply a style to, it also applies that same style to every element inside the selected element.

CSS selectors have a number of different ways to select elements. Let's look at three of these while working with Douglas the JavaScript Robot:

- ✒ **Element selectors:** Take a look at the first two rules in the JavaScript robot CSS panel:

```
body {
    font-family: Arial;
}
p {
    font-size: 1em;
}
```

These are both examples of element selectors. Element selectors select HTML elements using the name of the element. To use an element selector, just type the name of the element you want to select. In these cases, we're selecting the body element (which uses <body> and </body> tags) and the p element (which uses <p> and </p> tags).

✔ **Class selectors:** Take a look now at the third CSS rule in the JavaScript Robot CSS pane:

```
.eye {
    background-color: blue;
    width: 20%;
    height: 20%;
    border-radius: 50%;
}
```

The class selector starts with a period (.), followed by the value of an HTML attribute named class. In this case, we're selecting all the elements that have class="eye". If you look in the HTML pane, you can see that there are two elements with class="eye". These are used to make Douglas's two eyes.

Class selectors are ideal for times when you need to apply the same style to multiple elements. In this case, the robot has two eyes, and the two eyes have several things in common (they're both blue and the same size, for example).

✔ **ID selectors:** ID selectors start with a hash symbol (#) and select elements based on the value of the element's ID attribute. For example, Douglas's left eye and right eye have separate ID attributes:

```
#righteye {
    position: absolute;
    left: 20%;
    top: 20%;
}
#lefteye {
    position: absolute;
    left: 60%;
    top: 20%;
}
```

ID selectors are useful when you need to select a single element in an HTML document.

Every ID attribute must be unique within a document.

If you look in the HTML pane, you can see that Douglas's left and right eyes, in addition to both having class attributes, also have unique ID attributes. We added these attributes so that we could position the eyes individually on Douglas's face.

CSS declarations

CSS declarations go inside declaration blocks following CSS selectors. Declarations are made up of two parts:

- **Property:** The property part of a declaration tells what should be modified. For example, you can change the color, width, or position of an element. The property must be followed by a colon (:).

- **Value:** The value tells how the property should be changed.

Each declaration must end with a semicolon (;). You can have as many declarations within a declaration block as you need to get the job done.

The declaration block for the elements with the eye class, for example, contains four declarations:

```
.eye {
    background-color:blue;
    width:20%;
    height:20%;
    border-radius: 50%;
}
```

CSS Properties Give You Style

CSS properties are what change the characteristics of elements. Douglas the JavaScript Robot's beautiful eye color, the size of his body and arms, the roundness of the corners of his head, and the position of his different parts are all determined by the values of properties.

Let's make some changes to Douglas's looks by modifying the values of some different CSS properties:

1. Find the CSS rule for the p element.

   It's currently the second rule in the CSS pane.

2. Change the value of the font-size property to 2.5em.

   The complete rule should now look like this:

   ```
   p {
      font-size: 2.5em;
   }
   ```

   There are several different ways to specify text sizes. The most commonly used ways are by using pixels (px), percent (%), or ems (em). When you use percent or ems, the font size of the selected element is set based on the font size of the parent element. For example 2.5em is two and a half times the font size of the selected element's parent. We cover percent and pixels in more detail later in this chapter.

3. Click the Run button to see the change in the Results pane.

   Douglas should now look like Figure 6-1.

4. Find the CSS rule for the body element.

5. Change the value of the body element to the following, paying attention to the use of quotes:

   ```
   "Comic Sans MS", cursive, sans-serif
   ```

   The complete CSS rule should now look like this:

   ```
   body {
      font-family: "Comic Sans MS", cursive, sans-serif;
   }
   ```

Figure 6-1: Douglas with a bold message.

6. Click the Run button to see the results.

Douglas now has interesting letters on his shirt, as shown in Figure 6-2.

Figure 6-2: Douglas, now with fun letters!

Next, let's change Douglas's eye color to match your eye color!

7. Find the CSS rule that contains Douglas's eye color.

   It currently looks like this:

   ```
   .eye {
       background-color:blue;
       width: 20%;
       height: 20%;
       border-radius: 50%;
   }
   ```

8. Change the value of the `background-color` property to your eye color.

   For example, if your eyes are brown, you would change it to the following:

   ```
   background-color: brown;
   ```

9. Click the Run button to see the results.

The color that Douglas's eyes change to when you use the word brown doesn't look very brown to us, and the color that is used when you try to make Douglas's eyes green also isn't a color that anyone's eyes are likely to be. To get a more precise color, you can use another one of the CSS color names (see Chapter 4) or create your own custom color by using hexadecimal notation.

Using CSS colors

CSS colors describe the millions of possible colors that a web browser can display by using different combinations of red, green, and blue.

Here's an example of a CSS color in hexadecimal notation:

```
#9BE344
```

Let's take a closer look at this code.

The hash symbol (#) indicates that this is a hexadecimal code. After that, the first and second symbols (9B) indicate the shade of red to blend into the new color, the third and fourth symbols (E3) indicate the shade of green to blend in, and the fifth and sixth symbols (44) indicate the amount of blue. When these three parts are blended, the color you end up with is a nice green color.

At this point, you're probably wondering why hexadecimal notation combines letters and numbers. The answer is pretty simple: to get more possibilities.

Hexadecimal notation is how a monster with 16 fingers might count. For example, people have ten fingers, so we have ten different digits that we use for counting: 0, 1, 2, 3, 4, 5, 6, 7, 8, and 9.

If you had 16 fingers, however, you would need to invent new symbols to represent the additional fingers. Computers frequently count by 8 or 16 because bytes are made up of 8 digits, or bits. You could say that computers are like creatures with 16 fingers.

Instead of inventing new symbols, computers use letters for the digits after 9. So, A in hexadecimal is equivalent to 10, B is the same as 11, C is the same as 12, D is the same as 13, E is the same as 14, and F is the same as 15.

Two-digit hexadecimal codes start with 00, which is equivalent to 0, and end with FF, which is equivalent to 255.

When we say that the shade of red should be 00, we mean that it should have no red at all. If we say that it should be 01, we mean that it should have only the smallest amount of red (which probably wouldn't even be noticeable) When we say that the shade of red should be FF, we mean that it should be pure red.

Instead of guessing how much of each color to blend in, you can use an online tool such as the one at www.colorpicker.com to visually choose your colors.

Resizing elements with CSS

Every element in an HTML document is a rectangle. Even if an element looks like a circle (like Douglas's eyes), it's actually treated like a rectangle surrounding the circle. Because everything is a rectangle, you can change the size of elements with CSS by adjusting their width and height.

When we measure the width and height of things in the real world, we use units of measurement such as inches, centimeters, or meters. When we measure things in the CSS world, we have several different units of measurement. These include px (pixels) and % (percent):

- **Pixels:** The pixel is the smallest dot that can be displayed in your web browser. When you specify widths and heights using pixels, you tell the browser exactly how many pixels wide and tall an element should be. The problem with using pixels for measurements is that it always displays things the same size — even if the user's browser window is very large or very small.

- **Percent:** When you specify widths and heights with percent, you're telling the browser to make the element a certain percentage of the size of the element's parent.

We've specified all of Douglas's measurements using percent. This is beneficial because it means that regardless of whether you're looking at Douglas on a mobile phone or on the Jumbotron in Times Square, his size will adapt to fit the screen. To see the magic of relative sizing in action, drag the pane borders in JSFiddle to make the Result pane larger or smaller. Notice how Douglas changes size along with the size of the window.

You may have heard the term *responsive design*. Responsive design aims to create web content that is flexible and responds to the size of the user's screen. The way we specified Douglas's size is an example of responsive design.

Let's make a couple changes to some of Douglas's parts:

1. Find the CSS rule for the eye class.

2. Change the width to 30% and the height to 30%.

   You'll notice that Douglas's eyes get larger. But they're also no longer centered on his face, as shown in Figure 6-3! We'll fix that in a little bit.

Figure 6-3: Douglas's big eyes are off center.

3. Find the CSS rule for the arm class.

```
.arm {
    background-color: #cacaca;
    position: absolute;
    top: 35%;
    width: 5%;
    height: 40%;
}
```

The .arm CSS rule controls the color and size of both arms.

The .arm rule also controls the distance of the arms from the top of the window, as you'll learn about in the next section.

4. Change the width of the arms to 3% and then click Run to give Douglas skinny arms.

5. Find the CSS rule for Douglas's left arm.

6. Add properties to change the width to be larger than the height.

   For example:

```
#leftarm {
    position: absolute;
    left: 70%;
    width: 27%;
    height: 5%;
}
```

   Click run to see the change. Douglas is now pointing off screen, as you can see in Figure 6-4.

Figure 6-4: Douglas is pointing!

In the last step, you added a width and height to a rule with an ID selector, even though the selected element already had a width and height applied using a class selector.

Even though there was already a width and height for the left arm, the arm took on the new width and height from the rule with the ID selector.

This is an example of what we call *cascading* (and we finally learn where CSS gets its name!).

Understanding cascading

A robot's left arm can only be one width and height. So, what happens when two different CSS rules try to set the width and height of the arm separately? What happens is that the browser holds a competition between the two CSS rules.

The browser looks at factors such as which CSS rule was set last and which one is more specific to determine which width and height will actually be used.

In this cascading competition, ID attributes win over class attributes because they're unique to a single element and, therefore, more specific than class attributes.

Positioning elements with CSS

In addition to giving you the ability to change colors and how elements appear in a browser, CSS also lets you change where on screen an element will appear. Changing the place where an element will appear is called *positioning* an element.

Let's change the position of some of Douglas's parts:

1. Find the CSS rule that controls Douglas's right eye.

```
#righteye {
    position: absolute;
    left: 20%;
    top: 20%;
}
```

The first property, `position`, tells the browser how to interpret the specific location properties (such as `top` and `left`). When you use absolute positioning, the selected element (the eye in this case) can be positioned anywhere in the head without your needing to worry about whether another element in the head will push it out of the way. If two absolutely positioned elements are positioned in the same place, they'll simply overlap.

The right eye is set to show up 20% below (of the height of the head) from the top edge of the head element and 20% (of the width of the head) to the right of the left edge of the head.

2. Move the right eye to the left and up by changing the value of both `left` and `top` to smaller percentages.

For example:

```
#righteye {
    position: absolute;
    left: 10%;
    top: 10%;
}
```

Click Run to see the results, as shown in Figure 6-5.

Figure 6-5: Douglas raising his right eye.

Customize Your Own JavaScript Robot!

Now it's your turn! Using what you've learned in this chapter, make as many changes to Douglas as you like. Try changing colors, positions, and sizes of elements to make him look exactly like you want him to look!

Share your customized version of Douglas with us on Twitter or Facebook! We're looking forward to seeing what you come up with!

Building an Animated Robot

HTML, CSS, and JavaScript are a great team. Each piece works with the other two to make great things happen in web browsers.

In this chapter, we put all the pieces together to make Douglas the JavaScript Robot dance!

Changing CSS with JavaScript

Just as you can use JavaScript to change the HTML in a web page, you can also use it to change CSS styles. The process is very similar.

The first step is to select the element you want to apply or change a style on. In Chapter 5, we show you how to do this using `getElementById`. For example, to select Douglas's left eye, you can use the following code:

```
document.getElementById("lefteye")
```

Once you've selected an element, you can change its style by attaching the `style` property to the selector, followed by the style you want to change. To change the color of the left eye, you can use this JavaScript:

```
document.getElementById("lefteye").style.backgroundColor =
            "purple";
```

Do you notice anything strange about this code, compared to how you changed the background color with CSS? When changing styles with JavaScript, there are two rules:

- When the CSS property is just one word, such as `margin` or `border`, you can use the same CSS name to change the style in JavaScript.

- If the CSS property has dashes (-), the CSS property name gets converted to camelCase. So, `background-color` gets changed to `backgroundColor`.

Here are some examples of CSS properties, and how each property is spelled in JavaScript:

CSS Property	JavaScript Style Property
background-color	backgroundColor
border-radius	borderRadius
font-family	fontFamily

CSS Property	JavaScript Style Property
margin	margin
font-size	fontSize
border-width	borderWidth
text-align	textAlign
color	color

JavaScript cares a lot about capitalization. The capital letters in the JavaScript style properties need to be there in order for the properties to work.

Modifying Douglas with JavaScript

Modifying CSS using JavaScript makes it possible for the look and position of elements to change in response to user input.

We'll make Douglas dance in a little bit, but let's get some practice with making changes to him first:

1. Go to the public dashboard at `http://jsfiddle.net/user/forkids/fiddles`, find the program called Chapter 7: Start, and open it.

   You see the Douglas Robot project pretty much as we left it at the end of Chapter 6, as shown in Figure 7-1.

2. Click the Fork button to create a copy of this program in your own JSFiddle account.

3. Type the following into the JavaScript pane to change Douglas's left eye color:

   ```
   document.getElementById("lefteye").style.backgroundColor =
               "purple";
   ```

4. Click Run to see the result.

   Douglas's left eye will change to purple, as shown in Figure 7-2.

Figure 7-1: Douglas, the unanimated JavaScript robot.

Figure 7-2: Douglas's left eye is now purple.

5. Press Return (Mac) or Enter (Windows) to start a new line in the JavaScript panel and then type the following:

```
document.getElementById("head").style.transform =
        "rotate(15deg)";
```

6. Click Run to see the result.

Douglas now is tilting his head to his left. He looks ready to dance (see Figure 7-3)!

Figure 7-3: Douglas is ready to dance!

7. Open the Fiddle Options in the left menu and give your program a new name.

8. Click Update and then click Set as Base to save your program to your public dashboard.

Experimenting with Douglas

There are countless possibilities for customizing Douglas using JavaScript's style properties. To get started experimenting with a few, try adding each of the following statements to the JavaScript pane and then running them:

```
// Put a 2-pixel-wide, solid black border around his body.
document.getElementById("body").style.border = "2px black
        solid";

// Round the corners of his mouth.
document.getElementById("mouth").style.borderRadius = "4px";
```

```
// Put yellow dots around his right eye.
document.getElementById("righteye").style.border =
         "4px yellow dotted";

// Change his left arm's color.
document.getElementById("leftarm").style.backgroundColor =
         "#FF00FF";

// Change the text color.
document.getElementById("body").style.color = "#FF0000";

// Give Douglas hair.
document.getElementById("head").style.borderTop =
         "5px black solid";
```

Now it's your turn. Can you figure out how to make each of the following changes using JavaScript?

✔ Tilt Douglas's head to the other side.

✔ Make Douglas's nose round.

✔ Make Douglas's right arm green.

✔ Make Douglas's lips pink.

If you need help with any of these, visit our public dashboard on JSFiddle and look for the program named Chapter 7: Changing CSS with JS.

Keep in mind that JavaScript is very sensitive. If you have a typo, or forget a period, or spell `getElementById` wrong anywhere in the JavaScript pane, all the lines of JavaScript will fail to run, not just the statement where you made the mistake.

Make Douglas Dance!

Now that you know how to change CSS using JavaScript, let's put that knowledge to good use and make Douglas more animated!

1. With the latest version of your Robot Style program open in JSFiddle (or the Chapter 7: Start fiddle from our public dashboard), press the Fork button in JSFiddle.

2. Open Fiddle Options in the left menu and change the name of the fiddle to Animated Robot.

3. Click Update to save your work.

   Now you have a new fiddle for the new and improved dancing Douglas, and you can still get to the previous, nondancing, Douglas from your public dashboard.

Douglas isn't the greatest dancer, but he does have a few moves that he's very proud of. The first is one he calls the "eye bounce." His eye makes a quick movement upward and then floats back into place. Trust us, when he does it to the beat, it's almost hypnotic.

Figure 7-4 shows Douglas in the middle of one of his signature eye bounces.

In our program, you're going to control Douglas's dancing by clicking his different parts to animate them. We start with programming his right eye to bounce when you click it.

Figure 7-4: Douglas doing the eye bounce.

1. In the JavaScript pane, type the following statement:

```
var rightEye = document.getElementById("righteye");
```

This variable declaration creates a shortcut for us to refer to the right eye. Now that this has been created, every time you need to refer to Douglas's right eye in the rest of the program, you can just use the variable named `rightEye`.

2. Tell JavaScript to listen for mouse clicks on the right eye with this statement:

```
rightEye.addEventListener("click", moveUpDown);
```

Handling events

Event listeners are a way to tell JavaScript to watch an element for something to happen to it, and then to do something (handle it) when the event happens.

In JavaScript, we use a method called `addEventListener` to tell programs what to do when events happen. To listen for and handle events, you need three parts:

✏ **The event:** Whenever something happens in a web browser, it's called an *event*. Examples of events include clicking the mouse, pressing a key, dragging and dropping, hovering your mouse over something, and selecting text.

Events aren't just the things that people do with web browsers. Other events happen without your doing anything at all. These include the page loading, elements displaying, errors happening in the code, and animations completing. Here are the most common events that happen in a web browser.

- `click`: The user clicks the mouse.

- `submit`: A form is submitted.

- `drag`: An element is being dragged.

- `drop`: An element has been dropped after being dragged.

- copy: The user has copied content.

- paste: The user pastes content.

- mouseover: The mouse passes over an element.

- load: The page loads.

To listen for events, put the name of the event you want to listen for in quotes inside the addEventListener method. For example:

```
target.addEventListener("click", listener)
```

✔ **The event target:** The next step in creating an event handler is to attach the addEventListener method to an object. For example, to listen for the click event on Douglas's right eye, you would use the following:

```
rightEye.addEventListener("click", listener);
```

The element that JavaScript will listen for events on is called the event target. In this case, rightEye (which is a variable you created to stand for the value document.getElementBy Id("righteye") is the event target.

✔ **The listener:** The third part of an addEventListener statement is the actual listener. This is the object that should be notified when the event happens.

In the case of Douglas, we want to notify a function that we're going to write and that we're going to call moveUpDown. This function will serve the purpose of moving Douglas's eye up and down.

```
rightEye.addEventListener("click", moveUpDown);
```

The format of a typical event handler is as follows:

```
target.addEventListener("event", listener);
```

Now that you know how `addEventListener` works, let's get back to Douglas the JavaScript Robot and create the listener that we want to activate when someone clicks his eye.

Writing a listener

So far, the JavaScript pane should contain the following code:

```
var rightEye = document.getElementById("righteye");
rightEye.addEventListener("click", moveUpDown);
```

If you run your program now, you'll find that it doesn't do anything at all. That's because we haven't yet created the listener.

A listener is a *function,* or a smaller program within the larger JavaScript program. Whenever the event happens that the listener is attached to, the listener function runs.

The listener for the eye bounce animation will be called `moveUpDown`. Follow these steps to create the `moveUpDown` listener function.

1. After the last line of code in the JavaScript pane, press Return or Enter a couple times to insert some white space.

2. Type the following to start creating the listener:

```
function moveUpDown(e) {
```

This code starts your function and gives it a name. Note the `e` between the parentheses. When the function is called by the `addEventListener` function, the `e` will contain some information about the event that just happened, which we can use inside of the function. More on this in a moment!

3. Press Return or Enter after the open curly bracket ({) and type the rest of the function:

```
var robotPart = e.target;
var top = 0;

var id = setInterval(frame, 10) // draw every 10ms
```

```
function frame() {
  robotPart.style.top = top + '%';
  top++;
  if (top === 20){
    clearInterval(id);
  }
}


}
```

This may look complicated, but it's actually fairly simple. Before we explain, let's test it out to make sure it works.

4. Click Run.

   If you entered everything correctly, you should now be able to click Douglas's right eye and see it bounce, as shown in Figure 7-5.

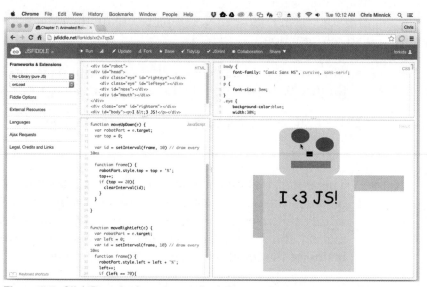

Figure 7-5: Click Douglas's eye to make it bounce.

If your program isn't working correctly, double-check your code. It should be exactly the same as Listing 7-1.

Listing 7-1   **The Code Required in the JavaScript Pane to Enable the Eye Bounce**

```
var rightEye = document.getElementById("righteye");
rightEye.addEventListener("click", moveUpDown);

function moveUpDown(e) {
  var robotPart = e.target;
  var top = 0;

  var id = setInterval(frame, 10) // draw every 10ms

  function frame() {
    robotPart.style.top = top + '%';
    top++;
    if (top === 20){
      clearInterval(id);
    }
  }
}
```

If you entered everything correctly and Douglas's eye does the bounce when you click it, read on to find out how it all works!

Creating animations with JavaScript

Computer animation, like film and video animation, is a trick. The trick relies on showing a series of pictures in a quick enough succession that the images appear to move.

Each picture in an animation is called a *frame.* The way Douglas's eye bounce animation works is that it shows his eye in a slightly different place, every 10 milliseconds (one-tenth of a second), starting with the position of the eye being at the top of the head, and ending with it at 20 percent from the top of the head.

Figure 7-6 shows the position of the eye at various points during the animation.

Figure 7-6: Douglas's eye at various points in the animation.

Now let's step through the code and see how this effect is created in JavaScript. We'll start with the first line after the function declaration:

```
var robotPart = e.target;
```

This statement uses the event object (that comes automatically from the addEventListener method) to find out what part of the robot (what element) was clicked on. It stores the information about that element (the rightEye in this case) in a new variable called robotPart.

This statement creates a new variable called top and gives it a value of 0:

```
var top = 0;
```

This top variable is what we'll use to position the eye in each frame of the animation.

The following line uses a command called setInterval to make the animation magic happen:

```
var id = setInterval(frame, 10); // draw every 10ms
```

The setInterval command will run the function listed first in the parentheses, and will do it on a schedule determined by the number in the parentheses.

The number is a number of milliseconds (thousandths of a second) to wait before doing the thing again. So, 1,000 milliseconds equal a second. The larger this number is, the slower the animation will go, and vice versa.

Here we're creating a new function (or mini-program) that is run by the `setInterval` command and that will handle the task of creating each new animation frame:

```
function frame() {
```

Here, we set the value of `top` to the value of our top variable and add % at the end, for the element that was clicked:

```
robotPart.style.top = top + '%';
```

So, when you first click the eye, top will be set to 0 percent, which will put it at the very top of Douglas's head.

The following line increases the value of top by 1 using a thing called the *increment operator:*

```
top++;
```

We cover the increment operator in more detail in Chapter 9.

Here, we check whether the final frame of the animation has been reached, by seeing if `top` is equal to 20:

```
if (top === 20){
```

If `top` is equal to 20, the next command is run.

The `clearInterval` statement ends the animation:

```
clearInterval(id);
```

Finally, we just clean everything up by closing all the curly brackets that we opened:

```
        }
    }
}
```

Animating another element

Now that we've written the moveUpDown function to animate one eye, animating the other eye is a simple matter of adding another event listener.

1. Click Update to save your work so far.

2. Insert the following new variable declaration just below the one for rightEye:

```
var leftEye = document.getElementById("lefteye");
```

3. Insert the following new event handler just below the rightEye one:

```
leftEye.addEventListener("click", moveUpDown);
```

4. Click Run.

Now, clicking either the left or right eye will cause the moveUpDown animation to happen on the clicked element.

Adding a second animation function

Douglas isn't a one-trick robot. He has at least one more dance move besides the eye bounce. He calls this one the "arm sweep." This classic move involves a smooth movement of the left arm from right to left across Douglas's body as his eyes stare straight ahead.

To create the arm sweep animation, we'll add a second listener function, based on the moveUpDown function, but we'll modify it slightly in order to animate the arm from right to left rather than from top to bottom.

1. Create a new variable, just under the two other variables, to represent the left arm:

```
var leftArm = document.getElementById("leftarm");
```

2. Write a new event handler, underneath the two other event handlers.

```
leftArm.addEventListener("click", moveRightLeft);
```

3. Select the moveUpDown function and press ⌘ +C (Mac) or Ctrl+C (Windows) to copy it.

4. Paste a copy of the moveUpDown function below the existing moveUpDown function.

Now, we'll modify the copy of moveUpDown() to create the new moveRightLeft function.

1. Change the name of the function from moveUpDown to moveRightLeft.

```
function moveRightLeft(e) {
```

2. Change the second line in the function body to the following:

```
var left = 0;
```

3. Change the first line inside of the frame function to the following:

```
robotPart.style.left = left + '%';
```

4. Change the second line of the frame function to the following:

```
left++:
```

5. Change the third line of the frame function to the following:

```
if (left === 70){
```

When you're finished with the changes, your new moveRight Left function should match the following code in Listing 7-2.

Listing 7-2 **The Finished moveRightLeft Function**

```
function moveRightLeft(e) {
  var robotPart = e.target;
  var left = 0;
  var id = setInterval(frame, 10) // draw every 10ms
  function frame() {
    robotPart.style.left = left + '%';
    left++;
    if (left === 70){
      clearInterval(id);
    }
  }
}
```

To save your work and test out the new animation, press Update. When you click Douglas's left arm now, you'll see the `moveRightLeft` animation work, as shown in Figure 7-7.

Figure 7-7: Douglas performs the arm sweep move.

The completed code in the JavaScript pane should now match Listing 7-3.

Listing 7-3 The JavaScript Required to Implement Both of Douglas's Dance Moves

```javascript
var rightEye = document.getElementById("righteye");
var leftEye = document.getElementById("lefteye");
var leftArm = document.getElementById("leftarm");

rightEye.addEventListener("click", moveUpDown);
leftEye.addEventListener("click", moveUpDown);
leftArm.addEventListener("click", moveRightLeft);

function moveUpDown(e) {
  var robotPart = e.target;
  var top = 0;
  var id = setInterval(frame, 10) // draw every 10ms
  function frame() {
    robotPart.style.top = top + '%';
    top++;
    if (top === 20){
      clearInterval(id);
    }
  }
}


function moveRightLeft(e) {
  var robotPart = e.target;
  var left = 0;
  var id = setInterval(frame, 10) // draw every 10ms
  function frame() {
    robotPart.style.left = left + '%';
    left++;
    if (left === 70){
      clearInterval(id);
    }
  }
}
```

Now it's your turn to have some fun making Douglas dance! Start out by turning on some music and clicking his eyes and arm to the beat! Next, try adding some new event handlers to animate different parts of Douglas, such has his nose, his mouth, or his right arm!

Part III
Getting Operations

```html
1  <div id="car">                         HTML
2      This <span id="modelyear"></span>
   dream car can be yours for just:
   $<span id="pricetag"></span>
3      <div id="body">
4      </div>
5      <div id="frontwheel"></div>
6      <div id="backwheel"></div>
7  </div>
```

```css
1  #car {                                  CSS
2      font-family: Arial;
3  }
4  #body {
5      position: absolute;
6      top: 50px;
7      width: 80%;
8      height: 100px;
9      background-color: #000000;
```

```javascript
1  var dreamCar = {                  JavaScript
2      make: "Oldsmobile",
3      model: "98",
4      color: "brown",
5      year: 1983,
6      bodyStyle: "Luxury Car",
7      price: 4500
8  };
9  document.getElementById("pricetag")
10     .innerHTML = dreamCar.price;
11
12 document.getElementById("modelyear")
13     .innerHTML = dreamCar.year;
14
15 document.getElementById("body")
16     .style.backgroundColor =
   dreamCar.color;
17
18 document.getElementById("body")
19     .innerHTML = dreamCar.make + " " +
   dreamCar.model;
20
21
```

This 1983 dream car can be yours for just: $4500

Oldsmobile 98

In this part . . .

■ Building Your Dream Car with Operands......... 125

■ Putting It Together with Operators 136

■ Creating Your Own JavaScript Word Game 153

For tips on naming JavaScript variables, go to
www.dummies.com/extras/
javascriptforkids.

Building Your Dream Car with Operands

When you speak or write in a human language, you typically string together nouns and verbs to create action. You might then spice things up with adjectives, adverbs, pronouns, conjunctions, prepositions, and interjections. However, the real work of a sentence is done by the nouns and verbs.

Forming JavaScript sentences is called *writing statements.* Statements are mostly made up of operands (which are like nouns) and operators (which are like verbs).

In this chapter, you learn about the different types of operands and you see examples of how to work with operands in JavaScript programs.

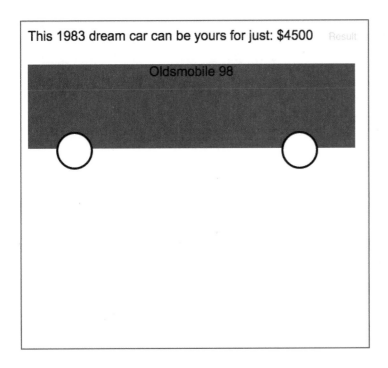

This 1983 dream car can be yours for just: $4500   Result

Oldsmobile 98

Knowing Your Operands

An expression in JavaScript is any valid piece of code that resolves to a value.

When we say that an expression "resolves to a value," what we mean is that when everything the computer needs to do is done, some sort of value is produced. For example,

- The expression 1 + 1 "resolves to" 2. Another way to say the same thing is that it has the value of 2.

- The expression x = 7 is a different kind of expression. It assigns its value (7) to the variable called x.

Expressions are made up of operands (such as the number 1 or the variable x) and operators (such as = or +). Operands can be any of the JavaScript data types that we talk about in Chapter 3, as well as objects or arrays.

In this chapter, we show you how to create and use your own objects. We show you how to create and use arrays in Chapter 11.

Instead of simply explaining the different types of possible data types that operands can use, let's play a game. We're going to list some valid JavaScript operands, and you'll determine which type of data each operand is.

We'll give you all the answers at first, until you get the hang of it. After that, we'll still give you all the answers, but we'll hide them a little better. Here we go!

For each of the following operands, tell us whether it's a number, a string, or a Boolean:

- **100:** This is, quite clearly, a number, because it's not surrounded by quotes and it's made entirely of numbers.

- **"Hello JavaScript World!":** This is a string, because it's surrounded by quotes.

✔ **false:** This is a Boolean, because it's true or false and it's not surrounded by quotes.

✔ **"true":** This is a string, because, even though it contains the word *true* (which would seem to make it a Boolean), the word is surrounded by quotes (which makes it a string).

Now it's your turn. For each of the following operands, decide whether it's a number, a string, or a Boolean:

✔ 187

✔ "007"

✔ "Number 9"

✔ true

✔ 86

✔ "It's 5 o'clock somewhere"

How do you think you did? Here are the answers:

✔ 187 is a number.

✔ "007" is a string.

✔ "Number 9" is a string.

✔ true is a Boolean.

✔ 86 is a number.

✔ "It's 5 o'clock somewhere" is a string.

Operands aren't always literal values. More often, in fact, programmers assign values to variables and use those variables as operands. Here are some statements that assign values to variables. For each of these, figure out the data type of the operand (number, string, or Boolean):

✔ distance = 3000

✔ distance = 800 * 4

✔ doTheMath = 7 + 8 + 36 + 18 + 12

✔ countrySong = "mama" + "truck" + "train" + "rain"

If you said that the first three of these are numbers and the last is a string, you got it right!

If you don't believe us, try the following exercise to find out for yourself!

1. Open the JavaScript console in Chrome by pressing ⌘+Option+J (Mac) or Ctrl+Shift+J (Windows).

   The JavaScript Console appears, as shown in Figure 8-1.

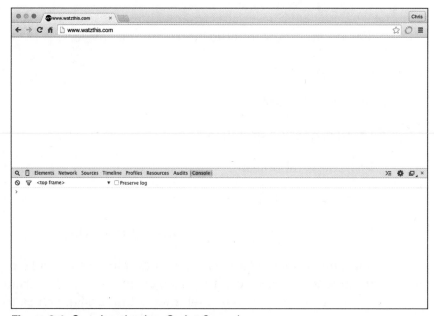

Figure 8-1: Opening the JavaScript Console.

2. Use the `typeof` command to find out the data type of a number.

   For example, type this:

   ```
   typeof 8
   ```

   The JavaScript Console returns `"number"`, as shown in Figure 8-2.

Figure 8-2: Finding out the type of an operand.

3. Type the following to create a variable and use an expression to set its value:

   ```
   var doTheMath = 7 + 8 + 36 + 18 + 12
   ```

   The console returns `undefined`, letting you know that it has done its job.

4. Find out the type of your new variable using the `typeof` command.

   ```
   typeof doTheMath
   ```

   The result, once again, is `"number"`.

5. Find out the type of a string with the following expression:

```
typeof "the cat's favorite toy"
```

The result, of course, is `"string"`.

6. Try finding the type of a word that's not in quotes, like this:

```
typeof automobile
```

The result of this expression will be `"undefined"`. What's happening here is that JavaScript treats a word that's not in quotes as if it's a variable. Because we haven't defined a variable named `automobile`, the result of asking for the type of the `automobile` variable is `"undefined"`.

Working with Objects

In addition to the basic data types (string, number, and Boolean), operands in JavaScript can also be of the object type. As we explain in Chapter 5, JavaScript objects can have *properties* (things that describe them) and *methods* (things that they can do).

Now, we're going to show you how to create your own objects! To create an object, start with the `var` keyword, just as you do to create any variable, followed by an equal sign (=):

```
var myObject =
```

After the equal sign is where things get a little different. When you create an object, you always start with curly braces ({ and }):

```
var myObject = {};
```

Inside the curly braces, you can put multiple properties and methods. Each property or method of an object starts with a name (on the left), followed by a colon (:), followed by a value. If an object contains multiple properties or methods, they're separated by commas.

Let's practice making some objects and looking at their values in JSFiddle:

1. Go to `http://jsfiddle.net` in your web browser.

   You should now have a blank fiddle, meaning that all four of the panes on the screen (HTML, CSS, JavaScript, and Result) are blank.

2. Enter the following into the JavaScript pane to create a `dreamCar` object:

   ```
   var dreamCar = {
       make: "Oldsmobile",
       model: "98",
       color: "brown",
       year: 1983,
       bodyStyle: "Luxury Car",
       price: 4500
   }
   ```

   Feel free to customize your dream car in any way that you want!

   Notice that, in an object, it's perfectly fine to mix properties with different data types. For example, in the `dreamCar` object, the `make`, `model`, `color`, and `bodyStyle` properties are all strings, and the year and price are numbers.

3. Type the following into the JavaScript pane after the object definition in order to find out the type of the `dreamCar` object:

   ```
   alert("The type of dreamCar is: " + typeof dreamCar);
   ```

4. Click Run.

   An alert appears, showing you that your `dreamCar` is an object, as shown in Figure 8-3.

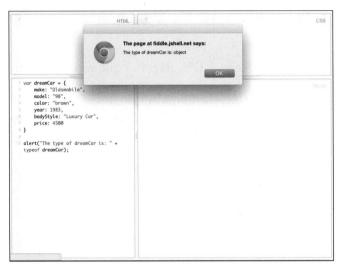

Figure 8-3: Your dream car is an object.

Configuring Your Dream Car

Enough talk! Let's configure our dream car and get this baby on the road!

The first step in building any car is to create the frame. We'll do that with HTML.

1. Enter the following HTML into the HTML pane in JSFiddle:

```
<div id="car">
    This <span id="modelyear"></span> dream car can be yours for
            just: $<span id="pricetag"></span>
    <div id="body">
    </div>
    <div id="frontwheel"></div>
    <div id="backwheel"></div>
</div>
```

This HTML simply creates a basic structure for our car — plus the price tag, of course. In the next step, we give the car some style.

2. Enter the following into the CSS pane:

```
#car {
  font-family: Arial;
}
#body {
    position: absolute;
    top: 50px;
    width: 80%;
    height: 100px;
    background-color: #000000;
    text-align: center;
}
#backwheel {
    position: absolute;
    left: 10%;
    top: 130px;
    background-color: #ffffff;
    border: 3px solid black;
    border-radius: 50%;
    width: 40px;
    height: 40px;
}
#frontwheel {
    position: absolute;
    left: 55%;
    top: 130px;
    background-color: #ffffff;
    border: 3px solid black;
    border-radius: 50%;
    width: 40px;
    height: 40px;
}
```

Great! We've built and styled a generic car, complete with a body, a price tag, and wheels.

3. Click Run to see where we're at so far.

The generic car design appears in the Result pane, as shown in Figure 8-4.

This dream car can be yours for just: $ Result

Figure 8-4: A generic car.

Now, let's get down to the business of customizing our car with JavaScript!

1. Create your `dreamCar` object in the JavaScript pane.

   Here's ours:

   ```
   var dreamCar = {
       make: "Oldsmobile",
       model: "98",
       color: "brown",
       year: 1983,
       bodyStyle: "Luxury Car",
       price: 4500
   };
   ```

2. Write a statement to update the price of the car when the program runs:

   ```
   document.getElementById("pricetag").innerHTML = dreamCar.price;
   ```

3. Write a statement to update the model year on the price tag:

```
document.getElementById("modelyear").innerHTML = dreamCar.year;
```

4. Write a statement to update the color of the car:

```
document.getElementById("body").style.backgroundColor = dreamCar.
    color;
```

5. Write a statement to write out the make and model of the car on the side of the car:

```
document.getElementById("body").innerHTML = dreamCar.make + " " +
    dreamCar.model;
```

Now, click Run to see your amazing new car! Ours is shown in Figure 8-5.

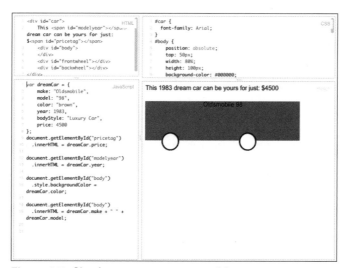

Figure 8-5: Check out our sweet new ride.

Try customizing your car with different settings, and then run the program to see how the properties of an object can be used to change the output of a program or the CSS styles of a web page.

Putting It Together with Operators

An operator is a symbol that performs a task (an operation) using operands. In this chapter, you learn about the different types of operators you can work with in JavaScript.

JavaScript has an operator for every need and a couple operators that you'll probably never need. Instead of simply listing all the operators, let's write a program that lets you choose operators and enter in operands and then see the results.

The program will be a Super-Calculator — it can work with words and letters as well as numbers.

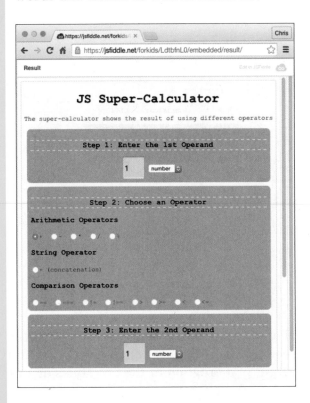

Introducing the Super-Calculator

You've never seen a calculator like this before. Friends, this calculator can do your everyday arithmetic — it can add, subtract, multiply, and even divide. But wait, there's more! It can also take any two numbers — that's right, ANY TWO NUMBERS — and tell you how much is left over when you divide one by the other. We call that amazing feature a modulo operation. Get your modulo operation done right here! Free!

But that's not all! This here Super-Calculator can take words and stick them together! Let's say you have the word *Java* and you have the word *Script* and you wanted to somehow glue them together. Impossible, you say? Hard to believe? Not with the Super-Calculator!

The Super-Calculator gives you the power to glue words together — heck, you can even glue entire sentences — using the *concatenation* operator. Don't let all the syllables scare you off. Concatenation is the best invention since socks, and the operator looks exactly like the operator for addition (a plus sign). How simple is that? Simply type in the first word, choose the concatenation operator, type in the second word and — BLAMMO! — you're concatenating like a pro.

If you order now, we'll also include the full range of comparison operators at no cost to you! Comparison operators take any two values — let's say 3 and 8 — and tell you if they're the same. If you want to know if one is bigger or if one is smaller, we've got an operation for that, too! And, talk about simple — the result of a comparison is always either true or false. No need to bother with other results like "kinda" or "almost" when you're comparing!

How does this amazing Super-Calculator work? How can you get one? We're about to tell you, and your world will never be the same again!

Forking the Super-Calculator

Follow these steps to open the Super-Calculator and to make your own version of it:

1. Open your web browser and log in at `http://jsfiddle.net`.

2. Go to our public dashboard at `http://jsfiddle.net/user/forkids/fiddles` and locate the program called Chapter 9 – Super-Calculator, or go directly to the Super-Calculator at `http://jsfiddle.net/forkids/LdtbfnL0`.

   The Super-Calculator fiddle opens, as shown in Figure 9-1.

3. Click the Fork button in the top menu to make a copy of the Super-Calculator in your own JSFiddle account.

4. Use the Fiddle Options in the left menu to change the name of your Super-Calculator to (Your Name)'s Super-Calculator.

5. Click Update in the top menu, and then click Set as Base.

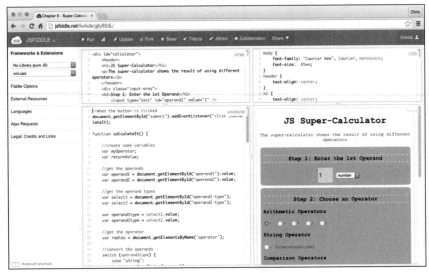

Figure 9-1: The JS Super-Calculator.

Now you have your own version of the Super-Calculator. You're ready to start learning how it works and using it to learn about operators!

Using the Super-Calculator

The Super-Calculator allows you to see the result of using different operators. It features two operand inputs, each with a drop-down menu where you can select the type of data you entered, and radio buttons for selecting a single operator to use in an operation involving those two operands.

Radio button is the name that HTML uses to refer to circular input buttons that can be grouped together. They're different from check boxes in that you can only select one option in a group of radio buttons, but you can select multiple options in a group of check boxes. We suspect they're called radio buttons because they work in the same way as car radio station selection buttons. Pressing one of them sets the station to that choice and deselects the others.

To get started with the Super-Calculator, take a look at the settings that are in the Result window when you first open it.

The input area at the top, shown in Figure 9-2, contains a single value, the number 1. The Data Type drop-down menu is set to number.

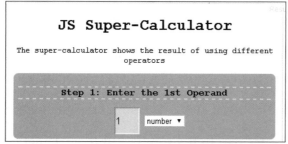

Figure 9-2: The default value of the first operand is the number 1.

Under the input area for the first operand is where you select an operator. The operators are divided into three groups: arithmetic operators, string operators, and comparison operators. We take a more in-depth look at each of these a little later in this chapter. For now, notice that the first operator in the group of arithmetic operators, +, is selected, as shown in Figure 9-3. This is the addition operator, of course.

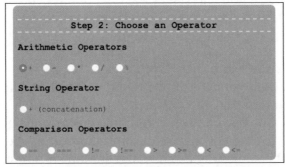

Figure 9-3: The addition operator is selected by default.

Underneath the operator choice area is the input area for the second operand. By default, this is set to the number 1 as well, as shown in Figure 9-4.

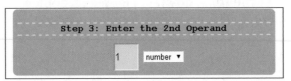

Figure 9-4: The second operand is set to the number 1.

So, putting it together, the default operation for the Super-Calculator is the world's most basic math problem: 1 + 1.

Click the Operate button at the bottom of the calculator.

The operation specified in the top part of the calculator and the return value of that operation (the result, in other words) will display in the Output section of the screen, as shown in Figure 9-5.

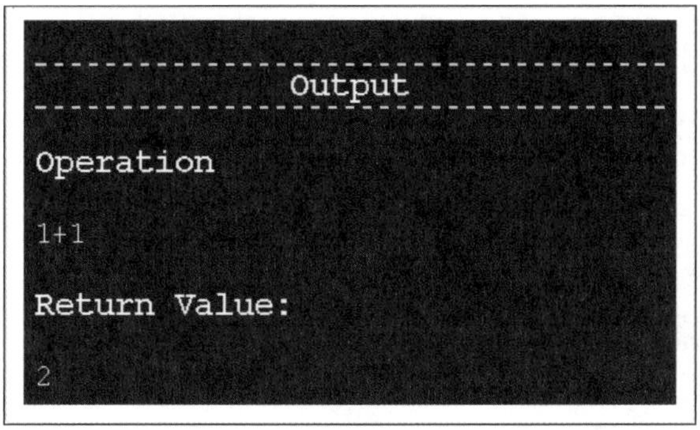

Figure 9-5: The return value of the operation displays in the Output area.

Of course, you already knew the answer to that operation! Right now you may be thinking that this Super-Calculator isn't so super after all. Not so fast! Move on to the next section to really see the power of the Super-Calculator!

Super-calculating with strings and arithmetic operators

Now let's try some operations that, while still simple (because they only involve two operands), will show you some interesting things about JavaScript.

1. Leave the values of the operands set to their default (1 and 1), but select the string operator, +, and change the data types for each operand to string.

   Now, when you click the Operate button, you see that the result is 11, as shown in Figure 9-6.

2. Leave the operator set to the concatenation operator, and leave the data types set to string. Change the first operand value to "Java" and the second operand to "Script".

   The result of concatenating "Java" and "Script" is shown in Figure 9-7.

Output
Operation
"1"+"1"
Return Value:
11

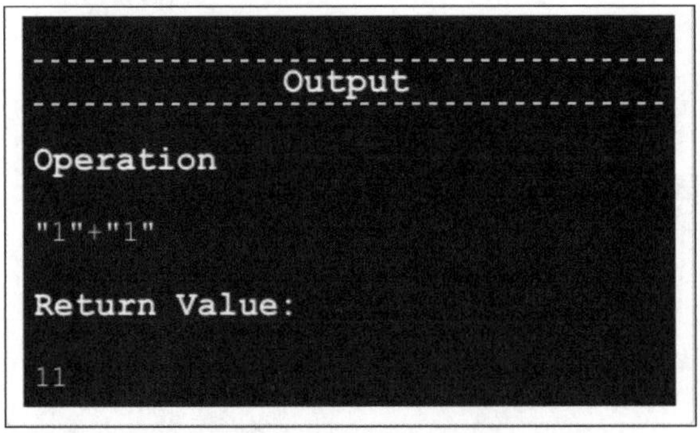

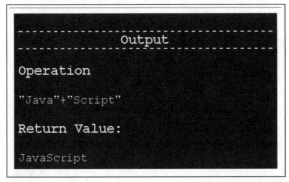

Figure 9-6: The result of concatenating 1 and 1.

Output
Operation
"Java"+"Script"
Return Value:
JavaScript

Figure 9-7: Concatenating `"Java"` and `"Script"`.

3. Leave the operator set to the concatenation operator and both data types set to string. Change the first operand to your first name, followed by a space, and change the second operand to your last name.

4. Press the Operate button.

   The result will be a string containing your first and last name, with a space between them. The important thing to learn from this example is that concatenation includes any spaces in the strings that are concatenated.

5. Change the operator from the concatenation operator to any of the arithmetic operators. Leave both data types set to string.

6. Press the Operate button.

   The result, shown in Figure 9-8, is NaN, which means "not a number." There's no way for JavaScript to perform arithmetic operations using letters, and NaN is its way of telling you that.

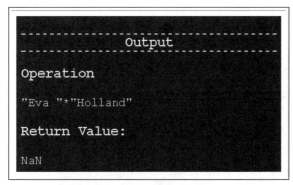

```
- - - - - - - - - - - - - - - - - - - - - - - - - - - - - - - - - -
                        Output
- - - - - - - - - - - - - - - - - - - - - - - - - - - - - - - - - -

Operation

"Eva "*"Holland"

Return Value:

NaN
```

Figure 9-8: Trying to do math with your name results in NaN.

7. Change the first operand to 9 and change its data type to number.

8. Change the operator to the arithmetic operator that looks like a percent sign (the modulus operator).

   The modulus operator is used to perform modulo operations, of course. A modulo operation tells you what the remainder is after dividing one number by another.

9. Change the second operator to 2 and change its data type to number.

10. Click the Operate button.

    The result of the operation is 1. Do you see why? The modulo (remainder) operator figures out how many times the first operand can be evenly divided by the second number, and returns what's left over.

11. Change the second operator to 2.5.

    Can you guess what the result will be?

12. Click the Operate button.

    The result is 1.5, because 9 can be divided by 2.5 three times, with a remainder of 1.5, as shown in Figure 9-9.

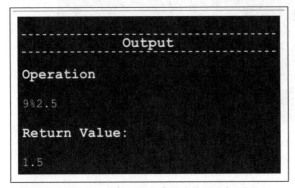

Figure 9-9: The remainder of dividing 9 by 2.5.

13. Change the value of the first operand to 1000000000000 (a 1 with 12 zeros, also known as 1 trillion).

    Note: Don't put commas in your number.

14. Change the operator to *.

15. Change the value of the second operand to 1000000000000.

16. Click Operate!

    The result, shown in Figure 9-10 looks unusual. This is called *scientific notation*. It's a way to show very large numbers in a more compact space. To convert this type of number to the type of number you're accustomed to seeing, move the decimal place to the right the number of times specified after the plus sign.

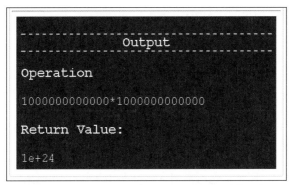

Figure 9-10: The result of multiplying 1 trillion by 1 trillion.

In this case, the result that JavaScript gives for 1 trillion × 1 trillion is 1e+24. This translates to a 1 with 24 zeros after it. Scientific notation is just a lot faster to read than 1000000000000000000000000.

Super-calculating with comparison operators

JavaScript's comparison operators are frequently used to test the values of variables and to make choices based on them. Most often, they're used in `if...else` statements. (We cover `if...else` statements in detail in Chapter 14.)

Comparison operators always return either `true` or `false`.

Let's go back into the Super-Calculator and try out some comparison operations:

1. Open your Super-Calculator program in JSFiddle.net.

2. Enter the number **5** into the input field for the first operand and select number from the Data Type drop-down menu.

3. Choose the equality operator (`==`) from the list of comparison operators.

4. Enter the same number (**5**) into the input field for the second operand and choose number as the data type.

5. Click the Operate button.

The result will be shown in the Output area, as shown in Figure 9-11.

Great! So, now you know that 5 is equal to 5.

Next, let's mix things up a bit and see some other interesting things that happen with comparisons.

1. Leave 5 in both operand input fields, but change the data type of the first input field to string.

2. Make sure that the equality operator (==) is still selected.

3. Click the Operate button.

What you're doing in this operation is to compare "5" to the number 5. The result is shown in Figure 9-11.

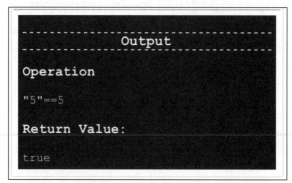

Figure 9-11: Comparing a string and number with the equality operator.

The result of this operation is interesting because the operator is called the equality operator, but it says that the number 5 and a string containing the number 5 are equal. What's happening is that the equality operator does something called *type conversion* to make the string containing 5 into a number before doing the comparison.

This type conversion feature of the equality operator can be a source for bugs in programs. Because of this, we recommend that you don't use the equality operator. Read on to find out what we do recommend using instead.

JavaScript has another comparison operator, the strict equality operator, that doesn't do type conversion for you. Follow these steps to try out the strict equality operator:

1. Set both of your operands to the same number.

   Any number will do, but we like 37.

2. Change the data type of the first operand to number, and change the data type of the second operand to string.

3. Select the === comparison operator.

   This is the strict equality operator.

4. Click the Operate button.

   The result is shown in Figure 9-12. Unlike the equality operator (==), the strict equality operator (===) considers a number and a string containing that number to be two completely different things.

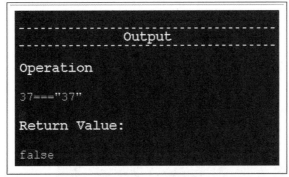

Figure 9-12: Strictly speaking, a number and a string are not the same.

Sometimes, you need to check whether things are not equal. For that, JavaScript has the inequality operators. These work the same way as the equality operators, except in reverse. Think of them as the equality operators' evil twins.

Just as the equality operator (==) should never be used, its evil twin, the inequality operator (!=) should also never be used in programs.

1. Enter a number as the first operand (say, 99) and set the data type to number.

2. Select the inequality operator (!=).

3. Enter **99** as the second operand and choose string as the data type.

4. Click the Operate button.

   The result, as shown in Figure 9-13, is false, meaning that the != operator doesn't consider 99 and "99" to be unequal.

5. Leave the operands the same, but change the operator to the strict inequality operator (!==).

6. Click the Operate button.

   The result, shown in Figure 9-14, is true, meaning that the strict inequality operator considers the two values to be not equal.

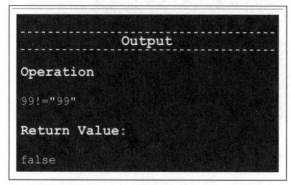

Figure 9-13: The != operator and different data types.

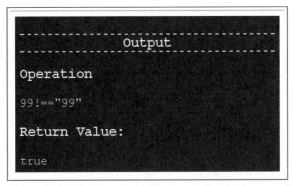

```
-------------------------------------------------
                    Output
-------------------------------------------------
Operation

99!=="99"

Return Value:

true
```

Figure 9-14: The ! == operator sees that strings and numbers are different.

Comparison operators can also be used to test whether one number is greater or less than another number. Let's take the comparison operators for a spin:

1. Change the first operand to 10 and select the number data type.

2. Change the operator to greater than (>).

Greater-than and less-than operators look like alligators. Alligators always want to eat the larger thing. If the alligator's mouth is open toward the larger thing, the result will be true!

3. Change the second operand to 5 and select the number data type.

4. Click the Operate button.

The result, as you would expect, is true; 10 is greater than 5.

JavaScript also lets you test whether a number is greater than or equal to another number. Follow these steps to try it out:

1. Change the first operand to 10 and select the number data type.

2. Change the operator to greater than or equal to (>=).

3. Change the second operand to 10 and select the number data type.

4. Click the Operate button.

The result, shown in Figure 9-15, is true, because 10 is greater than or equal to 10.

```
------------------------------------------------
                    Output
------------------------------------------------

Operation

10>="10"

Return Value:

true
```

Figure 9-15: Ten is greater than or equal to 10.

The less-than and less-than-or-equal-to operators work in the same way as the greater-than and greater-than-or-equal-to operators. Try them out on your own now if you like!

Super-Calculator Tricks

JavaScript holds a few surprises when it comes to how it works with operators. But when you understand the logic behind them, it all makes sense. To see a couple more interesting JavaScript operator behaviors in action, follow these steps:

1. Change the first operand to 1, with a number data type.

2. Change the operator to the addition (+) operator.

3. Change the second operand to 1, with a string data type.

4. Click the Operate button.

The result is 11. What happened is that JavaScript assumes that if one of the values in your addition operation is a string, you want both of them to be treated like strings. The result, then, is the result of concatenating "1" and "1".

5. Change the data type of the first operand to string and change its value to 10.

6. Change the operator to greater than (>).

7. Change the data type of the second operand to number, and change its value to 5.

8. Click the Operate button.

Interesting! The result, shown in Figure 9-16, is still true. Unlike with the equality operators, the greater-than and less-than comparison operators don't have a way of comparing values strictly. A number and a string containing a number will be compared as if both of them are numbers.

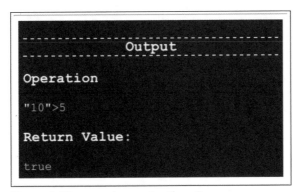

Figure 9-16: "10" is greater than 5.

The Super-Calculator has many other secrets to tell. Spend some time playing around with it and trying to break it. If you like, take a look at the JavaScript, CSS, and HTML that make it work. Read through the comments in the code and discover how it works.

Finally, try making some changes to the code. Can you make the Super-Calculator even more super?

As always, we're looking forward to seeing what you come up with! Share your creations with us on Facebook or Twitter!

Creating Your Own JavaScript Word Game

Word replacement games give you a basic story structure and ask you to supply different parts of speech: nouns, verbs, adjectives, adverbs, and so on. If you think about it, these games are very similar to JavaScript web apps. The basic structure is provided by the HTML, the CSS, and the JavaScript code. The variables in the JavaScript code are what make the results of the program different every time it's run.

In this chapter, we create a word replacement game by using the string concatenation operator to combine the words you enter with a story.

Result

fluffy

ADJECTIVE

practicing

VERB (ENDING IN "-ING")

dining room

ROOM IN A HOUSE

blue

COLOR

tooth brushes

PLURAL NOUN

threw

VERB (PAST TENSE)

milk

BEVERAGE

Douglas's Dance Party

One FLUFFY day, Douglas was PRACTICING in his DINING ROOM, reading a book about BLUE TOOTH BRUSHES.

As he THREW his MILK, he heard SMOOTH JAZZ music playing in the BATHROOM.

WOW! he exclaimed, as he ROLLED down the stairs to join the GOOFY party.

Douglas danced the SHARK Dance, the BELGRADE Shake, and took the prize for dancing the best Electric LIFT.

Creating a Variable Story

For this first version of the game, we wrote a story about Douglas the JavaScript Robot's adventures. Then we removed some of the words and replaced them with just a part of speech, so that the person playing the game can fill them in.

Here's our story about Douglas the JavaScript Robot, with certain words removed and replaced with the input expected (underlined):

> One <u>adjective</u> day, Douglas was <u>verb ending in "–ing"</u> in his <u>room in house</u>, reading a book about <u>color</u> <u>plural noun</u>.
>
> As he <u>past-tense verb</u> his <u>beverage</u>, he heard <u>type of music</u> music playing in the <u>different room in house</u>.
>
> <u>exclamation</u>! he exclaimed, as he <u>past-tense verb</u> down the stairs to join the <u>adjective</u> party.
>
> Douglas danced the <u>name of animal</u> Dance, the <u>name of city</u> Twist, and took the prize for dancing the best Electric <u>verb</u>.

Now that we have the story, let's build a JavaScript program around it that will accept input from a user and output a customized — and hilarious — story.

Creating the Word Replacement Game

The word replacement game makes use of everything you've learned so far in this book, including variables, operators, event handlers, HTML, CSS, input, output, and more!

Before we jump into the building of the game, let's try it out and see it in action:

1. Open your web browser and go to our JSFiddle Public Dashboard at `http://jsfiddle.net/user/forkids/fiddles`.

2. Locate the fiddle named Chapter 10 – Word Replacement Game, and click the title to open it.

   The finished Word Replacement Game project will open up.

3. Depending on your screen size, you may need to adjust the size of the Result pane so that it fits correctly.

   The labels for the underlined input areas on the left should all fit on the screen without wrapping to new lines. You should also see a very short rectangle with a dotted border to the right of the input questions. This is where the finished story will display.

4. Click the underline right above the first question to select the text input field.

5. Enter a value in the input field.

   After you've entered the desired value, press the Tab key or use your mouse to click the next input field on the page and fill that one out.

6. When you've finished filling out all the fields, click the Replace It button at the bottom of the form.

   The story of Douglas's adventure appears on the right with the words you entered into the input fields inserted, as shown in Figure 10-1.

Now that you've seen how the program works, let's start from scratch and build it. When you know how to build the game, you'll be able to add to it, improve it, and even change the story completely!

Follow these steps to begin creating your own version of the Word Replacement Game from scratch:

1. Open a new browser tab by selecting New Tab from the Chrome menu or pressing ⌘+C (Mac) or Ctrl+C (Windows) and go to `http://jsfiddle.net` in the new tab.

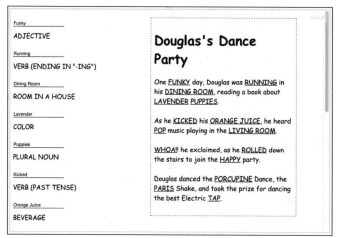

Figure 10-1: The finished story of Douglas's adventure.

2. Make sure that you're logged in to JSFiddle by checking whether your username is in the upper-right corner of the screen.

   When you're logged in, you're ready to go!

3. Click the Fiddle Options link in the left navigation bar and enter a name for your new program.

   For example, you might call it Douglas's Dance Party.

4. Click Save in the top menu.

Now you're ready to get started with the HTML for the program!

Writing the HTML

Our Word Replacement Game has three main areas, or sections:

✔ **The question area:** This is the input area where the program prompts you to enter words.

✔ **The button area:** This is the area at the bottom of the questions that contains the Replace It button that will add your input into the story.

✔ **The story area:** This is the area where the user input and the story appear together after the Replace It button is clicked.

The first thing we'll do is create these three areas. We'll create each section using a div element.

1. Enter three <div> elements into the HTML pane.

   Each <div> will have a unique id attribute that correlates with its purpose. Our first <div> will have an id of inputWords. We want the second <div> to be inside of the first <div>, and we'll give it an id of buttonDiv, as shown here:

   ```
   <div id="inputWords">

   <div id="buttonDiv"></div>

   </div>
   <div id="story"></div>
   ```

2. Next, create a structure for the input fields.

   We'll use an HTML unordered list to hold all the input fields. Use the following HTML markup inside the first div to create the structure:

   ```
   <ul>
     <li></li>
   </ul>
   ```

3. Create the first input field inside of the <li> element.

   Use the input element, with type=text" and id="adj1", like this:

   ```
   <input type="text" id="adj1" />
   ```

Notice that we put a slash (/) before the closing bracket in the input field. Although it's not required in HTML5, JSFiddle tends to format HTML markup better when you do use the slash at the end of elements like <input> and <br>.

4. Put a label underneath the input field by using a `<br>` tag, followed by the label, like this:

```
<br />Adjective
```

5. Finally, close the `<li>` element by putting the following ending tag after the word `Adjective`:

```
</li>
```

6. Put an HTML comment on the next line to serve as a placeholder for the other input fields that you'll add to the program later on.

```
<!-- put other input fields here -->
```

HTML comments start with `<!--` and end with `-->`.

7. Type the third `<div>` element underneath all the other markup in the HTML pane.

```
<div id="story"></div>
```

If you've entered everything correctly, your HTML pane should now look like the following:

```
<div id="inputWords">
  <ul>
    <li><input type="text" id="adj1" /><br />Adjective</li>
<!-- put other input fields here -->

  </ul>
<div id="buttonDiv"></div>
</div>
<div id="story"></div>
```

8. Click Update to see what the output of the web application is now.

It should look like Figure 10-2.

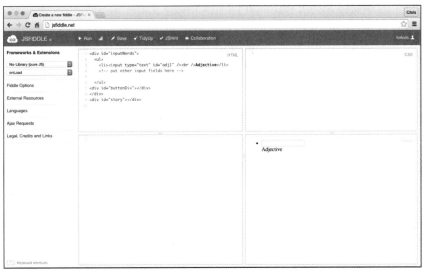

Figure 10-2: The beginning of the Word Replacement Game.

The final step that we'll do in the HTML pane for now is to create the button.

9. Place your cursor inside the `div` with the `id` of `buttonDiv`, and type the following:

```
<button id="replaceButton">Replace it!</button>
```

10. Click Update again.

You now have a single input field, a label under that field, and a button underneath both of them, as shown in Figure 10-3.

Figure 10-3: The essential components are in place.

Because all the rest of the input fields are just copies of this first one, we won't walk you through how to create all those. You can copy the first input field to create the rest of them, or feel free to copy them from the HTML pane in our finished version of the program.

Let's move on to the CSS pane!

Styling the word game

Before we jump right into styling, let's talk about organizing our CSS.

When you're using a lot of CSS for an application, it's important to organize it in some way so that you'll be able to easily find styles later on when you want to edit them.

One way to organize CSS files is by what section of the HTML document they apply to. Typically, this method will list CSS styles in roughly the same order as the elements that they apply to in the HTML.

Following this method, the first element for us to style is the body element, followed by the container for the input fields, followed by the list, followed by the input fields, and so on.

So, let's get styling. Follow these steps to apply styles to the Word Replacement Game:

1. To change the typeface of all the text in the document, apply a `font-family` style to the body element.

   We're going to use the super-fun Comic Sans typeface:

   ```
   body {
       font-family: "Comic Sans MS";
   }
   ```

   For a list of other common font families, visit www. w3schools.com/cssref/css_websafe_fonts.asp.

2. Style the section containing the input fields with the following rule:

```
#inputWords {
    float:left;
    width: 45%;
}
```

The `float:left` property in this rule causes the `<div>` to be placed along the left edge of its container (which is the document's body element in this case). Other elements will flow around it.

In practice, what `float:left` will do is to cause the `<div>` containing the input questions to be placed to the side of the `<div>` that will contain the finished story, rather than above it.

3. Style the list using the following two rules:

```
ul {
    list-style-type: none;
    padding: 0px;
    margin: 0px;
}
li {
    line-height: 2em;
    text-transform: uppercase;
    margin-top: 8px;
}
```

Here's what each of the properties in these rules does to the list:

- The `list-style-type` property removes the dot (bullet) from the left of each item in the list.

- Setting the `padding` and `margin` to `0px` makes the list left aligned with the other text on the page.

- Setting the line-height of the `<li>` creates more space between list items. Without this property, the elements would be uncomfortably close to each other.

The `text-transform` property of the `<li>` element causes all the input field labels underneath the input field to display as all capital letters.

The `margin-top` property creates yet more space between list items.

4. With these new CSS rules in place, click Update to see the latest version of the app.

The next few styles apply some formatting to the input fields, the button, and the story.

5. Type the following into the CSS pane:

```
input[type=text] {
    border-width: 0 0 1px 0;
    border-color: #333;
}
#buttonDiv {
    text-align: center;
}
#replaceButton {
    margin-top: 30px;
    width: 200px;
}
#story {
    margin-top: 12px;
    width: 45%;
    border: 1px dashed blue;
    padding: 8px;
    float: left;
}
.replacement {
    text-decoration: underline;
    text-transform: uppercase;
}
```

6. Click the Update button to save your work.

Your Result pane should now look like Figure 10-4.

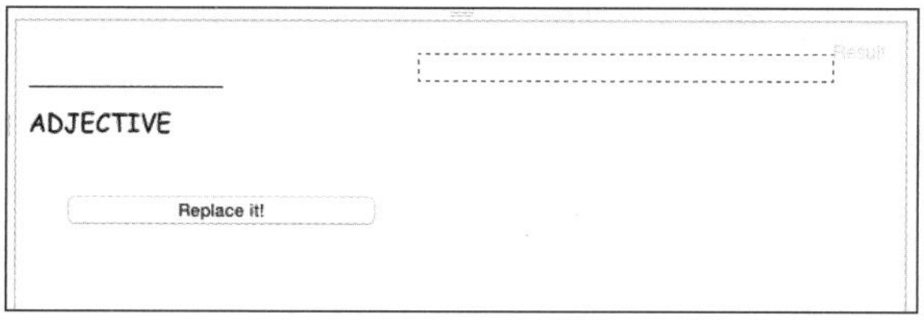

Figure 10-4: The Result pane with all the CSS styles applied.

There is much more to creating a good JavaScript web application than just JavaScript code. But now that we've got those pieces in place, we're ready to move on to the JavaScript!

Writing the JavaScript code

The first thing we'll do in the JavaScript pane is to create an event handler for the button. We'll use the addEventListener method covered in Chapter 7.

```
var replaceButton =
        document.getElementById("replaceButton");
replaceButton.addEventListener("click",replaceIt);
```

This first line creates a variable (replaceButton) to hold a reference to the button element. The second line uses that reference to attach a function (replaceIt) to an event (click).

Now let's create the replaceIt function.

1. Write an empty function definition for the function named replaceIt.

```
function replaceIt() {}
```

2. Inside the curly brackets, enter a line break and then create a variable to reference the <div> element where the finished story will appear.

```
var storyDiv = document.getElementById("story");
```

We'll come back and use the `storyDiv` variable in a moment. For now, our next task is to retrieve the values from the HTML input fields.

3. Create a variable to hold the value of the first HTML input field.

```
var adj1 = "<span class='replacement'>"+ document.
          getElementById("adj1").value + "</span>";
```

Notice that we're using the string concatenation operator to surround the value (which we get using `document.getElementById`) with an HTML `<span>` element. The program uses this `<span>` element to style user input differently from the other text in the story.

4. Write a comment after the creation of the `adj1` variable.

```
/* Insert more variable definitions here */
```

The comment will remind you that you need to come back to this spot later to put a variable for every other HTML input field that you add to the HTML pane later.

5. Create a variable that will be used to put the story together.

We'll call the variable `theStory`.

```
var theStory;
```

6. Put the title of the story into `theStory`, and put the title into an `<h1>` element.

```
theStory = "<h1>Douglas's Dance Party</h1>";
```

7. Add the first part of the story to `theStory` by using the combination concatenation/assignment operator, `+=`.

This operator adds the new value to any value that's already stored in the variable.

```
theStory += "One " + adj1 + " day,";
```

8. Once again, leave a comment for yourself to remind you that you need to come back and add the rest of the story after you get the basic functionality all working.

```
/* .Put the rest of the story here, using the += operator */
```

9. Use `innerHTML` to display the value of `theStory` inside the `div` we created for the story.

```
storyDiv.innerHTML = theStory;
```

With this line written, the code inside the JavaScript pane should now look like the following:

```
var replaceButton = document.getElementById("replaceButton");
replaceButton.addEventListener("click", replaceIt);

function replaceIt() {
    var storyDiv = document.getElementById("story");
    var adj1 = "<span class='replacement'>" + document.
            getElementById("adj1").value + "</span>";
    /* Insert more variable definitions here */
    var theStory = "<h1>Douglas's Dance Party</h1>";
    theStory += "One " + adj1 + " day,";
    /* Put the rest of the story here, using the += operator */
    storyDiv.innerHTML = theStory;
}
```

 If your code isn't as nicely formatted as this JavaScript code, click the TidyUp button in the top menu. This button does exactly what you would think: It cleans everything up, sets all the tabs nicely, and makes your code easier to read and work with.

Now, the moment you've been waiting for! Press Update in the top menu to see the first version of the Word Replacement Game in action!

Try entering a word into the input field and then press the Replace It button to see the results of your hard work, as shown in Figure 10-5.

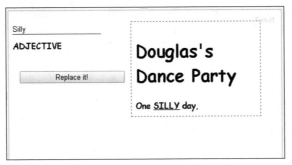

Figure 10-5: The generated story.

Finishing the program

You now have all the components of the Word Replacement Game in place. Finishing it is just a matter of repeating the following three steps for each additional word that the player needs to input.

1. Make a copy of an input field and update the value of the `id` attribute and the label.

2. Make a copy of the JavaScript statement containing `getElementById` and change the variable name and the value in parentheses.

3. Add more text, containing the new variable, to the `theStory` variable.

Let's try out these three steps to add the next part of the story (a verb ending in "–ing") to the game.

1. Select the following code in your HTML pane and make a copy of it.

   ```
   <li><input type="text" id="adj1" />
   <br />Adjective</li>
   ```

2. Paste the copy of your code on the line after the original.

3. Change the value of the `id` attribute to `verbIng`.

4. Change the label after the input field to the following:

```
Verb (ending in "-ing")
```

5. In the JavaScript pane, make a copy of the following statement:

```
var adj1 = "<span class='replacement'>"+
document.getElementById("adj1").value + "</span>";
```

6. Paste the code you copied onto the line after the original.

7. Change the variable name to `verbIng` and change the value inside the parentheses after `getElementById` to `verbIng`.

The new statement should now look like this:

```
var verbIng = "<span class='replacement'>"+
document.getElementById("verbIng").value + "</span>";
```

8. Make a copy of the following statement:

```
theStory += "One " + adj1 + " day,";
```

9. Paste your copy on the next line and modify it to match the following:

```
theStory += " Douglas was " + verbIng;
```

10. Save your work by clicking Update.

When you test out the program now, it should look like Figure 10-6. Congratulations, you've added a second question to the game!

Repeat the preceding ten steps to add more questions to your game. When it's complete, the markup in your HTML pane should match the markup in Listing 10-1, and the code in your JavaScript pane should match Listing 10-2.

Listing 10-1 The Completed Markup in the HTML Pane

```html
<div id="inputWords">
    <ul>
        <li><input type="text" id="adj1" /><br>Adjective</li>
        <li><input type="text" id="verbIng" /><br>Verb (ending
            in "-ing")</li>
        <li><input type="text" id="roomInHouse" /><br>Room in a
            house</li>
        <li><input type="text" id="color" /><br>Color</li>
        <li><input type="text" id="nounPlural" /><br>Plural
            noun</li>
        <li><input type="text" id="pastVerb" /><br>Verb (past
            tense)</li>
        <li><input type="text" id="beverage" /><br>Beverage</li>
        <li><input type="text" id="musicType" /><br>Type of
            music</li>
        <li><input type="text" id="diffRoom" /><br>Different room
            in a house</li>
        <li><input type="text" id="exclamation"
            /><br>Exclamation</li>
        <li><input type="text" id="pastVerb2" /><br>Verb (past
            tense)</li>
        <li><input type="text" id="adjDance" /><br>Adjective</li>
        <li><input type="text" id="animal" /><br>Animal</li>
        <li><input type="text" id="city" /><br>City</li>
        <li><input type="text" id="verb" /><br>Verb</li>
    </ul>
<div id="buttonDiv">
<button id="replaceButton">Replace it!</button>
</div>
</div>

<div id="story"></div>
```

Listing 10-2 The Completed Code in the JavaScript Pane

```javascript
var replaceButton = document.getElementById("replaceButton");
replaceButton.addEventListener("click",replaceIt);

function replaceIt() {
    var storyDiv = document.getElementById("story");
    var adj1 = "<span class='replacement'>"+ document.
            getElementById("adj1").value + "</span>";
```

```
var verbIng = "<span class='replacement'>"+ document.
      getElementById("verbIng").value + "</span>";
var roomInHouse = "<span class='replacement'>"+ document.
      getElementById("roomInHouse").value + "</span>";
var color = "<span class='replacement'>"+ document.
      getElementById("color").value + "</span>";
var nounPlural = "<span class='replacement'>"+ document.
      getElementById("nounPlural").value + "</span>";
var pastVerb = "<span class='replacement'>"+ document.
      getElementById("pastVerb").value + "</span>";
var beverage = "<span class='replacement'>"+ document.
      getElementById("beverage").value + "</span>";
var musicType = "<span class='replacement'>"+ document.
      getElementById("musicType").value + "</span>";
var diffRoom = "<span class='replacement'>"+ document.
      getElementById("diffRoom").value + "</span>";
var exclamation = "<span class='replacement'>"+ document.
      getElementById("exclamation").value + "</span>";
var pastVerb2 = "<span class='replacement'>"+ document.
      getElementById("pastVerb2").value + "</span>";
var adjDance = "<span class='replacement'>"+ document.
      getElementById("adjDance").value + "</span>";
var animal = "<span class='replacement'>"+ document.
      getElementById("animal").value + "</span>";
var city = "<span class='replacement'>"+ document.
      getElementById("city").value + "</span>";
var verb = "<span class='replacement'>"+ document.
      getElementById("verb").value + "</span>";

var theStory = "<h1>Douglas's Dance Party</h1>";
theStory += "One " + adj1 + " day,";
theStory += " Douglas was " + verbIng;
theStory += " in his " + roomInHouse;
theStory += ", reading a book about " + color;
theStory += " " + nounPlural + ".<br><br>";
theStory += "As he " + pastVerb;
theStory += " his " + beverage;
theStory += ", he heard " + musicType;
theStory += " music playing in the " + diffRoom + ".<br><br>";
theStory += exclamation + "! he exclaimed, as he ";
theStory += pastVerb2 + " down the stairs to join the ";
theStory += adjDance + " party.<br><br>";
```

(continued)

Listing 10-2 *(continued)*

```
        theStory += "Douglas danced the " + animal;
        theStory += " Dance, the " + city + " Shake,";
        theStory += " and took the prize for dancing the best Electric
                " + verb + ".<br><br>";

        storyDiv.innerHTML = theStory;

    }
```

After you've finished entering all the questions and the JavaScript code to generate the whole story, it will replace all the blanks in the story with words you enter into the input fields, as shown in Figure 10-6.

Now that you have a working copy of our Word Replacement Game, feel free to use the Fork button in the top menu to make a copy and try customizing it to tell your own story!

If your program doesn't work as you expect it, check your code carefully and compare it with ours line by line. The problem is probably just a small typo. Visit www.dummies.com/extras/ javascriptforkids to read our tips on debugging JavaScript programs.

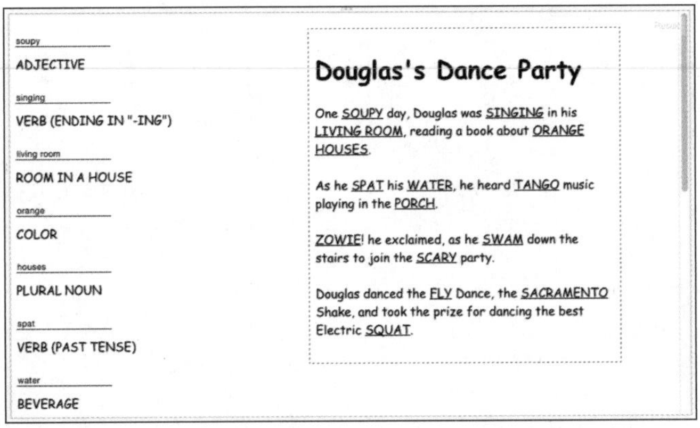

Figure 10-6: The working Word Replacement Game.

Part IV
Arrays and Functions

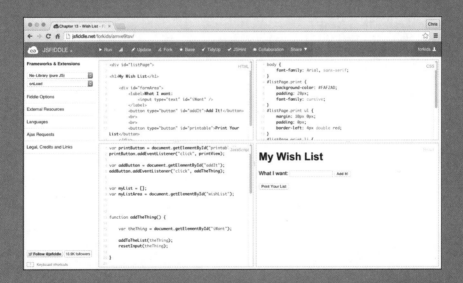

In this part . . .

■ Creating and Changing Arrays 173

■ Making It Functional 190

■ Creating a Wish List Program 206

For information on working with anonymous functions in JavaScript, go to www.dummies.com/
extras/javascriptforkids.

Creating and Changing Arrays

Who doesn't like lists? Lists are everywhere and we use them all the time in our day-to-day lives. Whether you're keeping track of your favorite songs, writing down everything you have to get done today, or viewing the top ten cutest animal pictures on the Internet, lists help us organize and make sense of the world.

In computer programming, we use something called an *array* to store lists of data. In this chapter, we show you how to create arrays, how to change the values in arrays, and how to work with arrays to do useful things inside your programs.

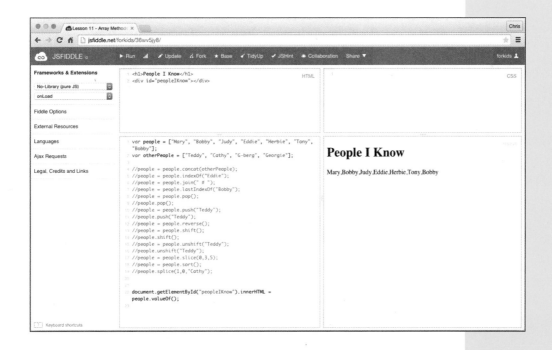

What Are Arrays?

Arrays are a special kind of variable that can hold multiple values using the same name. You can picture an array as being similar to a dresser with multiple drawers. Each drawer can hold something different, but the whole thing is still your dresser.

If you want to tell someone which drawer to look in for socks, you can say, "The socks are in the top drawer." If they're in the next drawer down, you'd say, "They're in the second drawer from the top." If you were to make a list showing what's in each drawer of your dresser, you would do something like this:

Top drawer: Socks

Second drawer: Shirts

Third drawer: Pants

If you understand how your dresser organizes your clothes, you have a good start on understanding how JavaScript arrays organize data.

If we wanted to create a JavaScript array to describe the contents of the dresser, we could use the following code:

```
var dresser = ["socks","shirts","pants"];
```

This statement creates three "drawers" (or *elements,* as they're called in JavaScript). When you want to know what's in each of the elements, you can simply ask JavaScript. For example, to find out what's in the third element, you use the following:

```
dresser[2]
```

The value of `dresser[2]` is `pants`.

As we talk about in Chapter 3, JavaScript starts counting from zero. So, the first element of an array is number 0, the second is 1, and the third is 2.

The maximum number of elements that a JavaScript array can hold is 4.29 billion. So, pretty much anything that you want to list will fit into an array!

Now that you understand how arrays work, let's talk a bit more about how to create them.

Creating and Accessing Arrays

Creating an array starts the same way as any variable: with the var keyword. However, in order to let JavaScript know that the object you're making isn't just a normal variable, you put square brackets after it.

To create an array with nothing inside it, just use empty brackets, like this:

```
var favoriteFoods = [];
```

To create an array with data inside it, put values inside the brackets, separated by commas, like this:

```
var favoriteFoods = ["broccoli","eggplant",
            "tacos","mushrooms"];
```

Storing different data types

Arrays can hold any of the different data types of JavaScript, including numbers, strings, Boolean values, and objects.

In fact, a single array can contain multiple different data types. For example, the following array definition creates an array containing a number, a string, and a Boolean value:

```
var myArray = [5, "Hi there", true];
```

Just as when you create regular variables, string values in arrays must be within either single or double quotes.

Getting array values

To get the value of an array element, use the name of the array, followed by square brackets containing the number of the element you want to retrieve. For example:

```
myArray[0]
```

Using the array definition that we created in the last section, this will return the number 5.

Using variables inside arrays

You can also use variables within array definitions. For example, in the following code, we create two variables and then we use that variable inside an array definition:

```
var firstName = "Neil";
var middleName = "deGrasse"
var lastName = "Tyson";
var Scientist = [firstName, middleName, lastName];
```

Because variables are stand-ins for values, the result of these three statements is exactly the same as if we were to write the following statement:

```
var Scientist = ["Neil","deGrasse" "Tyson"];
```

To find out more about arrays, let's practice setting, retrieving, and changing array elements in the JavaScript Console.

Changing Array Element Values

JavaScript gives you several ways to modify arrays.

The first way is to give an existing array element a new value. This is as easy as assigning the value. Follow these steps in your JavaScript Console to see how this works:

1. Create a new array with the following statement:

   ```
   var people = ["Teddy","Cathy","Bobby"];
   ```

2. Print out the values of the array elements with this statement:

   ```
   console.log(people);
   ```

   The JavaScript Console returns the same list of elements that you put in in the previous step.

3. Change the value of the first element by entering this statement, and then press Return or Enter:

   ```
   people[0] = "Georgie";
   ```

4. Print the values of the array's element now, using the following statement:

   ```
   console.log(people);
   ```

   The value of the first array element has been changed from "Teddy" to "Georgie".

Now it's your turn. Can you modify the array so that it contains the following list of names, in this order?

```
Mary, Bobby, Judy, Eddie, Herbie, Tony
```

When you have lists of names, or lists of anything, there are many things that you can do with them, such as sorting them, adding to and removing from them, comparing them, and much more. In the next section, we talk about how JavaScript simplifies many of these tasks with array methods.

Working with Array Methods

Array methods are built-in things that can be done with or to JavaScript arrays. These methods are perhaps the best part about working with arrays in JavaScript. Once you know how to use them, you'll save yourself a lot of time and effort. Plus, they can also be a lot of fun!

JavaScript's built-in array methods are listed in Table 11-1.

Table 11-1	JavaScript Array Methods
Method	**Description**
concat()	A new array made up of the current array, joined with other array(s) and/or value(s).
indexOf()	Returns the first occurrence of the specified value within the array. Returns −1 if the value is not found.
join()	Joins all the elements of an array into a string.
lastIndexOf()	Returns the last occurrence of the specified value within the array. Returns −1 if the value is not found.
pop()	Removes the last element in an array.
push()	Adds new items to the end of an array.
reverse()	Reverses the order of elements in an array.
shift()	Removes the first element from an array and returns that element, resulting in a change in length of an array.
slice()	Selects a portion of an array and returns it as a new array.
sort()	Returns an array after the elements in an array are sorted. (The default sort order is alphabetical and ascending.)
splice()	Returns a new array comprised of elements that were added to or removed from a given array.
tostring()	Converts an array to a string.
unshift()	Returns a new array with a new length by the addition of one or more elements.

Learning the Ways of Arrays

Array methods can be difficult to understand without seeing them in action, so let's go into JSFiddle and try some of them out!

1. Go to JSFiddle.net in your web browser and log in.

2. Open the public dashboard at `http://jsfiddle.net/user/forkids/fiddles`.

3. Locate the program named "Lesson 11 – Array Methods – Start" and click the title to open it.

4. Click the Fork link in the top menu to create your own version of the program.

5. Change the name of your program under Fiddle Options to "(Your Name) Array Methods."

6. Click Update and then click Set as Base in the top menu to save your program.

   The program should look like Figure 11-1, with two arrays in the JavaScript pane, two HTML elements in the HTML pane, and a header displaying in the Result pane.

In this example, we create a simple program that, when run, uses an array method to modify an array or create a new array. The program then outputs the array as a list in the Result pane.

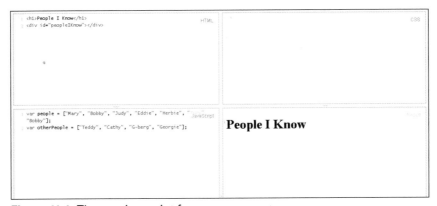

Figure 11-1: The starting point for our program.

toString() and valueOf()

The toString() and valueOf() methods both do the same thing: They convert the array to a string, with each element separated by a comma.

Our program will use toString() in the statement that tells the browser where to display the array values.

Follow these steps to create the output statement:

1. Click inside the JavaScript pane and press Return or Enter to insert a couple of line breaks after the statement that creates the otherPeople array.

2. Type the following on a new line:

```
document.getElementById("peopleIKnow").innerHTML =
                people.toString();
```

   This statement writes out the values in the people array as a list.

3. Click the Update button.

   The values in the people array display in the Result pane, as shown in Figure 11-2.

4. Replace toString() with valueOf() in the JavaScript pane.

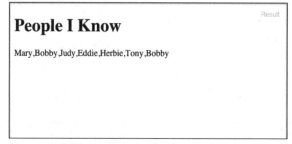

People I Know

Mary,Bobby,Judy,Eddie,Herbie,Tony,Bobby

Figure 11-2: The values in the people array.

5. Click Update.

The Result pane should be unchanged, demonstrating that `toString()` and `valueOf()` do the same thing to arrays.

concat()

Follow these steps to use the `concat()` method to join together two arrays:

1. Type the following statement below the array definitions, but above the output statement:

```
people = people.concat(otherPeople);
```

2. Click Update.

The `concat()` method has added together the `people` array and the `otherPeople` array. We then used the assignment operator (=) to store the result of this operation in the `people` array. The resulting array is shown in Figure 11-3.

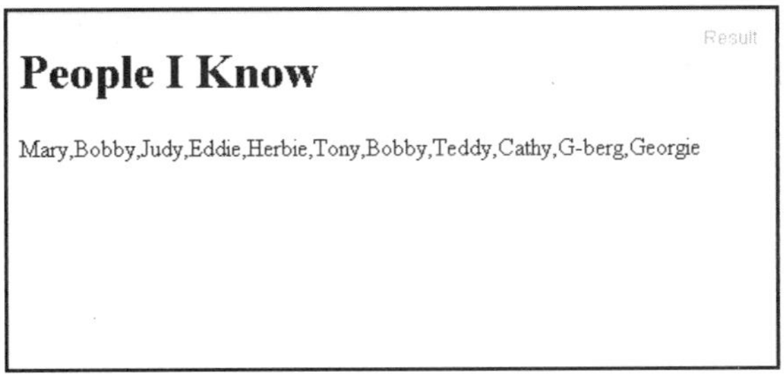

Result

People I Know

Mary,Bobby,Judy,Eddie,Herbie,Tony,Bobby,Teddy,Cathy,G-berg,Georgie

Figure 11-3: The result of using the `concat()` operator to add together the two arrays.

indexOf()

The `indexOf()` array method looks for a value among an array's elements and returns the position of that array. To try it out with the `people` array, follow these steps:

1. Comment out the statement using the `concat()` method by putting two slashes before the line, as shown in Figure 11-4.

Commenting out the statement will cause it to not run, but the code will still be there if you want to use it again later.

```
1  var people = ["Mary", "Bobby", "Judy", "Eddie", "Herbie", "Tony",
   "Bobby"];
2  var otherPeople = ["Teddy", "Cathy", "G-berg", "Georgie"];
3
4  //people = people.concat(otherPeople);
5
6  document.getElementById("peopleIKnow").innerHTML =
   people.valueOf();
```

Figure 11-4: Commenting out a statement.

2. Type the following statement, which will look for the string `"Eddie"` in the `people` array.

```
people = people.indexOf("Eddie");
```

3. Click the Update button to save and run the program.

The Result window displays the position in the array of the string, as shown in Figure 11-5.

Result

People I Know

3

Figure 11-5: Finding Eddie.

join()

The `join()` array method behaves like the `toString()` and `valueOf()` methods, in that it joins the elements of an array together. However, the `join()` method has one very special feature: It lets you specify the character or characters that should come between the elements of the array.

To try out `join()`, follow these steps:

1. Comment out the statement using the `indexOf()` method.

2. Type the following statement underneath the commented statements:

```
people = people.join(" # ");
```

3. Click the Update link to save your work and run the program.

   The Result pane should now display the elements in the people array, separated by #, as shown in Figure 11-6.

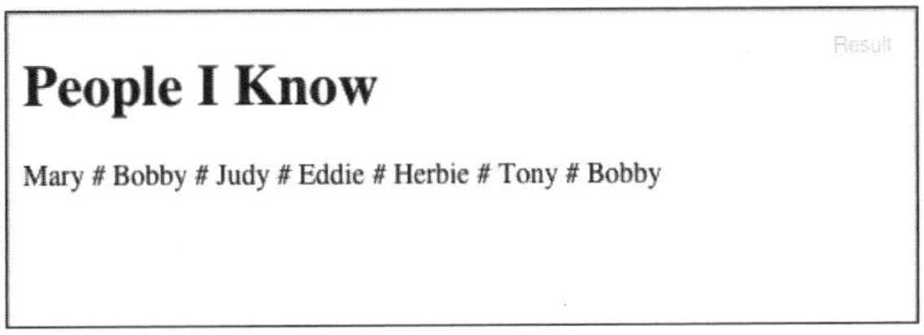

Result

People I Know

Mary # Bobby # Judy # Eddie # Herbie # Tony # Bobby

Figure 11-6: Using `join()`.

lastIndexOf()

The `lastIndexOf()` array method tells you the last array element that contains the specified value.

Notice that our people array contains the name Bobby in both the second and seventh positions (array elements numbers 1 and 6). What value do you think running `lastIndexOf()` will print out? Use these steps to find out:

1. Comment out the previous statement, the one using `join()`.

2. Enter the following statement underneath the commented statements:

```
people = people.lastIndexOf("Bobby");
```

3. Click Update to save your work and run your code.

The result window should display the last position of the string "Bobby" in the array, as shown in Figure 11-7.

```
                                                    Result
 People I Know

 6
```

Figure 11-7: The last position of "Bobby".

pop()

The pop() array method removes the last element in an array and returns that element. Do the following steps to see it in action:

1. Comment out the previous statement.

2. Enter the following statement underneath the commented ones:

   ```
   people = people.pop();
   ```

3. Click Update to save your work and run your code.

   The Result pane displays the last item that was in the original people array.

   Notice that our statement not only removed the last item from the people array, but also set the value of the people array to just that one item. If you want to just remove the last item from an array, continue with the following steps.

4. Comment out the previous statement.

5. Type the following underneath the commented statements:

   ```
   people.pop();
   ```

6. Click Update to see the result.

Now, the people list has all the same elements, but with the last one removed (or "popped off"), as shown in Figure 11-8.

Figure 11-8: Bobby has been popped off the list.

push()

The push() array method adds an element, or elements, to the end of an array and returns the new number of elements of the array (in other words, its length).

To try out push(), follow these steps:

1. Comment out the previous statement.

2. Type the following statement underneath the commented statements:

```
people = people.push("Teddy");
```

3. Click Update.

The result window now shows the new length of the people array: 8. By setting the value of people equal to the return value of the push() method, however, we've deleted all the elements of the people array. Let's use push() again, but preserve the elements of the people array this time.

4. Comment out the previous statement.

5. Enter the following in order to modify the array without changing its value to the return value:

```
people.push("Teddy");
```

6. Click Update to see the result.

A list of the elements in the `people` array is displayed, with Teddy added to the end, as shown in Figure 11-9.

Figure 11-9: The `people` array with Teddy pushed onto the end.

reverse()

The `reverse()` method flips your array over. What was the first element becomes the last, what was the last becomes the first, and everything in between reverses, too.

Follow these steps to see `reverse()` do its thing.

1. Comment out the previous statement.

2. Type this statement after the commented statements:

```
people = people.reverse();
```

3. Click Update.

The result will display in the Result pane, as shown in Figure 11-10. If you compare the result with the original array, you'll see that everything is in opposite order.

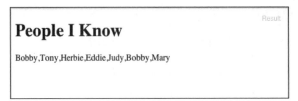

Figure 11-10: Reversing the elements in an array.

shift() and unshift()

The `shift()` method removes the first element from the array. To try it out, follow these steps:

1. Comment out the previous statement.

2. Type this statement after the commented statements:

   ```
   people.shift();
   ```

3. Click Update.

   The Result pane displays the new array, with Mary removed from the beginning, as shown in Figure 11-11.

   People I Know

   Bobby,Judy,Eddie,Herbie,Tony,Bobby

Figure 11-11: The `shift()` method removes the first element.

The `shift()` method has a twin, called `unshift()`, which adds an element to the beginning of an array. To use it, follow these steps:

1. Comment out the previous statement.

2. Type the following statement after the commented statements:

   ```
   people.unshift("Teddy");
   ```

3. Click Update.

   The Result pane shows the people list, with Teddy added at the beginning.

slice()

The slice() method lets you pick certain elements from your array to create a new array. Follow these steps:

1. Comment out the previous statement.

2. Type the following after the commented statements:

   ```
   people = people.slice(0,3);
   ```

3. Click Update.

   The Result pane shows the elements in the people array after the slice() method, as shown in Figure 11-12.

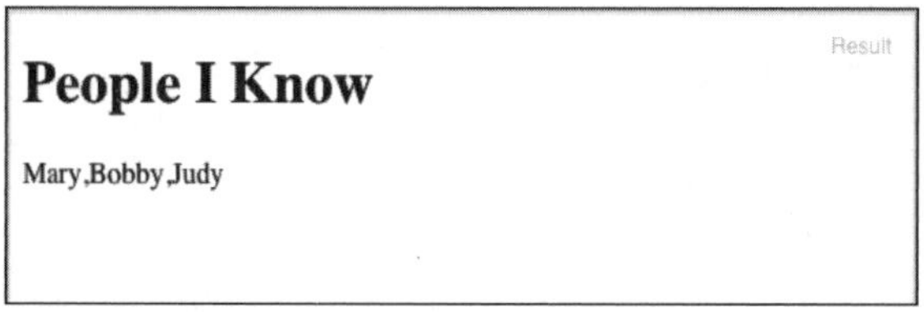

Result

People I Know

Mary,Bobby,Judy

Figure 11-12: The slice() method selects certain elements.

sort()

The sort() method sorts the elements in an array alphabetically. To use sort(), follow these steps:

1. Comment out the previous statement.

2. Type the following on a line after the commented statements:

   ```
   people = people.sort();
   ```

3. Click the Update link.

   The Result pane shows you that the elements have been re-sorted, alphabetically, as shown in Figure 11-13.

Figure 11-13: The elements have been re-sorted.

splice()

The `splice()` method lets you add or remove elements at certain positions. To try it out, follow these steps:

1. Comment out the previous statement.

2. Enter the following after the last commented statement:

    ```
    people.splice(1,0,"Cathy");
    ```

    What this is saying is to insert the value after the first element, don't remove any elements (that's what the 0 means), and insert `Cathy`.

3. Click Update.

    In the Result pane, you see that `Cathy` has been added after Mary, as shown in Figure 11-14.

Figure 11-14: Using `splice()`.

12 Making It Functional

Functions are the building blocks of JavaScript programs. They help you to keep from having to repeat yourself, and they make your programs neater and more flexible!

In this chapter, we use functions to create a game called Function Junction.

- Click the train to make it go faster.
- Click the Stop button to stop it.
- Try to stop it as close to the edge as possible, without crashing.

Stop!

Understanding Functions

Functions are programs inside of programs. Functions are great at handling tasks that may be required multiple times by different parts of a program. They're also a great way to keep things organized within your program.

Built-in functions

Some functions are built into JavaScript, such as the methods of arrays, strings, numbers, and other objects. You can tell that something's a function because it has parentheses after it.

When a function is part of an object (such as the `document` object, for example) we call it a *method*. But it's still a function.

Here are some of the functions that are built into JavaScript that you've already used:

```
getElementById()
toString()
addEventListener()
indexOf()
```

Can you think of other functions you've seen?

Custom functions

In addition to the functions that are built into JavaScript, you can also create your own, using the steps and information that we're about to show you!

You can't spell *function* without "fun," and you can't write JavaScript code without using functions. Therefore, you can't write JavaScript code without having fun!

If you've read through the previous chapters, you've already seen functions in action in the demonstration programs. Here's an example of a function that adds a smiley face to any text you give it:

```
function smileyIt(theText) {
    theText += " :)";
    return theText;
}
```

Follow these steps to try out this function:

1. Open JSFiddle.net in your web browser.

   You should have a blank project. If it's not blank, click the JSFiddle logo in the upper-left corner of the screen.

2. Type the code for the `smileyIt()` function into the JavaScript pane.

3. Click the Run button.

   Notice that nothing happens. Unlike JavaScript code that's outside a function, code inside functions doesn't run until the function is called.

4. Add the following statement underneath the function:

   ```
   smileyIt("Hi There!");
   ```

5. Click the Run link.

   Once again, nothing appears to have happened. But this time, something actually did happen. We just didn't report the results of running the function back to you.

6. Modify the statement you wrote in the last step to put the result of running the function into an alert popup, like this:

   ```
   alert(smileyIt("Hi there!"));
   ```

7. Click the Run link.

   If you entered everything correctly, you should get an alert popup saying Hi there! :), as shown in Figure 12-1.

Figure 12-1: Outputting the result of the function to an alert.

alert() is another example of a built-in JavaScript function!

Knowing What Functions Are Made Of

Functions have a special vocabulary and way that they must be written and used. To really understand functions, you need to be able to speak their language. So, let's look at a couple words and take apart a function to see what's inside!

Defining a function

When you write a function, that's called *defining* it. Defining a function makes the code inside that function available to be run.

There are a couple different ways to define a function. The most common way is to use the function keyword, followed by the name of the function, followed by parentheses and then curly braces, like this:

```
function myFunction() {
  // statements go here
}
```

Another way to define a function is by using the new Function technique. That looks like this:

```
var myFunction = new Function() {
  // statements go here
}
```

Both methods get the job done, but we recommend using the first, more common, technique.

Giving the function a head

The first part of a function definition is called the *function head*. The function head includes the function keyword, the name of the function, and the parentheses:

```
function myFunction()
```

Filling out the function body

Next up is the *function body*. The function body is made up of statements, surrounded by curly braces. For example:

```
{
  // this is the function body
}
```

Calling a function

When you run the code within a function body, that's called *calling* the function. To call a function, you simply write the name of the function, followed by parentheses. For example:

```
myFunction();
```

Defining parameters

Parameters are values that can be included between the parentheses when a function is called. To define a parameter, simply give the parameter a name and put it between the parentheses in the function definition. For example:

```
function myFunction(theText) {

}
```

You can define multiple parameters by separating them with commas.

Passing arguments

When you call a function using a value between the parentheses, it's called *passing an argument.* For example:

```
myFunction("This is some text");
```

In this case, the argument is the string `"This is some text"`.

When you're defining a function, the values between the parentheses are called *parameters.* When passing values into a function, they're called *arguments.*

When you pass an argument into a function, the function automatically creates a new variable with the name of the parameter and gives it the value of the argument that you passed.

Returning a value

When you call a function and (optionally) pass it an argument, the function starts doing its thing. After the function completes its task, it stops running and produces some sort of value. The value that a function produces when it finishes running is called its *return value.*

You can set what the return value is by using the *return statement.* For example, the following function will always return the number 3000:

```
function whatsTheNumber(){
  return 3000;
}
```

To find out or use the return value of a function, you can call the function as part of an operation. For example, to do math with the result of a function, you just include the function as a normal operand (see Chapter 8), like this:

```
var theTotal = whatsTheNumber() + 80;
```

When you run this statement, a value equal to the return value of whatsTheNumber() plus 80 (or 3080) will be assigned to theTotal.

If you don't specify a return value for a function, the function will return undefined.

Building Function Junction

Now that you know the basics of how functions are created and used, let's write a game. We call this game Function Junction. The goal is to get a train as far along a track as quickly as possible without it crashing at the end of the track.

Before we explain how it works and show you how to build it, let's try it out!

1. Open your web browser and go to http://jsfiddle.net/ user/forkids/fiddles.

2. Find the program named "Chapter 12 – Function Junction" program in our public dashboard and click the title to open it.

To play the game, click the train. It starts moving down the track at a very slow pace. If you click the train again, it picks up a little bit of speed. Click several more times and it picks up even more steam. But if you keep clicking, the train will eventually be moving so fast that you'll feel like you're going off the rails on this crazy train.

If you don't do something before the train reaches the end of the track, it will crash. All you need to do to bring the train to a screeching halt is to click the Stop button. But can you get to it quickly enough?!

Like so many computer games, the actual game play isn't nearly as exciting as the narrative description. But with the skills you learn in this chapter, you'll be able to make improvements and maybe even turn Function Junction into the next big thing!

Now, let's see how to build Function Junction.

Start by going to our partially built version of the program, named "Chapter 12 – Function Junction – Start." You can find it in our public dashboard in JSFiddle.

When you've located it and opened it, follow these steps:

1. Click the Fork button to create your own copy of the program.

2. Open the Fiddle Options and change the name of your new program.

3. Click Update and then Set as Base to save your program.

Now we're ready to get started!

Touring the HTML

The HTML for Function Junction is pretty simple, and we've included everything you need already.

Tiptoeing through the CSS

Now let's move on to the CSS pane. We've already included all the CSS you need for the game. Before we show you that, take a look at Figure 12-2. This is what the game looks like without any CSS.

Pretty big difference, huh? Listing 12-1 shows all the styles that we apply to the game to make it look the way it does.

Figure 12-2: Function Junction without any CSS.

Listing 12-1   The Function Junction CSS

```css
body {
    font-family: Arial, sans-serif;
}
#container {
    padding: 10px;
    width: 360px;
    height: 80%;
    background-color: #00FF00;
}
#track {
    width: 340px;
    border-top: 2px solid white;
    border-bottom: 2px solid white;
    margin: 20px auto;
}
#train {
    height: 92px;
    width: 100px;
    position: relative;
    left: 0px;
}
```

```
#stopButton {
    padding-top: 15px;
    margin: 10px auto;
    background-color: white;
    width: 100px;
    height: 50px;
    color: red;
    text-align: center;
    font-size: 24px;
    line-height: 30px;
}
```

Take a look at each of the selectors. Notice that, except for the font-family style that we've applied to the body element, we're using all ID selectors, which begin with #.

We used most of these same styles in previous programs, so we won't go over them all again. However, there are a couple styles that you should know about so that you can customize your version of the game later on.

Find the styles for the container element. These control the size and color of the background. Currently set to green, you can experiment with making this a different color. Also, if you want to make the game wider (and the train travel farther), you'll need to adjust the width here (as well as in a couple other spots that we'll show you in a moment).

Now find the styles for the track element. These style the white train tracks. We've created the two lines of the tracks by putting a top border and a bottom border on a rectangle that contains the train. If you want to make the train travel farther, this is another spot where you'll need to make an adjustment (to the width property).

If you'd like, spend a few minutes changing the styles and then clicking Run to see what they do in the Result pane.

If you end up doing something that you don't like or that breaks the look of the game, go to your Public Dashboard and reopen your base version of the program.

Writing the Function Junction JavaScript

Now, move over to the JavaScript pane.

We've removed most of the JavaScript from our starting version of the program and replaced it with JavaScript comments telling what needs to be done, as shown in Listing 12-2.

Many of the comments begin with `todo:`. This is a commonly used way that programmers leave notes to themselves or to other programmers to indicate what needs to be done to finish or to improve their JavaScript code.

Listing 12-2   **The JavaScript Pane with Comments Indicating What to Do**

```
/*
todo: Create three global variables:
* trainSpeed (initial value = 250)
* trainPosition (initial value = 0)
* animation (no initial value)
*/


/*
todo: Listen for click events on the train element and
        call a function named speedUp when they happen.
*/


/*
todo: Listen for click events on the stop button element
        and call a function called stopTrain when they
        happen.
*/


function speedUp() {
    /*
```

```
        todo: Check whether the train is already going as fast
              as it can. If not, increase the speed.
    */


    /*

    If the train is already moving, stop it and then
              restart with the new speed by calling a
              function called frame.
    */



    function frame() {
        /*
        todo: Reposition the train and check whether the
              train is crashed.
        */
    }
}


function stopTrain() {
    /*
    todo: Test whether the train is already crashed. If
              not, stop the train.
    */
}

function checkPosition(currentPosition) {
    /*
    todo: Check the train's current position and crash it
              if it's at the end of the line.
    */
}
```

Read through these instructions now. If you'd like, try to complete as many of the items as you can before moving on to our step-by-step instructions.

Now, let's start at the top and get this train moving!

1. The first instruction is to create three variables, so underneath this comment, type the following statements:

```
var trainSpeed = 250;
var trainPosition = 0;
var animation;
```

2. The next instruction says to listen for click events on the train. This just means to use the same addEventListener function that we use in earlier chapters to attach a click event handler to the element with an id = "train". Use this code:

```
var train = document.getElementById("train");
train.addEventListener("click", speedUp);
```

3. Next, we need to add an event listener to the stop button. The code is similar to the last statement:

```
var stopButton = document.getElementById("stopButton");
stopButton.addEventListener("click", stopTrain);
```

4. Now we're getting to the good stuff. Inside the speedUp() function, the first instruction is to check whether the train is already going at top speed. Here's the code for that:

```
if (trainSpeed > 10) {
        trainSpeed -= 10;
}
```

This code tests the value of the trainSpeed variable. If it's greater than 10, the train can still go faster, so the next line subtracts 10 from the value of trainSpeed.

The speed of the animation is determined by the second parameter of setInterval, which is how long to wait (in milliseconds) between steps in the animation. So, a smaller number means that there will be less time between steps, which will make the train move faster.

5. The next thing to do inside the speedUp function is to restart the loop that does the animation, but with the new speed. Type these two lines underneath the previous statement.

```
clearInterval(animation);
animation = setInterval(frame, trainSpeed);
```

The first statement, clearInterval, temporarily stops the animation. The second statement starts up a new setInterval loop using the new value trainSpeed. The setInterval function will call a function called frame().

6. Next, we need to create the frame() function. This function is very similar to the frame() function that we use in Chapter 7 to animate Douglas the JavaScript robot. We just need to make a few adjustments to it for our particular circumstances. Modify the frame() function in your Function Junction program so that it looks like this:

```
function frame() {
   trainPosition += 2;
   train.style.left = trainPosition + 'px';
   checkPosition(trainPosition);
}
```

This function first increases the value of the trainPosition variable; then it updates the location of the train according to the current value of trainPosition. After the train has been moved, it makes a call to another function, called checkPosition() and passes it the currentPosition variable.

7. Next, let's take a look at the checkPosition() function. Update the checkPosition() function to match the following:

```
function checkPosition(currentPosition) {
    if (currentPosition === 260) {
        alert("Crash!");
        console.log("Crash!");
        clearInterval(animation);
    }
}
```

This function accepts a single argument, currentPosition. It tests whether currentPosition is equal to 260 (because 260 pixels is the distance from the left edge of the tracks that we've determined to be the point where the train crashes). If you want to make your train tracks longer, this is another spot where you'll need to change a value.

8. Finally, move down to the stopTrain() function and make it match the following:

```
function stopTrain() {
    if (trainPosition < 260) {
        clearInterval(animation);
    }
}
```

The stopTrain() function runs when the Stop button is clicked. It first tests to make sure that the train hasn't already crashed, by comparing the trainPosition with the "end of the line" number, which is 260 in this case.

If you want to increase the length of the tracks, this is the final place where you'll need to make an adjustment.

9. Click Update to save your work and then click the train to see if the game works as it should.

If you did everything right, the train will start to move! If it doesn't budge, check your work carefully. You can also check in the JavaScript Console to see if there are any error messages that might be helpful with tracking down the problem.

Your turn: Lengthening the tracks!

Throughout this chapter, we told you the places where you need to make changes in order to make the train tracks longer. Now it's your turn to try it out!

Go through the CSS and the JavaScript and increase the values that need to be increased in order to make the train tracks longer. When you're finished, click the Update link to try it out! Does your train still crash at the very edge of the background. If not, can you find what you need to change to make it work correctly?

Creating a Wish List Program

The JavaScript genie came to us and told us that we can have not three, but unlimited, wishes if we just use arrays and functions to build a Wish List application. It seemed like quite a deal to us, until the genie reminded us that wishing doesn't make it true. There's always a catch! In this chapter, we show you how you can build a Wish List application.

My Wish List

A Birthday Party
A Puppy
Friends
New Clothes
To Become a JavaScript Expert
World Peace

Introducing the Wish List Program

The Wish List application uses an HTML form to accept input from a user, which it adds to an array and to an HTML list. A Print button allows a user to create a nicely formatted and sorted list that she can print out and deliver to the genie of her choice.

Viewing the finished program

To get an idea of how the finished Wish List program will look and function, follow these steps:

1. Open our Public Dashboard in JSFiddle.net by going to `http://jsfiddle.net/user/forkids/fiddles`.

2. Find the program named "Chapter 13 – Wish List – Finished" and click the title to open it.

   You should see the finished Wish List program, as shown in Figure 13-1.

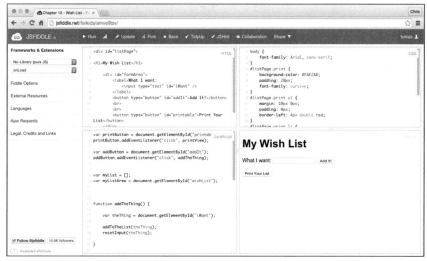

Figure 13-1: The finished Wish List program.

3. Enter something into the HTML input field — World Peace, for example — and click the Add It button.

   The item you entered will be added as a list item and removed from the input field.

4. Add a few more items to your list.

   When you get to about five or six items, move on to the next step.

5. Click the Print Your List button.

   A nicely formatted list appears, sorted in alphabetical order, as shown in Figure 13-2.

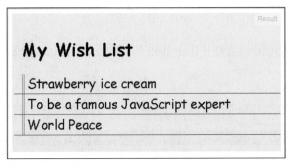

Figure 13-2: The printable wish list.

Forking the Code

Let's get started! To start building the Wish List program, follow these steps:

1. Go to our Public Dashboard in JSFiddle.net, locate the program called "Chapter 13 – Wish List – Start" and click its title to open it.

   The starting point for building the Wish List application will open, as shown in Figure 13-3.

Figure 13-3: The starting point for the Wish List program.

2. Click the Fork link in the top menu bar to create your own copy of the program.

3. Give your copy a new name by clicking the Fiddle Options menu item on the left.

4. Click Update, and then click Set as base to save your work.

The starting point for this application is a bare-bones HTML document, some CSS styles, and some instructions and an outline for the JavaScript that needs to be written.

If you want a challenge, try writing the program using only the instructions found in the comments, how you saw the finished version of the program working, and what you've learned elsewhere in this book. Go ahead and try it out before reading on! We'll still be here, and we'll give you detailed instructions for building this app when you return.

Writing the HTML

As with the other programs you've written, the first step in building the Wish List program is to create the structure using HTML. The first line of the HTML is the beginning tag of the `<div>` element that will surround everything else in the program.

```
<div id="listPage">
```

We've already written this tag for you, so there's no need to add it. Follow these steps to complete the HTML:

1. Use an `<h1>` element to give the page a header.

   ```
   <h1>My Wish List</h1>
   ```

   Notice that the beginning section, containing the form we'll use to input our wishes into, is already included in the HTML pane. It looks like this:

   ```
   <div id="formArea">
   ```

2. Within the section containing the form, put the text input field, where users will enter list items. We'll surround it with a `<label>` element that puts the words "What I want:" to the left of it.

   ```
   <label>What I want:
         <input type="text" id="iWant" />
   </label>
   ```

3. Next, type the first button element (labeled "Add It!") onto the next line.

   ```
   <button type="button" id="addIt">Add It!</button>
   ```

   This element puts a button on the same line as the input field.

4. Write the Print Your List button on the next line.

   ```
   <button type="button" id="printable">Print Your List</button>
   ```

5. In order to have the Print Your List button show up underneath your Add It button, type two `<br />` elements after the first button and before the next one:

```
<br /><br />
```

6. Next, create an empty `<div>` element with an ID of `"wishList"`.

```
<ul id="wishList"></ul>
```

7. Finally, close the `<div>` element that you opened back in Step 1 , that encloses all the program's HTML.

```
</div>
```

8. Click the Update button to save your work and to see the HTML in the Result pane.

   It should look like Figure 13-4.

Figure 13-4: The Wish List program with the HTML finished.

If you haven't already, you can remove the HTML comments that were in the code as placeholders, or you can change them to anything you want that will help you to remember what the different sections of the page are.

The finished HTML is shown in Listing 13-1.

 Even if you entered everything correctly, your markup may not look exactly like ours due to differences in spacing. Click the TidyUp link in the top toolbar to make JSFiddle clean everything up a bit.

Listing 13-1   **The HTML for the Wish List Program**

```
<div id="listPage">

    <h1>My Wish List</h1>

    <div id="formArea">
        <label>What I want:
            <input type="text" id="iWant" />
        </label>
        <button type="button" id="addIt">Add It!</button>
        <br /><br />
        <button type="button" id="printable">Print Your
            List</button>
    </div>
    <ul id="wishList"></ul>

</div>
```

Writing the JavaScript Code

We're done with the HTML pane now, and we're going to shift our focus to the JavaScript pane. You may want to resize your JavaScript pane to give yourself more room to work, as shown in Figure 13-5.

All the functions and JavaScript code for the Wish List program are described in the JavaScript pane. Take a moment to read through these comments.

In this section, we look at these comments one by one and replace them with functioning JavaScript code.

Creating the event listeners

The Wish List program has two buttons. In this section, we create event listeners to wait for and respond to click events on each of these buttons:

Figure 13-5: Make the JavaScript pane larger.

1. Find the JavaScript comment that shows how to start the event listener for the print button. It looks like this:

```
// var printButton =
```

2. Uncomment this line (remove the two slashes from the beginning of the line) to create a variable declaration. Create a reference to the Print button element and store it in the new variable, like this:

```
var printButton = document.getElementById("printable");
```

3. Finish the event listener, using the `addEventListener` method.

```
printButton.addEventListener("click",printView);
```

4. Find the JavaScript comment that shows how to start writing the event listener for the Add It button. It looks like this:

```
// var addButton =
```

5. Uncomment this line to create a variable declaration. Create a reference to the `addIt` button element and store it in the new `addButton` variable, like this:

```
var addButton = document.getElementById("addIt");
```

6. Finish the event listener by using the `addEventListener` method.

```
addButton.addEventListener("click",addTheThing);
```

You now have both event listeners in place. You can remove the comments telling you how to create them, if you'd like. Excellent! Your first four statements should now look like Listing 13-2.

Listing 13-2 **The Event Listeners**

```
var printButton = document.getElementById("printable");
printButton.addEventListener("click", printView);

var addButton = document.getElementById("addIt");
addButton.addEventListener("click", addTheThing);
```

Declaring global variables

With the listeners in place, let's move on to create a couple of variables that will be used throughout the program.

When you create a variable in your JavaScript code, but not inside of a function, it's called a *global variable*. Global variables can be used anywhere within a JavaScript program.

Variables that you declare inside of functions can only be used inside of the functions in which they're declared. These variables are called *local variables*.

Follow these steps to create the global variables for the Wish List program:

1. Find the comment that says to create a blank array named `myList` and replace it with the following array declaration:

   ```
   var myList = [];
   ```

   When you assign empty square brackets to a variable, it creates an array with no elements. It will then be ready for you to add elements as needed.

2. Find the next comment that says to create a variable called `myListArea`.

   Underneath this comment is another one that starts the variable declaration for you.

3. Uncomment the `myListArea` variable declaration and finish the statement as follows:

   ```
   var myListArea = document.getElementById("wishList");
   ```

Now you have the global variables in place. The finished part of your JavaScript code should look like Listing 13-3.

Listing 13-3   The Event Listeners and Global Variables

```
var printButton = document.getElementById("printable");
printButton.addEventListener("click", printView);

var addButton = document.getElementById("addIt");
addButton.addEventListener("click", addTheThing);


var myList = [];
var myListArea = document.getElementById("wishList");
```

Writing the functions

The rest of the program consists of functions that handle the actions of the program, such as adding items to the list, clearing out the input field so that you can add more items, and creating the printable list.

We'll start with the function that runs when you click the Add It button, addTheThing(). The addTheThing() function creates a reference to the input field when the Add It button is clicked and then passes it as an argument to the two other functions in the program.

Follow these steps to write addTheThing():

1. Create a variable called theThing and assign to it the input field element:

```
var theThing = document.getElementById("iWant");
```

An important thing to keep in mind here is that this statement doesn't actually get the value of the input field — it just stores a reference to the element, which we can use later to get the value.

2. Pass theThing as an argument to the function addToTheList():

```
addToTheList(theThing);
```

This function gets the value and adds it to the list, addToTheList().

3. Pass theThing as an argument to the function that resets the value of the input field to blank, resetInput().

```
resetInput(theThing);
```

These three statements are all that you need for the addTheThing() function. When it's done, the function should look like Listing 13-4.

Listing 13-4   The Finished addTheThing( ) Function

```
function addTheThing() {

    var theThing = document.getElementById("iWant");

    addToTheList(theThing);
    resetInput(theThing);


}
```

This might be a good time to click the Update button to save your work.

Let's test out the program now and see what happens. What do you think will happen when you test it? If you guess nothing, you're partially right.

When you try to run the program in its current form, as it is now, you get an error.

Open the JavaScript Console in your browser (by selecting it from the Chrome ⇨ More Tools ⇨ JavaScript Console) and see what happens when you click Update or Run. The resulting error is shown in Figure 13-6.

Figure 13-6: Running the Wish List with incomplete functions returns an error.

The error indicates that the printView function, which one of our event listeners references, doesn't exist.

We're not quite ready to write the `printView` function yet, but let's remove this error by creating an empty function called `printView`.

1. In the JavaScript pane of JSFiddle, find the comment that holds a placeholder for the `printView` function.

   It looks like this:

   ```
   /*function printView, which outputs a nicely formatted
   view of the list
   function printView() {

   }
   */
   ```

2. Remove the comment from before the function, and the ending comment characters from after the function.

   It should now look like this:

   ```
   function printView() {

   }
   ```

   The `printView` function is now a perfectly valid function, although its body is empty and it won't do anything at all when it's run.

3. In your JavaScript Console, click the Clear Console Log button (which looks like a circle with a line through it) to clear all the previous messages from the console.

4. Click Update to see whether the error is now resolved in the JavaScript Console.

   If you've done everything correctly so far, you shouldn't see any errors, as shown in Figure 13-7.

Figure 13-7: The Wish List program doesn't return any errors when run.

5. With the JavaScript Console still open, type something into the input field and click the Add It button.

You'll see a new error in the console, as shown in Figure 13-8.

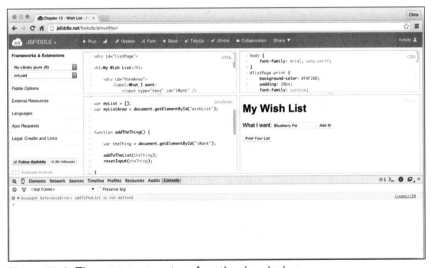

Figure 13-8: The `addToTheList` function is missing.

Let's resolve this error now, by creating the `addToTheList` function.

The purpose of `addToTheList` is to accept an argument, add it to an array, and then add it to an unordered list in the browser window. Follow these steps to create the function:

1. Find the comment that describes the `addToTheList` function and remove the comment before it and the ending comment characters from the end.

   The empty function should now look like this:

   ```
   function addToTheList(thingToAdd) {


   }
   ```

2. Write the first line inside the function body.

   ```
   myList.push(thingToAdd.value);
   ```

   This statement uses the `push()` array method to add the current value of the input field to the `myList` array.

   The `push()` array method adds values to the end of an array.

3. Write the next statement, which creates a new `<li>` element.

   ```
   var newListItem = document.createElement("li");
   ```

   The `createElement()` method causes a new element to be created in the current browser window. It's not displayed anywhere just yet; it's just an empty `<li>` element, which we've stored inside a new variable called `newListItem`.

4. The next statement changes the `innerHTML` property of the new element to put the current value of the input field into it.

   ```
   newListItem.innerHTML = myList[myList.length - 1];
   ```

Take a close look at the statement you just entered. Remember that each variable inside it is a stand-in for something else. Let's walk through it, starting with the value between the square brackets of the `myList` array:

```
myList.length - 1
```

This expression returns the length of the `myList` array, and then subtracts 1 from it. What we want to find out here is the index number of the last element of the array (the element we just added). We subtract 1 from the length of the array, because arrays start counting at 0.

If we have only one thing on our list, what the program is really saying when we say `myList[myList.length - 1]`, is `myList[0]`, which contains the value of the single item on our list.

If you entered World Peace into the input field, this whole statement could now be rewritten as:

```
newListItem.innerHTML = "World Peace";
```

This looks a lot more familiar now. Recall that setting the value of an element's `innerHTML` property changes everything between its starting and ending tags.

Since `newListItem` contains a reference to a new `<li>` element, this whole statement creates the following element if you entered World Peace into the form field:

```
<li>World Peace</li>
```

This element doesn't exist anywhere in the HTML document yet. To make it display, we need to write another statement in our `addToTheList()` function.

5. On the next line, type the following:

```
myListArea.appendChild(newListItem);
```

This statement uses another new method, `appendChild` to add our brand-new `<li>` element to the end of the contents of the element referenced by the `myListArea` variable.

If you look back in the code, you'll see that we created the `myListArea` global variable to hold a reference to the `<ul>` element with an ID attribute of `"wishList"`.

What this statement does is add a new list item to the `<ul>` element, which displays the new item in the browser window.

6. Click the Update button to save your work.

   The finished `addToTheList()` function is shown in Listing 13-5.

Listing 13-5   The Finished addToTheList() Function

```
function addToTheList(thingToAdd) {
    myList.push(thingToAdd.value);
    var newListItem = document.createElement("li");
    newListItem.innerHTML = myList[myList.length - 1];

    myListArea.appendChild(newListItem);
}
```

7. Enter something in the input field now, and click the Add It button.

   The new item will be added to a list below the input field.

8. Add a few more items and see how each item gets added to the end of the list, as shown in Figure 13-9.

The form doesn't work quite right yet. Each time you add a new value to the list, your old value stays in the form field.

To fix this problem, we'll write a new function, called `resetInput()`. The `resetInput()` function is called by the `addTheThing()` function after each item is added to the list. The purpose of `resetInput()` is simply to clear out the value of the input field for you to enter your next item.

Figure 13-9: New items get added to the end of the list.

Follow these steps to write the resetInput() function.

1. Find the commented-out resetInput() function in the JavaScript pane.

   It looks like this:

   ```
   /* function resetInput, which resets the value of the
   input field to blank ("")
   function resetInput(inputToReset) {


   }
   */
   ```

2. Uncomment the empty function.

   It should look like this:

   ```
   function resetInput(inputToReset) {


   }
   ```

3. Enter the following between the curly braces:

   ```
   inputToReset.value = "";
   ```

The `resetInput()` function contains only one statement here. This statement changes the value property of the element referenced by the `inputToReset` variable (the input field) to an empty string. The result is that the text in the input field empties out.

4. Click the Update link to save your work.

The finished `resetInput()` function is shown in Listing 13-6.

Listing 13-6   The Finished resetInput() Function

```
function resetInput(inputToReset) {
    inputToReset.value = "";
}
```

5. Test out your program by entering several items into the text field and pressing the Add It button.

The basic functionality of the Wish List program is done now. You can enter items into the text field and those items are added to the HTML list and to the array.

The final function we need to create is the handler for the Print Your List button. The purpose of the `printView()` function is to hide the form and to display each of the elements in the `myList` array in a nice format that can be printed and given to your genie!

Follow these steps to write the body of the `printView()` function. Find the empty `printView()` function in the JavaScript pane. It should look like this:

```
function printView() {
}
```

1. Create a new variable to hold a reference to the entire page.

```
var listPage = document.getElementById("listPage");
```

2. Create a new variable to hold a reference to the form area of the page.

```
var formArea = document.getElementById("formArea");
```

3. Hide the form by changing the value of the CSS display property to "none".

```
formArea.style.display = "none";
```

4. Add a new class attribute to the listPage element, with a value of "print".

```
listPage.className = "print";
```

What this statement does is to modify the first div element in the document from this:

```
<div id="listPage">
```

to this:

```
<div id="listPage" class="print">
```

The print class is used in the CSS to style the page differently. In other words, when the print class is assigned to the listPage div, it changes the way elements in the document are styled, using the style properties set for print in the CSS.

5. Clear all the items from the list with this statement:

```
myListArea.innerHTML = "";
```

6. Sort the array, using the sort() array method, using this statement:

```
myList.sort();
```

This statement sorts the items on your list alphabetically.

7. Next, we use a loop to print out each value in the array. Type this statement:

```
for (var i = 0; i < myList.length; i++) {
```

We cover loops in detail in Chapter 17. What this statement does is to run the statements between its curly braces one time for every item in the array.

8. Type the following to write the statement to print out the array element:

```
wishList.innerHTML += "<li>" + myList[i] + "</li>";
```

This statement adds a list item to the `wishList` and displays it in the browser window.

9. Close the loop by typing a final closing curly brace on the next line.

```
}
```

10. Save your work by clicking the Update button.

The finished `printView()` function is shown in Listing 13-7.

Listing 13-7   The Finished printView() Function

```
function printView() {
    var listPage = document.getElementById("listPage");
    var formArea = document.getElementById("formArea");

    formArea.style.display = "none";
    listPage.className = "print";
    myListArea.innerHTML = "";
    myList.sort();

    for (var i = 0; i < myList.length; i++) {
        wishList.innerHTML += "<li>" + myList[i] +
            "</li>";
    }
}
```

11. Add several items to your wish list, and then click the Print Your List button.

    You see a nicely formatted printable list, as shown in Figure 13-10.

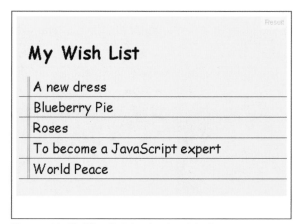

Figure 13-10: The finished printable list.

Opening the Print dialog box

Now that our list is formatted nicely, let's create the command that will cause the program to automatically open your browser's Print dialog box when you click the Print Your List button.

Follow these steps to enable the automatic printing:

1. After the loop in the `printView()` function, insert the following statement:

    ```
    window.print();
    ```

    This statement runs a built-in method, called `print()`, which belongs to the window object. The purpose of the `print()` method is to tell the browser to open the Print dialog box with the default settings.

    The `window` object represents the current browser window within JavaScript.

2. Click Update to save your changes.

3. Add as many items as you'd like to your wish list and then click Print Your List to generate the printable view.

   Your browser's Print dialog box appears, as shown in Figure 13-11.

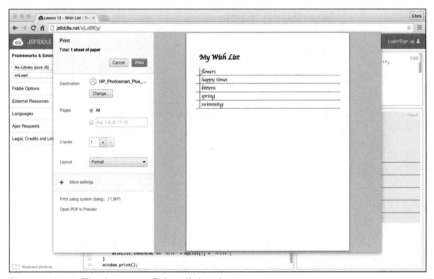

Figure 13-11: The browser Print dialog box.

4. If you have a printer connected to your computer, try printing out your wish list.

Enhancing the Wish List

We designed the application using functions and an array in order to make it super-customizable and expandable. Future enhancements could include the following:

✔ Adding an input field for a link, and storing the link in a second array

✔ Saving the list items to the user's computer so they can come back and view it later

✔ The ability to email the list to someone else

Can you think of other enhancements that you might want to add?

Part V

Freedom of Choice

JavaScript Pizzeria

How many pizzas do you want? 50

What kind of pizzas? Cheese

Where do you live? Sacramento

Is it your birthday? Yes

Place Order

Thank you for your order.

You get free delivery!

Your total is: $500

In this part . . .

Making Decisions with the If. . .Else Statement.. 233

Doing Different Things with Switch 252

Choose Your Own Adventure 267

For JavaScript troubleshooting tips, go to
www.dummies.com/extras/
javascriptforkids.

Making Decisions with the If...Else Statement

When you need to make an either/or or yes/no decision, the `if...else` statement is your best friend. In this chapter, you learn how to use `if...else` statements to create and navigate choices in JavaScript programs.

Result

JavaScript Pizzeria

How many pizzas do you want? | 1

What kind of pizzas? | Pepperoni ⬍

Where do you live? | Sacramento ⬍

Is it your birthday? | Yes ⬍

| Place Order |

Thank you for your order.

You get free delivery!

Your total is: $10

Boolean Logic

In Chapter 9, we talk about JavaScript's comparison operators and show you how they work in the JavaScript Super-Calculator. Let's briefly review the comparison operators here.

Equality

The equality operators are == and ===. The difference between the two is that the double equals will convert values between different types. For example, if you compare 3 with "3", the == operator will say that they're equal, while the triple equals operator will say that they aren't.

The triple equals operator is called the *strict equality operator.* We recommend that you always use the strict equality operator in order to avoid bugs.

Not equal

The not equal operators are formed by putting an exclamation point (!) before the equality operators. They tell you whether two values are different. The strict not equal operator (!==) compares values without converting their type and the not equal operator (!=) converts between data types before comparing. We recommend that you always use the strict not equal operator.

Greater than and less than

The greater than (>) and less then (<) operators compare numeric values. Remember that the greater than and less than operators look like alligators, and the alligators want to eat the larger number. If the "mouth" of the alligator is open toward the larger number, the result will be true.

Greater than or equal and less than or equal

The greater than or equal and less than or equal operators work the same as the greater than or less than operators except that they also return true if the values are equal to each other.

The greater than or equal and less than or equal operators are formed by putting an equal sign to the right of the greater than or less than operators. For example:

```
3 >= 4 // returns false
4 >= 4 // returns true
4 >= 3 // returns true
3 <= 3 // returns true
3 <= 4 // returns true
4 <= 3 // returns false
```

Not greater than and not less than

Putting an exclamation point after the greater than or less than signs converts them into not greater than (>!) or not less than operators (<!).

If you're like us, you may find not greater than and not less than operators to be confusing. Our advice: Don't use the not operator with greater than and less than. In truth, not greater than does exactly the same thing as the simple less than, and not less than is precisely the same as greater than.

Table 14-1 shows all the comparison operators that you need to know and shows examples of each.

Table 14-1	All the Comparison Operators You Need	
Operator	**What It Does**	**True Example**
===	Tests whether the value on the left is exactly equal to the one on the right.	14 === 14
!==	Tests whether the value on the left is not exactly equal to the one on the right.	14 !== 15
>	Tests whether the value on the left is greater than the one on the right.	15 > 14
<	Tests whether the value on the left is less than the one on the right.	14 < 15
>=	Tests whether the value on the left is either greater than or equal to the one on the right.	14 >= 14

(continued)

Table 14-1 *(continued)*

Operator	What It Does	True Example
<=	Tests whether the value on the left is either less than or equal to the one on the right.	14 <= 14

Introducing if...else Statements

Comparison operators aren't really very useful by themselves. Most of the time, they're used to make decisions inside of if... else statements.

The if...else statement looks like this:

```
if ([comparison]) {
    // statements to run if the comparison is true
} else {
    // statements to run if the comparison is false
}
```

The else part of the statement is optional. It's perfectly valid and common to only have an if condition followed by the statement or statements that will run if the comparison is true.

Listing 14-1 shows an example of how you might use if...else in a program.

Listing 14-1   **Using if...else**

```
var language = prompt("What language do you speak?");

if (language === "JavaScript") {
    alert("Great! Let's talk JavaScript!");
} else {
    alert("I don't know what you're saying.");
}
```

To try out this program, follow these steps:

1. Open JSFiddle in your web browser.

2. Create a new blank program by clicking the JSFiddle logo.

3. Type the code from Listing 14-1 into the JavaScript pane.

4. Click Run or Update to execute the code.

   A pop-up window appears, asking you to input text.

5. Type the word **JavaScript** (watch your capitalization!) into the pop-up and click OK.

   The first pop-up disappears and a second one opens that reads `"Great! Let's talk JavaScript!"`, as shown in Figure 14-1.

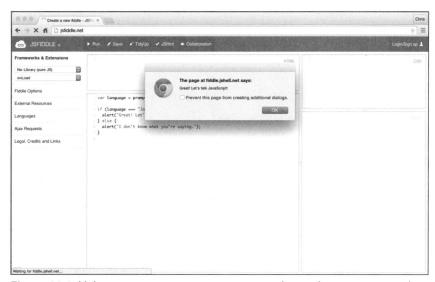

Figure 14-1: Using an `if...else` statement to choose between two paths.

Variables without operators

Sometimes, you may want to take a certain action only if a particular variable has a value or has been declared. To do this, you can just put the name of the variable in the parentheses after `if`. If the variable doesn't exist or doesn't have a value, it will result in a value of `false`.

Listing 14-2 expands the program from Listing 14-1 to create a variable called `speaksJavaScript` when you enter **JavaScript** into the prompt.

If you type in **JavaScript** correctly, the statement within the `if` block will execute, displaying a special message for JavaScript speakers only. If you enter anything other than **JavaScript**, the statement within the `else` block will execute, so that a different message will display.

Listing 14-2   Using Single-Word Operators

```
var language = prompt("What language do you speak?");

if (language === "JavaScript") {
  alert("Great! Let's talk JavaScript!");
  var speaksJavaScript = true;
} else {
  alert("I don't know what you're saying.");
}

if (speaksJavaScript) {
  alert("It's great to meet you.");
}
```

Combining Comparisons with Logical Operators

Logical operators allow you to combine more than one comparison operation. For example, let's say you own a pizza parlor. Your policy is that if a customer's order is more than $10 and they live within the city limits, they get free delivery.

In JavaScript, this rule requires two comparisons:

✔ Is the order over $10?

✔ Is the customer located within the city limits?

In order for the customer to get free delivery, both of these conditions have to be true. If one of these conditions is not true, the delivery charge is $5.

In JavaScript, you can specify that two conditions both need to be true by using the *and operator* (&&). To use the and operator in an if...else statement, you put it between two comparison expressions. Then you surround the whole combination expression with parentheses.

Listing 14-3 shows how you might write your pizza parlor's delivery rule in JavaScript.

Listing 14-3   Pizza Parlor Free Delivery Rule in JavaScript

```
if ((deliveryCity === "Anytown") && (orderPrice > 10)) {
      var deliveryPrice = 0;
    } else {
      var deliveryPrice = 5;
    }
```

As a special deal, you might decide to offer free delivery to people when it's their birthday, no matter how far away they live or the size of their order. In order to do this, you need to use the *or operator* (||). You type the or operator by holding down the Shift key and pressing the backslash (\) character on your keyboard twice.

Listing 14-4 shows how to write the new free delivery policy in JavaScript.

Listing 14-4   Free Delivery on Your Birthday

```
if (((deliveryCity === "Anytown") && (orderPrice > 10)) ||
          (birthday === "yes")) {
      var deliveryPrice = 0;
    } else {
      var deliveryPrice = 5;
    }
```

In the next section, we start with this free delivery policy and create a program for managing several different parts of your pizza parlor.

Freshening Up the JavaScript Pizzeria

The JavaScript Pizzeria is a little mom-and-pop place in Anytown, USA. They pride themselves on making good pizzas at a good price and keeping things simple.

Currently, they have a web page where you can order one of their two kinds of pizza — cheese or pepperoni — and have it delivered to you for free if you live inside the city limits of Anytown, USA.

Customers are demanding more, though! They want additional pizza options. And people in other cities have been hearing about JavaScript Pizzeria, and they want pizza delivered, too! Some people have even asked for a special deal on their birthday!

As the JavaScript programmer for the JavaScript Pizzeria, it's your job to whip up these new features so that the business continues to thrive! Don't worry, we're here to help.

Running the app

To test out the current version of the JavaScript Pizzeria website, follow these steps:

1. Go to our public dashboard on JSFiddle at
   `http://jsfiddle.net/user/forkids/fiddles`.

2. Find the program named "Chapter 14 – JavaScript Pizzeria – Start" and click its title to open it.

3. Enter a number of pizzas, select a pizza type, and press the Place Order button.

   The total (at $10 per pizza) will display below the form.

That's all there is to it! Move on to the next section to create your own version of the JavaScript Pizzeria that you can add new features to.

Forking the code (or just using your hands)

Follow these steps to create your own copy of the JavaScript Pizzeria program that you can add new features to:

1. Open the program named "Chapter 14 – JavaScript Pizzeria – Start."

2. Click the Fork button in the top menu bar.

3. Change the name of the program in the Fiddle Options on the left menu.

4. Click Update to save your changes, and then click Set as Base.

Great! You're ready to get started!

Planning the pizza parlor program improvements

Here are the three changes that we'll make to the JavaScript Pizzeria program:

- Add a new kind of pizza and charge extra for it.

- Add new cities and calculate delivery charges for them.

- Display the delivery charge.

- Add a birthday special.

Each of these changes requires an `if...else` statement, as well as some small changes to the HTML.

Adding the new item to the menu

The most important new feature at this point is to spruce up the menu. The cook has invented a new kind of pizza that has bacon, arugula, apples, 14 different kinds of cheese, and a corn dog on top. He calls it the Supreme pizza.

The problem is, the Supreme pizza is very expensive to make — mostly because of that corn dog! It's so difficult to find a gourmet corn dog in Anytown! So, the owner has decided to charge an extra $2 for each Supreme pizza.

Your job is to add the Supreme pizza to the menu and update the price when it gets ordered. Follow these steps to get started:

1. Look in the HTML pane to find the place where the list of pizzas is created.

   It currently looks like this:

   ```
   <label>What kind of pizzas?
       <select id="typePizza">
           <option value="cheese">Cheese</option>
           <option value="pepperoni">Pepperoni</option>
       </select>
   </label>
   ```

2. Add a new `option` element inside the `select` element to create the Supreme pizza option.

   It should have a value of `"supreme"`, and the label (between `<option>` and `</option>`) should read Supreme.

3. Click Update to save your work, and then test to make sure that Supreme shows up as a new option in the pizza type dropdown list, as shown in Figure 14-2.

4. Find the `calculatePrice()` function.

   It looks like this:

   ```
   function calculatePrice(numPizzas, typePizza) {
       var orderPrice = Number(numPizzas) * 10;
       var extraCharge = 0;

       // calculate extraCharge, if there is one

       orderPrice += extraCharge;
       return orderPrice;
   }
   ```

Figure 14-2: The new option has been added.

5. Right below the comment that reads `calculate extraCharge, if there is one`, type the following `if...else` statement:

```
if (typePizza === "supreme") {
    extraCharge = Number(numPizzas) * 2;
}
```

This statement checks the `typePizza` variable to see if the Supreme was selected. If so, it will multiply the number of pizzas by two in order to get the number of dollars to add to the price.

6. Save your work by clicking Update, and then try it out!

If you select the Supreme pizza, you should now see that the total will be equal to $12 times the number of pizzas your ordered, as shown in Figure 14-3.

Delivering to other cities

The pizzeria has to grow! But the population of Anytown can only eat so many pizzas, so management has decided to start delivery service to other, carefully chosen, cities.

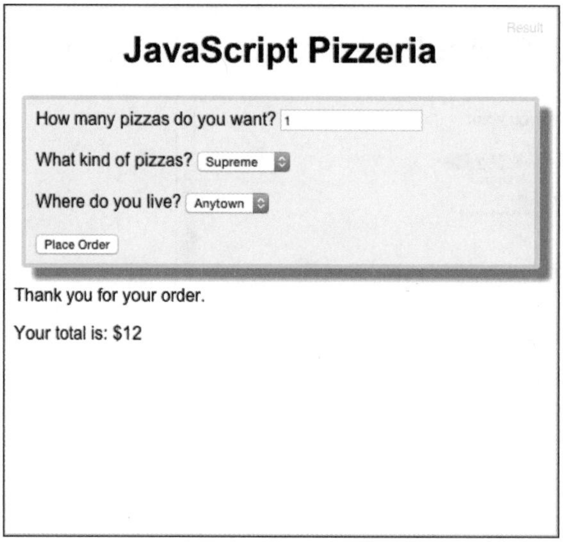

Figure 14-3: The new pie has been added!

There's a catch, though! It's not profitable to deliver just a single pizza or to deliver to Beverly Hills for free. We'll need to charge $5 for delivery of orders less than or equal to $10 and for out-of-town delivery.

Follow these steps to put the new rules into place!

1. In the HTML pane, locate the drop-down menu for the delivery city.

   It currently only has one option, Anytown.

2. Add at least two more options to the drop-down.

   When it's finished, it should look like this:

   ```
   <label>Where do you live?
     <select id="deliveryCity">
       <option value="Anytown">Anytown</option>
       <option value="Sacramento">Sacramento</option>
       <option value="Your Town">Your Town</option>
     </select>
   </label>
   ```

   You can replace Your Town with anything you like.

3. Click Update to save your work and see your changes in the Result pane.

4. In the JavaScript pane, find the `calculateDelivery()` function.

   It currently just sets everyone's `deliveryPrice` to 0.

5. Under the comment that reads `calculate delivery price, if there is one`, insert the following `if...else` statement.

```
if ((deliveryCity === "Anytown") && (orderPrice > 10))
  {
    deliveryPrice = 0;
  } else {
    deliveryPrice = 5;
  }
```

6. Save your work by clicking the Update button, and try out the form in the Result pane.

   If you select a city other than Anytown, or your order price is $10, a delivery fee of $5 will now be added to the total.

Displaying the delivery fee

Next, we need to display the delivery fee above the total, so that people know what they're getting into.

To display the delivery fee, follow these steps:

1. In the `placeOrder()` function, find the comment that reads `todo: output the delivery price, if there is one`.

2. Below that comment, type the following `if...else` statements:

```
if (deliveryPrice === 0) {
  theOutput += "<p>You get free delivery!</p>";
} else {
  theOutput += "<p>Your delivery cost is: $" + deliveryPrice;
}
```

This `if...else` prints out a free delivery message if the `deliveryPrice` is 0. Otherwise, it prints out the delivery charge.

3. Click Update to save your changes. Then try out the form in the Result pane.

   The new free delivery message is shown in Figure 14-4.

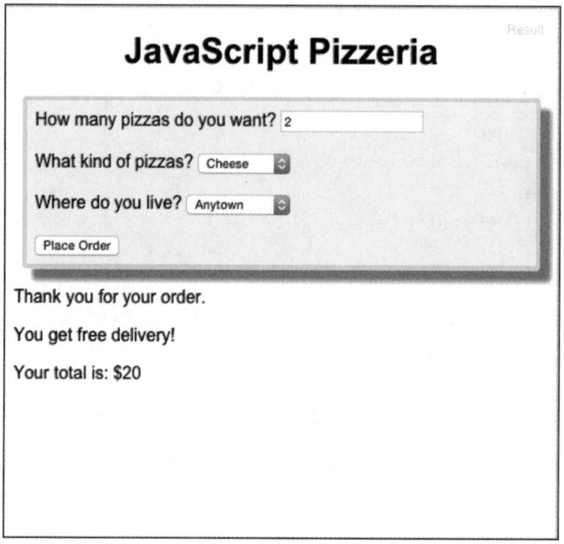

Figure 14-4: Telling the customer that they get free delivery is great for marketing!

Programming the birthday special

The final change that we'll make to the program is to give people free delivery on their birthdays.

To program this change, follow these steps:

1. In the HTML pane, add the birthday question to the form by typing this markup after the delivery city question:

```
<label>Is it your birthday?
  <select id="birthday">
    <option value="yes">Yes</option>
```

```
      <option value="no">No</option>
   </select>
</label>
```

2. Click Update to save your work and to see your changes in the Result pane.

   If your Result pane doesn't look like Figure 14-5, check your code carefully. You may also need to insert `<br/>` tags in order to put in the right amount of spacing between questions.

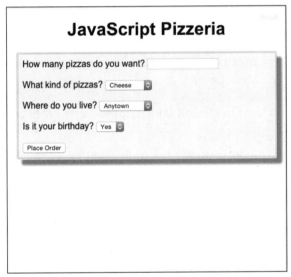

Figure 14-5: The Result pane with the new birthday question.

3. Add the following to the `placeOrder()` function, below the other `getElementById` statements to get the value of the birthday form field:

   ```
   var birthday = document.getElementById("birthday").value;
   ```

4. Add a third parameter to the `calculateDelivery` function definition for the birthday variable.

   ```
   function calculateDelivery(orderPrice, deliveryCity, birthday)
   ```

5. Add an `or` operator and a new expression to the `if...else` statement in the `calculateDelivery` function to test whether the value of birthday is yes.

```
if (((deliveryCity === "Anytown") && (orderPrice > 10)) ||
        (birthday === "yes")) {
```

6. Modify the statement in the `placeOrder()` function that calls `calculateDelivery`, to pass birthday as an argument:

```
var deliveryPrice = calculateDelivery(orderPrice, deliveryCity,
        birthday);
```

7. Click Update to save your work.

Listing 14-5 shows the completed JavaScript code for the JavaScript Pizzeria program.

Listing 14-5 The Completed JavaScript Pizzeria Program

```
// listen for button clicks
document.getElementById("placeOrder").addEventListener
        ("click", placeOrder);

/**
 * gets form values
 * calculates prices
 * produces output
 */
function placeOrder() {
    // get form values
    var numPizzas =
            document.getElementById("numPizzas").value;
    var typePizza =
            document.getElementById("typePizza").value;
    var deliveryCity =
            document.getElementById("deliveryCity").value;
    var birthday =
            document.getElementById("birthday").value;

    // get the pizza price
    var orderPrice = calculatePrice(numPizzas, typePizza);
```

```
            // get the delivery price
            var deliveryPrice = calculateDelivery(orderPrice,
                    deliveryCity, birthday);

            // create the output
            var theOutput = "<p>Thank you for your order.</p>";

            // output the delivery price, if there is one
            if (deliveryPrice === 0) {
                theOutput += "<p>You get free delivery!</p>";
            } else {
                theOutput += "<p>Your delivery cost is: $" +
                    deliveryPrice;
            }

            theOutput += "<p>Your total is: $" + (orderPrice +
                    deliveryPrice);

            // display the output
            document.getElementById("displayTotal").innerHTML =
                    theOutput;
        }

        /**
         * calculates pizza price
         */
        function calculatePrice(numPizzas, typePizza) {
            var orderPrice = Number(numPizzas) * 10;
            var extraCharge = 0;

            // calculate extraCharge, if there is one
            if (typePizza === "supreme") {
                extraCharge = Number(numPizzas) * 2;
            }

            orderPrice += extraCharge;
            return orderPrice;
        }

        /**
```

Listing 14-5 *(continued)*

```
 * calculates delivery price
 */
function calculateDelivery(orderPrice, deliveryCity,
        birthday) {
   var deliveryPrice = 0;

   // calculate delivery price, if there is one
   if (((deliveryCity === "Anytown") && (orderPrice >
        10)) || (birthday === "yes")) {
      deliveryPrice = 0;
   } else {
      deliveryPrice = 5;
   }
      return deliveryPrice;
}
```

Listing 14-6 shows the completed HTML markup for the JavaScript Pizzeria.

Listing 14-6 **The Final HTML**

```
<h1>JavaScript Pizzeria</h1>

<div id="orderForm">
   <label>How many pizzas do you want?
      <input type="number" id="numPizzas" />
   </label>
   <br />
   <br />
   <label>What kind of pizzas?
      <select id="typePizza">
         <option value="cheese">Cheese</option>
         <option value="pepperoni">Pepperoni</option>
         <option value="supreme">Supreme</option>
      </select>
   </label>
   <br />
   <br />
   <label>Where do you live?
      <select id="deliveryCity">
```

```
                        <option value="Anytown">Anytown</option>
                        <option value="Sacramento">Sacramento</option>
                        <option value="Beverly Hills">Beverly
                    Hills</option>
                </select>
            </label>
            <br />
            <br />
            <label>Is it your birthday?
                <select id="birthday">
                    <option value="yes">Yes</option>
                    <option value="no">No</option>
                </select>
            </label>
            <br />
            <br />
            <button type="button" id="placeOrder">Place
                    Order</button>
        </div>
        <div id="displayTotal"></div>
```

Figure 14-6 shows the final program's Result pane after placing our lunch order today.

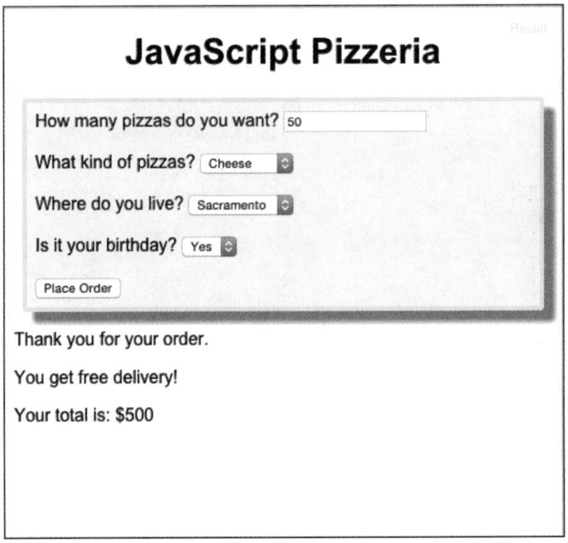

Figure 14-6: Our lunch order.

15

Doing Different Things with Switch

Switch statements are like highways with many different exits. The `switch` statement chooses among multiple cases by evaluating an expression. These values are like the exits. Each of these values in a `switch` statement is called a *case*.

In this chapter, we use a `switch` statement to write a calendar program that gives you suggestions for things to do, based on what day of the week it is.

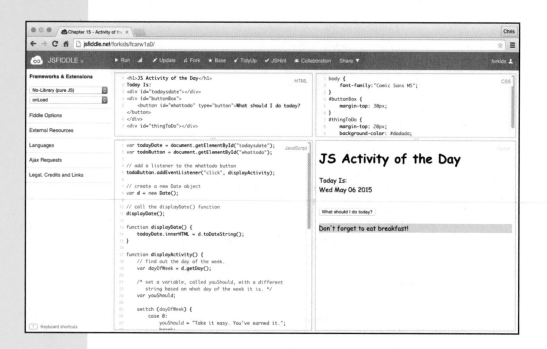

Writing a Switch

The switch statement starts with the switch keyword, followed by an expression in parentheses and then a series of different options (called *cases*).

The syntax for the switch statement looks like this:

```
switch (expression) {
  case value1:
    //statements to execute
    break;
  case value2:
    //statements to execute
    break;
  case default:
    //statements to execute
    break;
}
```

You can have as many cases inside a switch statement as you'd like. The switch statement will try to match the expression to each case until it finds one that matches. Then it runs the statements within that case until it gets to the break statement, which causes it to exit the switch statement. Each case must end with a break statement or semicolon (;). This tells the program to do everything inside the case up until the break statement and then stop.

A default case will run if no case matches the result of the expression.

Let's take a look at an example! The code in Listing 15-1 asks the user to enter his favorite day of the week. The program then uses a switch statement to produce a different output based on possible values that the user might enter. If the user enters anything other than a day of the week, the default switch statement will run.

Listing 15-1 Produce Different Results for Different Input

```javascript
var myNumber = prompt("Enter your favorite day of the
            week!");
var theResponse;

switch (myNumber) {
  case "Monday":
    theResponse = "Ack!";
    break;
  case "Tuesday":
    theResponse = "Taco day!";
    break;
  case "Wednesday":
    theResponse = "Halfway there!";
    break;
  case "Thursday":
    theResponse = "It's the new Friday!";
    break;
  case "Friday":
    theResponse = "TGIF! Yeah!";
    break;
  case "Saturday":
    theResponse = "What a day!";
    break;
  case "Sunday":
    theResponse = "Sunday = Funday!";
    break;
  default:
    theResponse = "I haven't heard of that one!";
    break;
}
alert (theResponse);
```

Follow these steps to try out this program in JSFiddle:

1. Open JSFiddle and create a new blank project by clicking the JSFiddle logo in the upper left.

2. Type the code from Listing 15-1 into the JavaScript pane.

3. Click the Run link in the top menu.

   A JavaScript prompt appears, asking you to enter your favorite day of the week.

4. Enter a day of the week and click OK.

   The switch statement runs. You should see a result based on the value that you entered, as shown in Figure 15-1.

Figure 15-1: Determining a response by evaluating different cases.

Building the Activity-of-the-Day Calendar

If you're like most people, you sometimes wake up thinking, "What day is it?" The next thing you may think is, "Of all the great things that I could be doing today, what is the one thing that I'm going to do first?" Here's where most people's days go wrong. They start off on the wrong foot, or get up on the wrong side of the bed, or set off on the wrong track.

Don't you wish you had a web page or mobile app that would tell you what day it is and exactly one thing that you should do on that day. Well, wish no more, because you're about to build it! If you use this program first thing in the morning, your odds of hitting the ground running and having a real whiz-bang kind of a day will be 110 percent greater! Guaranteed!

Using the Activity Calendar program

Before we start building it, let's check out the finished Activity Calendar and see what it does. Follow these steps to run it:

1. Visit our public dashboard at `http://jsfiddle.net/user/forkids/fiddles`.

2. Find the program named "Chapter 15 – Activity of the Day" and click its title to open it.

   You see the standard JSFiddle editor with the date and time and a button in the Result pane, as shown in Figure 15-2.

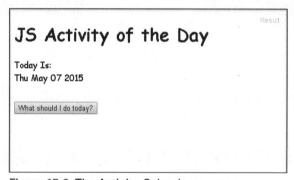

Figure 15-2: The Activity Calendar program.

3. Click the button labeled "What should I do today?"

   A message appears below the button, telling you what you should do, as shown in Figure 15-3. The message is different for every day of the week.

Forking the Activity Calendar program

To get started with the Activity Calendar, follow these steps:

1. Go to our JSFiddle public dashboard at `http://jsfiddle.net/user/forkids/fiddles` and locate the program named "Chapter 15 – Activity of the Day – Start."

2. Click the title of the program to open it in the editor.

Figure 15-3: The activity of the day.

3. Open the Fiddle Options in the left toolbar and change the name of the program to *Your Name*'s Activity Calendar (replacing *Your Name* with — you guessed it! — your name).

4. Click Update and Set as Base to save your work.

5. Test out the program by pressing the button in the Result pane.

   Nothing happens because the JavaScript hasn't been completed yet.

Before we show you how to complete the Activity Calendar, let's talk about an important built-in JavaScript object that we use in this chapter, the Date object.

Using the Date object

The JavaScript Date object represents a single moment in time within a JavaScript program. To create an instance of the Date object, use the new keyword and assign the result to a variable name, like this:

```
var myDate = new Date();
```

Creating a new `Date` object in this way will assign the current date to the variable.

To test this out, follow these steps:

1. Open the JavaScript Console in Google Chrome.

2. Type the following into the console, and then press Return (Mac) or Enter (Windows).

    ```
    var myDate = new Date();
    ```

    The console prints out `undefined` to acknowledge that the command has been run.

3. Type the following, and then press Return or Enter.

    ```
    myDate
    ```

    The console prints out the exact date and time that your `Date` object was created.

Like other JavaScript objects we talk about in this book, the `Date` object has a bunch of built-in functions (also known as methods) that you can use to do different things with the `Date` object.

Table 15-1 lists the methods that can be used to get information from the `Date` object. When you use a method to get information from an object, it's called a *getter method.*

Table 15-1	Getter Methods of the Date Object
Method	**What It Does**
`getDate()`	Gets the day of the month (1–31).
`getDay()`	Gets the day of the week as a number (0–6).
`getFullYear()`	Gets the year (yyyy).

Method	What It Does
getHours()	Gets the hour (0–23).
getMilliseconds()	Gets the fraction of a second (0–999).
getMonth()	Gets the month (0–11).
getSeconds()	Gets the seconds (0–59).
getTime()	Gets the time, in Unix time (milliseconds since January 1, 1970).

To use the getter methods of the Date object, attach them to an instance of the object using a period (or dot).

For example, after you've created a variable to hold a Date object in the Chrome Developer Console, follow these steps to use some of the getter methods.

1. Get the day of the week, as a number, with this statement:

   ```
   myDate.getDay()
   ```

   The JavaScript Console responds with a number from 0 to 6, where 0 is equal to Sunday and 6 is equal to Saturday.

2. Get the day of the month, as a number, with this statement:

   ```
   myDate.getDate();
   ```

3. Get the month of the year, as a number, with this statement:

   ```
   myDate.getMonth();
   ```

   Notice that both getMonth and getDay start with 0. In JavaScript, the number for January is 0.

   The numbers for both getDate and getFullYear, on the other hand, are returned how you would expect them. The second day of May is returned as the number 2, and the year 2020 is returned as 2020.

In addition to being able to get values from Date objects, JavaScript also allows you to set values. Table 15-2 lists the methods that can be used to set information in a Date object. When you use a method to set information in an object, it's called a *setter method*.

Table 15-2	Setter Methods of the Date Object
Method	**What It Does**
setDate()	Sets the day of the month (1–31).
setDay()	Sets the day of the week as a number (0–6).
setFullYear()	Sets the year (yyyy).
setHours()	Sets the hour (0–23).
setMilliseconds()	Sets the fraction of a second (0–999).
setMonth()	Sets the month (0–11).
setSeconds()	Sets the seconds (0–59).
setTime()	Sets the time, in Unix time (milliseconds since January 1, 1970).

To try using some of the setter methods in the JavaScript Console, follow these steps:

1. Create a new Date object using this statement:

   ```
   var myNewDate = new Date();
   ```

2. Find out the initial value of the Date object by typing its name into the console:

   ```
   myNewDate
   ```

   The console prints out the current value of the myNewDate object as a string.

3. Change the month to August using this statement:

   ```
   myNewDate.setMonth(7);
   ```

The console returns a giant number. This number is the new value of the `myNewDate` object in Unix time. Unix time is how JavaScript stores dates internally. It's equal to the number of milliseconds (thousandths of a second) since January 1, 1970.

4. Type the name of the object to see the new date as a human-readable string.

```
myNewDate
```

Now that you understand how to use the `Date` object, let's combine it with a `switch` statement to build the Activity Calendar program.

Building the Activity Calendar program

When you first load the starting point program for this chapter, the JavaScript pane contains the starting code and the comments that describe what the program will do. Listing 15-2 shows what our starting point code should look like.

Listing 15-2   The Starting JavaScript for the Activity Calendar

```
var todayDate = document.getElementById("todaysdate");
var todoButton = document.getElementById("whattodo");

// add a listener to the whattodo button
todoButton.addEventListener("click", displayActivity);

// create a new Date object
var d = new Date();

// call the displayDate() function
displayDate();

function displayDate() {
    // todo: display the current date in the todaysdate
            div
}

function displayActivity() {
    // todo: find out the day of the week
```

(continued)

Listing 15-2 *(continued)*

```
/* todo: set a variable, called youShould, with a
        different string based on what day of the
        week it is. */


// todo: output the value of youShould into the
        thingToDo div

}
```

Let's go over what the program does so far. Try following along in the code and pick out which statements do each of the following items:

✔ Define two new variables to hold references to HTML elements we'll be working with in the program.

✔ Create an event listener to handle clicks on the button.

✔ Create an instance of the Date object to hold the current date.

✔ Call a function that will display the current date.

After these things have been done, the program just sits and waits for someone to click the What To Do button. When it detects a click of the button, it runs the function associated with the event listener, displayActivity().

Your job is to finish the two functions in this program.

Before moving on to the step-by-step instructions, can you figure out how to do them yourself? Give it a try and when you're ready, move on and we'll walk you through how it works!

1. Find the displayDate() function and add this statement just below the comment:

   ```
   todayDate.innerHTML = d;
   ```

   This statement sets the innerHTML property of the div element referenced by the todayDate variable to the value of d (which we created as a Date object).

2. Click Update to see the date displayed in the Result pane.

3. To make the date displayed in the Result pane easier to read, change it to the following:

```
todayDate.innerHTML = d.toDateString();
```

Now when you run it, it will display a shorter date, with just the day of the week, the month, the date, and the year.

4. Find the function called `displayActivity()` and add a statement inside of it to get the current day of the week from the d variable.

```
var dayOfWeek = d.getDay();
```

5. Initialize a variable to hold the string that will contain the message for each day.

```
var youShould;
```

6. Write the condition part of a `switch` statement that will evaluate the value of the `dayOfWeek` variable, followed by an opening curly bracket:

```
switch (dayOfWeek) {
```

7. Write the first case, which will be for the value 0, or Sunday:

```
case 0:
```

8. Write a statement to set the value of `youShould` when it's Sunday, for example:

```
youShould = "Take it easy. You've earned it!";
```

9. Write a break statement to end the `switch` statement when this case is true.

```
break;
```

10. Write a case for each of the other days of the week.

11. After you've done the case for day 6, write a default case that should run in the (very remote) chance that the day of the week is something other than a number from 0 to 6.

```
default:
   youShould = "Hmm. Something has gone wrong.";
   break;
```

12. Finish the `switch` statement with a closed curly bracket on a line by itself.

```
}
```

13. Under the `switch` statement, write a statement to output the `youShould` string into the `div` with an ID of `thingToDo`.

```
document.getElementById("thingToDo").innerHTML = youShould
```

When all the statements are written, the JavaScript pane should look like Listing 15-3.

Listing 15-3   The Finished Program

```
var todayDate = document.getElementById("todaysdate");
var todoButton = document.getElementById("whattodo");

// add a listener to the whattodo button
todoButton.addEventListener("click", displayActivity);

// create a new Date object
var d = new Date();

// call the displayDate() function
displayDate();

function displayDate() {
   todayDate.innerHTML = d.toDateString();
}

function displayActivity() {
   // find out the day of the week
   var dayOfWeek = d.getDay();
```

```
/* set a variable, called youShould, with a different
        string based on what day of the week it is */

var youShould;

switch (dayOfWeek) {
  case 0:
    youShould = "Take it easy. You've earned it.";
    break;
  case 1:
    youShould = "Gotta do what ya gotta do!";
    break;
  case 2:
    youShould = "Take time to smell the roses!";
    break;
  case 3:
    youShould = "Don't forget to eat breakfast!";
    break;
  case 4:
    youShould = "Learn something new today!";
    break;
  case 5:
    youShould = "Make a list of things you like to do.";
    break;
  case 6:
    youShould = "Do one thing from your list of things
          you like to do.";
    break;
  default:
    youShould = "Hmm. Something has gone wrong.";
    break;
  }

// output the value of youShould into the thingToDo div
document.getElementById("thingToDo").innerHTML =
        youShould;
}
```

When it's done, try running it and pressing the button. The output in the Result pane should look like Figure 15-4.

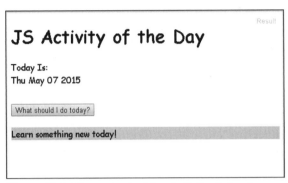

Figure 15-4: The output of the Activity Calendar program.

Now that you have your basic Activity Calendar, here are some ideas for making it even more awesome:

- Write your own activities, if you haven't already!

- Make it have a different activity for every day of the month instead of every day of the week.

- Have multiple messages — one for the day of the week, one for the day of the month, one for the month, and one for the year.

- Write CSS styles to customize the look of your Activity Calendar.

Can you think of other ideas for improving the Activity Calendar?

Choose Your Own Adventure

Imagine you're climbing a tree. If you climb up one branch, you'll see certain things, such as a bird's nest or a balloon that got stuck up there during your birthday party. If you climb a different branch, you might see other things, like the neighbor's garage. In JavaScript, the technique of using `if...else` or `switch` statements to choose between two or more paths is called *branching*.

In this chapter, we use branching to write a choose-your-own-adventure game that asks for user input at key moments to change the story.

You are the captain of a spaceship named "The Flying Hippo." One day, you're working on tuning up your ship's engines when you get an urgent message on your space phone:

"Captain, one of our Mars robots is sick. We need you to go to Mars immediately and retrieve it so that we can fix it and download the results of its important experiments."

You remember that you're supposed to go to a meeting of the Space Scouts tonight, and you were really looking forward to it. But, on the other hand, the other Space Scouts would understand that this mission is very important.

What do you do? Go to Mars, or stay home?

Go to Mars, or stay home?

Enter your answer: [   ] Go!

Planning the Story

Any good story needs a plot. The plot is the outline of events that happen over the course of the story. When writing a story where the user's input influences the plot, the writer needs to pay close attention to managing the different plot lines. Each plot line has the same beginning, but the middle and ending are different based on input from the user.

Creating a flow chart

Considering all of the different options — and planning for each possibility — in a branching program is a valuable skill to have as a programmer.

We'll begin by creating a simple story that poses a question. This creates two branches. Each of these branches will have a question that creates two more branches. Eventually, every choice will lead back to one of two possible endings.

A useful tool for visualizing branches of a story or of a program is a flowchart. Figure 16-1 shows a flow chart for our interactive story.

The next step in developing our story and program is to fill in the plot with some details.

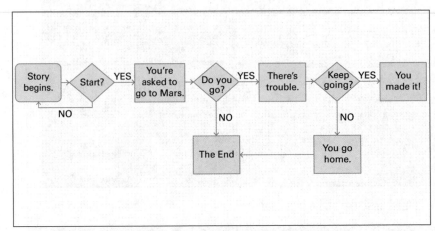

Figure 16-1: A flow chart showing the basic outline of the story.

Writing the story

Our story takes place on a spaceship in the not-too-distant future. You're the captain of the ship, and your mission is to fly to Mars to pick up an old robot that has stopped functioning so that it, and its valuable experiments, can be returned to Earth and studied.

The launch of the ship goes perfectly, but one week into the 260-day voyage, you discover that your cat has stowed away on your ship. Unless something changes, you might not have enough food for the both of you. You need to decide whether to turn your ship around, or keep going for Mars and hope for the best.

If you turn the ship around, the mission ends with the cat being returned to Earth and your boss yelling at you because you don't have the Mars robot.

If you continue toward Mars, you get very nervous about your food situation, but you feed the cat half of your meals each day, because you're a good person. You reach Mars and discover that the last person to visit the Mars robot left a large cooler full of delicious sandwiches. You pack them into the spaceship along with the robot and head home, where you're greeted as a hero.

Playing the Game

The most fun part about a game like this one, in which your choices decide how the story unfolds, is in exploring all the different possibilities. Interactive stories tend to be short, because reading and writing each of the different possibilities takes much more effort and time than writing or reading a story with just a single storyline.

To see how the Martian Rescue! game works, follow these steps:

1. Go to our public dashboard in JSFiddle, at `http://jsfiddle.net/user/forkids/fiddles`.

   You see a list of all the projects that we've created for this book.

2. Open the "Chapter 16 – Martian Rescue!" project by clicking its title in the public dashboard.

The project opens, as shown in Figure 16-2, and the Result pane asks you to answer the first question.

3. Enter your answer to the first question into the input field, and click the Go button.

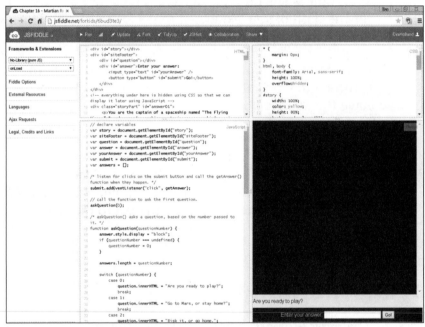

Figure 16-2: The Martian Rescue! program.

Depending on how you respond, new text displays in the Result pane and you're asked another question.

4. Respond to the new question.

Once again, the program will respond to your question by continuing the story.

5. Answer questions and view the results until the game ends.

6. Click Run in the JSFiddle top menu to start the program over.

   The text from the first time you ran the program will be removed from the Result pane and you see the first question again.

7. Play the game again, but answer questions differently this time in order to see the alternate messages and story ending.

Now that you've seen how the game works, move on to the next section, where we show you how to program it, and how you can customize it with your own stories!

Forking the Code

We've created a starting point for the program, with all the HTML and CSS necessary, but only part of the JavaScript written. Follow these steps to make a copy of the starter program in your own JSFiddle account.

1. Log into JSFiddle if you aren't already logged in.

2. Go to our JSFiddle Public Dashboard at `http://jsfiddle. net/user/forkids/fiddles` and find the "Chapter 16 – Martian Rescue – Start" project.

3. Open the starter project by clicking the title.

4. Click the Fork link in the top menu to save a copy in your own JSFiddle account.

5. Change the name of the project to "(Your Name)'s Martian Rescue."

6. Click Update and Set as Base in the top menu to save your work.

Tiptoeing through the HTML and CSS

The HTML and CSS for Martian Rescue! are finished in the starter program. Let's take a look at them now before we move on to finishing the JavaScript. We'll start with the HTML pane.

The HTML is made up of two parts, separated by an HTML comment. The first part of the HTML creates the top section, where the story will be displayed, and the bottom section, where questions and answers will be displayed.

Listing 16-1 shows this top section of the HTML.

Listing 16-1   **The Beginning of the HTML**

```
<div id="story"></div>
<div id="siteFooter">
    <div id="question"></div>
    <div id="answer">Enter your answer:
        <input type="text" id="yourAnswer" />
        <button type="button" id="submit">Go!</button>
    </div>
</div>
```

Everything that you see in the Result pane when the program first starts is the result of these lines of HTML, combined with the CSS.

Figure 16-3 shows the Result pane for the Martian Rescue! project before the JavaScript has been completed.

Notice that there are three differently colored sections:

✔ The top, dark gray part where the story will display

✔ The light gray part, where the question will display

✔ The white part, where the form and user input area will display

Figure 16-3: The initial Result pane.

If you look at the HTML and compare it with the Result pane, however, you'll notice that something's not right. The HTML clearly contains an input field and button, but those aren't displaying in the Result pane. Why?

Turning off elements with display:none

Because we only want to show the input field and button when we're asking a question, we've hidden the user input field and button using CSS.

Listing 16-2 shows the complete CSS for Martian Rescue!

Listing 16-2 **The CSS for Martian Rescue!**

```
* {
    margin: 0px;
}
html, body {
    font-family: Arial, sans-serif;
    height: 100%;
    overflow:hidden;
}
```

(continued)

Listing 16-2 *(continued)*

```css
#story {
    width: 100%;
    color: yellow;
    height: 80%;
    background-color: #333;
    overflow-y:scroll;
}
#site-footer, .story:after {
    position:static;
    bottom: 0;
    height: 20%;
}
#question {
    padding: 10px 0;
    width: 100%;
    background-color: #CCC;
    color: #333;
}
#answer {
    padding: 10px 0;
    width: 100%;
    background-color: #333;
    color: #FFF;
    text-align: center;
    display: none;
}
.storyPart {
    display: none;
}
p {
    margin-top: 1em;
}
```

If you look again at the HTML, you'll see that the input field and the button are inside of a `div` element with an ID of `answer`.

To see the styles applied to this `div` element, find the style rules with the ID selector of `answer` in the CSS pane.

The first five properties in this style rule set the background color, the text color, the padding, and the text alignment of the element. The last one, however, sets the display property, like this:

```
display: none;
```

When `display` is set to `none`, it turns off the display of the element — in other words, the element just doesn't display.

Often, programmers will use `display: none` in order to hide elements that they want to hide or show using JavaScript. When you want to display an element that's been hidden with CSS you can use JavaScript to change the value of the display property to any of its visible values, like this:

```
document.getElementById("answer").style.display = "block";
```

Looking at (or not looking at) the story parts

Underneath the basic HTML that creates the three sections of the Martian Rescue! program, you'll see several more `div` elements. Each of these contains text that may become part of the story, based on the choices that you make within the program.

Listing 16-3 shows the first one of these `div` elements.

Listing 16-3   The First storyPart div

```
<div class="storyPart" id="answer01">
    <p>You are the captain of a spaceship named "The
        Flying Hippo." One day, you're working on
        tuning up your ship's engines when you get an
        urgent message on your space phone:</p>
    <p>"Captain, one of our Mars robots is sick. We need
        you to go to Mars immediately and retrieve it
        so that we can fix it and download the results
        of its important experiments."</p>
```

(continued)

Listing 16-3 *(continued)*

```
    <p>You remember that you're supposed to go to a meeting
        of the Space Scouts tonight, and you were
        really looking forward to it. But, on the other
        hand, the other Space Scouts would understand
        that this mission is very important.</p>
    <p>What do you do? Go to Mars, or stay home?</p>
  </div>
```

Each of the parts of the story has a class attribute set to storyPart and a unique ID attribute.

The same class attribute value can be applied to multiple elements in an HTML document, but each ID attribute must be unique.

Can you guess why none of the div elements with class attribute values of storyPart are displaying in the Result pane when you open the program? If you guessed that it's because their CSS display properties are set to none, you're right!

Take a look at the CSS pane. Find the .storyPart selector and notice that it has only one style rule inside of it: display: none;.

By setting the display property to none for every element with the storyPart class, we've hidden them all. Then, when the time comes, we can display the correct part of the story using JavaScript.

That just about covers everything that you need to understand about the CSS and HTML. Now let's talk about the JavaScript.

Writing the Martian Rescue! JavaScript

When you first open the starter program for Martian Rescue!, the JavaScript pane contains the code shown in Listing 16-4.

Let's step through this skeletal code and finish it up!

Listing 16-4 The Starter JavaScript for Martian Rescue!

```javascript
// declare variables
var story = document.getElementById("story");
var siteFooter = document.getElementById("siteFooter");
var question = document.getElementById("question");
var answer = document.getElementById("answer");
var yourAnswer = document.getElementById("yourAnswer");
var submit = document.getElementById("submit");

// todo: make an empty array called answers

/* todo: listen for clicks on the submit button and call
         the getAnswer() function when they happen. */

// todo: call the function to ask the first question

/* askQuestion() asks a question, based on the number
         passed to it */
function askQuestion(questionNumber) {
}

/* getAnswer() gets the answer from the text field and
         pushes it into the answers array, then calls
         the continueStory function */
function getAnswer() {
}

/* continueStory() displays part of the story or an error
         based on the value of an item in the answers
         array */
function continueStory(answerNumber) {
}

/* theEnd() ends the story and hides the input field */
function theEnd() {
}
```

Creating element shortcuts

The first section of the code defines some global variables that we need to use throughout the rest of the program. The ones that are already finished for you are variables that create references to HTML elements. You'll use these variables as shortcuts to save you from having to type **document.getElementById** over and over again in the program.

When you use the following statement, it makes it possible for you to use `myElement` in place of `document.getElementById ("myElement")`:

```
var myElement = document.getElementById("myElement");
```

This can make your code much easier to type, and must easier to read later on, too.

Creating an empty array

After the element shortcuts is a comment telling you to create an empty array.

Recall from Chapter 11 that the way to create an empty array (one with no values stored in it) is to set the value of a variable to square brackets with nothing between them. To create an empty array called `answers`, type the following code on the next line after the comment telling you to create it.

```
var answers = [];
```

Now you have an array with no elements. Because you created this array outside of all the functions in your program, this array will be usable anywhere in the program.

A variable that can be used anywhere inside a program is called a *global variable*.

Creating an event listener

The next to-do item in the JavaScript pane says to listen for clicks on the submit button. The word *listen* is a clue for how to write this code. Can you guess what JavaScript method we'll use to listen for clicks? If you guessed that we'll use `addEventListener`, that's correct!

To write the event handler, follow these steps:

1. Under the comment telling you to listen for clicks on the submit button, first type the shortcut to the submit button, followed by a period:

   ```
   submit.
   ```

2. Right after the period, type the `addEventListener` keyword, followed by parentheses.

   ```
   submit.addEventListener()
   ```

3. Inside the parentheses after `addEventListener()`, pass the two arguments: the event you want to listen for and the function that will be called when the event happens.

   ```
   submit.addEventListener("click",getAnswer);
   ```

Great! Now you have the array that will be used to store the user's responses, and you have an event handler set up for the button. But, if you run the program now, you'll see that it doesn't appear to do anything that it couldn't do before. It just shows the same three blank sections in the Result pane.

In order to make this program do something useful, we need to kick off some sort of action. In the Martian Rescue! program, we start the action with a call to the `askQuestion()` function, as indicated in the next to-do item in the JavaScript pane.

Calling the askQuestion() function

The `askQuestion()` function takes a single parameter, the
`questionNumber`. The `questionNumber` is the number of the
question to ask the user. We'll call the first question question #0.

To call the function and ask the first question, type this after the
comment asking you to:

```
askQuestion(0);
```

As you complete to-do items, it's helpful to remove the word `todo`
so that you know that the item is done.

Congratulations, you've now completed the parts of the program
that aren't inside of functions. The beginning of your JavaScript
should now look like Listing 16-5.

Listing 16-5 The Beginning of the JavaScript

```
// declare variables
var story = document.getElementById("story");
var siteFooter = document.getElementById("siteFooter");
var question = document.getElementById("question");
var answer = document.getElementById("answer");
var yourAnswer = document.getElementById("yourAnswer");
var submit = document.getElementById("submit");
var answers = [];


/* listen for clicks on the submit button and call the
    getAnswer() function when they happen */

submit.addEventListener("click", getAnswer);

// call the function to ask the first question
askQuestion(0);
```

If you run the program now, you'll see that it still doesn't do
anything in the Result window.

To make the program actually do something, we need to finish the functions.

Writing the functions

The first function that we'll work on is the one that prompts users to answer questions, the askQuestion() function.

To complete the askQuestion() function, follow these steps.

1. Change the value of the display property of the answer div so that the input field and button appear, using this code:

```
answer.style.display = "block";
```

This statement causes the form to show up in the Result pane.

2. Change the length of the answers array to match the number of the question being asked, using this code:

```
answers.length = questionNumber;
```

This statement uses the argument passed to the function to set the length property of the answers array. We do this so that answers are always stored within their question in the array. In the event that a user enters an invalid value, such as "Maybe," when a question asks for a "Yes" or a "No," setting the length of an array to the number of the question will cause the invalid values to be overridden when the question is asked again.

When you set the length property of an array to a number that's less than the actual length of the array, elements after the new length will be deleted.

3. Write a switch statement that will use the argument passed into the function to determine which question to answer.

Here's the code for the `switch` statement:

```
switch (questionNumber) {
        case 0:
                question.innerHTML = "Are you ready to play?";
                break;
        case 1:
                question.innerHTML = "Go to Mars, or stay home?";
                break;
        case 2:
                question.innerHTML = "Risk it, or go home.";
                break;
        default:
                break;
    }
```

It's not technically necessary to use a `break` statement after the default clause of a `switch` statement, since the switch will exit after the default clause anyway. It's also not necessary to specify a default clause at all if it doesn't do anything, as in this case. But we think it's still a good idea to do both of these things for consistency.

4. After the `switch` statement, end the function with a closing curly brace, like this:

```
    }
```

5. Save your work by clicking the Update link.

The finished `askQuestion()` function is shown in Listing 16-6.

Listing 16-6   The Finished askQuestion() Function

```
/* askQuestion() asks a question, based on the number
        passed to it. */
function askQuestion(questionNumber) {
    answer.style.display = "block";

    //make sure the array is the right length
    answers.length = questionNumber;
```

```
switch (questionNumber) {
    case 0:
        question.innerHTML = "Are you ready to play?";
        break;
    case 1:
        question.innerHTML = "Go to Mars, or stay
        home?";
        break;
    case 2:
        question.innerHTML = "Risk it, or go home.";
        break;
    default:
        break;

    }
}
```

With the askQuestion() function finishes, the Result pane now does something. You'll see that the first question displays, and the input field and button display beneath it, as shown in Figure 16-4.

At this point, however, you can put any value into the input field and press the Go button and nothing will happen. In order to make the game work, we need to write the next two functions.

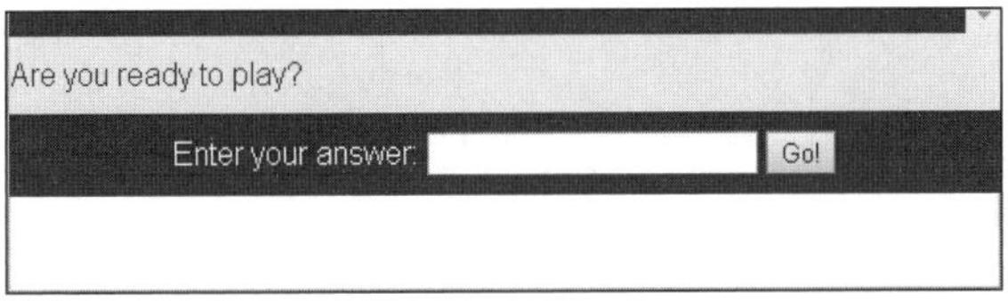

Figure 16-4: The first question displays.

Follow these steps to write the getAnswer() function.

1. Get the value from the input field and convert it to uppercase letters with this statement:

```
cleanInput = yourAnswer.value.toUpperCase();
```

2. Use the `push` array method to add the user's answer as a new element at the end of the `answers` array, like this:

```
answers.push(cleanInput);
```

3. Reset the input field, clearing the current value out of it, like this:

```
yourAnswer.value = "";
```

4. Call the `continueStory()` function, passing it the number of the last element in the `answers` array, using this code:

```
continueStory(answers.length - 1);
```

Because arrays start counting at 0, the *length* (number of elements in the array) will always be one more than the number of the last element, which is why we subtract 1 from the length above.

5. Finish the `getAnswer()` function with a closing curly bracket.

```
}
```

The finished `getAnswer()` function is shown in Listing 16-7.

Move on to the next section to write the `continueStory()` function.

Listing 16-7   The Finished getAnswer() Function

```
/* getAnswer() gets the answer from the text field and
            pushes it into the answers array, then calls
            the continueStory function */
function getAnswer() {
    cleanInput = yourAnswer.value.toUpperCase();
    answers.push(cleanInput);
    yourAnswer.value = "";
    continueStory(answers.length - 1);
}
```

Writing continueStory()

The `continueStory()` function uses `if...else` statements to determine whether the user entered a valid value and then to show the correct part of the story based on that input.

Follow these steps to write `continueStory()`:

1. Write a `switch` statement to use the value of the argument to find out what question is being asked.

   The basic switch statement, without the `if...else` statements for each question, looks like this:

   ```
   switch (answerNumber) {
     case 0:
       //insert statements
       break;
     case 1:
       // insert statements
       break;
     case 2:
       // insert statements
       break;
     default:
       // insert statements
       break;
   }
   ```

2. Write `if...else` statements for the first question in the game: "Are you ready to play?"

   When it's finished, the first case in the `switch` statement should look like this:

   ```
   case 0:

   if (answers[0] === "YES") {
     story.innerHTML = document.getElementById("answer01").
           innerHTML;
     askQuestion(1);
   ```

```
        } else if (answers[0] === "NO") {

            story.innerHTML = document.getElementById("answer02").
                    innerHTML;
            askQuestion(0);

        } else {

            story.innerHTML = document.getElementById("err0").innerHTML;
            askQuestion(0);

        }

        break;
```

Let's step through this code line-by-line:

```
    case 0:
```

This line says that if the user responded to the first question, run the following statements.

```
    if (answers[0] === "YES") {
```

This line is saying that if the first element in the array (which corresponds to the first question) is set to "YES", run the following statements. Remember that in the getAnswer() function, we converted the user's input to uppercase before pushing it into the array. So, the user can enter **yes**, **Yes**, or even **yeS** and this statement will still be true.

```
story.innerHTML = document.getElementById("answer01").
        innerHTML;
```

This statement gets the HTML from inside the div element with an ID of answer01 and overwrites the contents of the div with the ID of story. If you locate the div with the ID equal to answer01 in the HTML pane, you'll see that it's the beginning of the story.

When you answer "Yes" to the question "Are you ready to play?," the first part of the story will display.

```
askQuestion(1);
```

This statement calls the askQuestion function and tells it to ask question #1. This causes the askQuestion function to ask "Go to Mars, or stay home?"

```
} else if (answers[0] === "NO") {
```

If the user didn't answer "yes," the else clause will run. But here we put another if statement inside of the else clause so that we can test for a value of "NO", but only if the answer wasn't "YES".

```
story.innerHTML = document.getElementById("answer02").innerHTML;
```

If the answer is "NO", set the story div's innerHTML equal to the appropriate message.

```
askQuestion(0);
```

Because they said they aren't ready to play, ask them the first question again until they are ready.

```
} else {
```

Do the following if the user didn't enter Yes or No.

```
story.innerHTML = document.getElementById("err0").innerHTML;
```

Set the value of the story div to an error message, telling them to enter either Yes or No.

```
askQuestion(0);
```

Ask the first question again, and hopefully they'll provide a good answer this time!

3. Write the cases for the other two questions in the game, like this:

```
case 1:
if (answers[1] === "GO TO MARS") {
    story.innerHTML = document.getElementById("answer11").
            innerHTML;
    askQuestion(2);
} else if (answers[1] === "STAY HOME") {
    story.innerHTML = document.getElementById("answer12").
            innerHTML;
    theEnd();
} else {
    story.innerHTML = document.getElementById("err1").innerHTML;
    askQuestion(1);
}
    break;
case 2:
    if (answers[2] === "RISK IT") {
    story.innerHTML = document.getElementById("answer21").
            innerHTML;
    theEnd();
} else if (answers[2] === "GO HOME") {
    story.innerHTML = document.getElementById("answer22").
            innerHTML;
    theEnd();
} else {
    story.innerHTML = document.getElementById("err2").innerHTML;
    askQuestion(2);
}
    break;
default:
    story.innerHTML = "The story is over!";
    break;
}
```

4. Finish the function with a closing curly bracket.

```
    }
```

5. Save your work by clicking the Update link.

The completed `continueStory()` function is shown in Listing 16-8.

Listing 16-8 The continueStory() Function

```
/* continueStory() displays part of the story or an error
          based on the value of an item in the answers
          array. */
function continueStory(answerNumber) {
    switch (answerNumber) {
        case 0:
            if (answers[0] === "YES") {
                story.innerHTML = document.
        getElementById("answer01").innerHTML;
                askQuestion(1);
            } else if (answers[0] === "NO") {
                story.innerHTML = document.
        getElementById("answer02").innerHTML;
                askQuestion(0);
            } else {
                story.innerHTML = document.
        getElementById("err0").innerHTML;
                askQuestion(0);
            }
            break;
        case 1:
            if (answers[1] === "GO TO MARS") {
                story.innerHTML = document.
        getElementById("answer11").innerHTML;
                askQuestion(2);
            } else if (answers[1] === "STAY HOME") {
                story.innerHTML = document.
        getElementById("answer12").innerHTML;
                theEnd();
            } else {
                story.innerHTML = document.
        getElementById("err1").innerHTML;
                askQuestion(1);
            }
            break;
```

(continued)

Listing 16-8 *(continued)*

```
            case 2:
                if (answers[2] === "RISK IT") {
                    story.innerHTML = document.
                getElementById("answer21").innerHTML;
                    theEnd();
                } else if (answers[2] === "GO HOME") {
                    story.innerHTML = document.
                getElementById("answer22").innerHTML;
                    theEnd();
                } else {
                    story.innerHTML = document.
                getElementById("err2").innerHTML;
                    askQuestion(2);

                }
                break;
            default:
                story.innerHTML = "The story is over!";

                break;
        }
    }
```

The final function we need to write is the function that runs when
the story comes to the end.

Writing theEnd()

The function called `theEnd()` prints out the final line of the story
and hides the contents of the answer `div` — including the question as well as the input field and button. To write the `theEnd()`
function, follow these steps:

1. Type the following statement in the function body of
   `theEnd()` to print out "The End" after the last text in the
   story div:

   ```
   story.innerHTML += "<p>The End.</p>";
   ```

2. Erase the last question asked from the `question` div, using this statement:

```
question.innerHTML = "";
```

3. Hide the input field and button with this statement:

```
answer.style.display = "none";
```

4. Click Update to save your work.

The final `theEnd()` function is shown in Listing 16-9.

Listing 16-9   The theEnd() Function

```
/* theEnd() ends the story and hides the input field */
function theEnd() {
    story.innerHTML += "<p>The End.</p>";
    question.innerHTML = "";
    answer.style.display = "none";
}
```

That completes the Martian Rescue! program. Click Update and Set as Base and then try it out!

If you did everything correctly, you should be able to play through the game in any way that you want. Figure 16-5 shows the Result pane of a game in progress.

Do you have ideas for other interactive stories? Can you think of other ways to modify our story to make it longer, more exciting, or funnier? Experiment with the program and share your work with your friends or with us online! We're looking forward to seeing what you come up with!

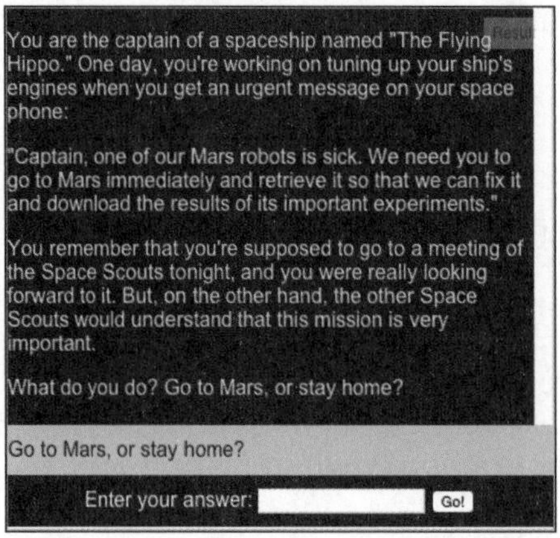

You are the captain of a spaceship named "The Flying Hippo." One day, you're working on tuning up your ship's engines when you get an urgent message on your space phone:

"Captain, one of our Mars robots is sick. We need you to go to Mars immediately and retrieve it so that we can fix it and download the results of its important experiments."

You remember that you're supposed to go to a meeting of the Space Scouts tonight, and you were really looking forward to it. But, on the other hand, the other Space Scouts would understand that this mission is very important.

What do you do? Go to Mars, or stay home?

Go to Mars, or stay home?

Enter your answer: [   ] [Go!]

Figure 16-5: Playing Martian Rescue!

Part VI

Loops

Lunch Game!

You get a weekly allowance of $20 to buy lunch. Sandwiches are always between $1 and $5, but you never know the price until you get to school.

Your goal is to be able to buy lunch every day of the week.

How many sandwiches do you want per day?

| 2 | Place Order |

On day 1, sandwiches are: $2.89. You have $14.22 left.

On day 2, sandwiches are: $2.12. You have $9.98 left.

On day 3, sandwiches are: $3.94. You have $2.10 left.

Today, sandwiches are: $2.65. You don't have enough money. Maybe your sister will give you some of her sandwich.

You bought 3 lunches this week.

In this part . . .

- What's This Loop For? 295
- Using While Loops 309
- Building a Lemonade Stand 326

For information on advanced looping with JavaScript, go to www.dummies.com/extras/ javascriptforkids.

What's This Loop For?

`for` **loops are useful** for when you know in advance how many times you need to do something. You can use a `for` loop to count to 10, or to count to 1,000,000. It's all the same to JavaScript!

In this chapter, we look at one of the most popular types of loops in JavaScript: the `for` loop. We use `for` loops to create our own weather forecasting app.

Forecast for Monday:	Forecast for Tuesday:	Forecast for Wednesday:	Forecast for Thursday:	Forecast for Friday:
Thunderstorm and 35 degrees.	Cloudy and 55 degrees.	Partly Cloudy and 80 degrees.	Sunny and 17 degrees.	Cloudy and 11 degrees.

Introducing the for Loop

The `for` loop is the most commonly used type of loop in JavaScript. Here's a sample `for` loop that prints out the words `Hello, JavaScript!` 500 times to the JavaScript console.

```
for (var counter = 0; counter < 500; counter++) {
    console.log(counter + ": Hello, JavaScript!");
}
```

Figure 17-1 shows what this code looks like when it's run in the JavaScript console.

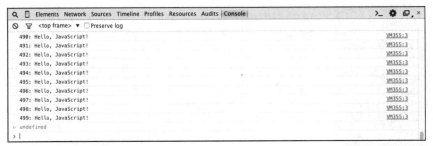

Figure 17-1: Saying "Hello, JavaScript!" 500 times.

This isn't the most exciting use for a loop, but you can certainly see that it's easier to use a loop than it would be to type out 500 `console.log` statements!

Let's take a closer look at how to write `for` loops.

The three parts of the for loop

The `for` loop is made up of three different statements:

✔ **Initialization:** The initialization statement declares a variable that the loop will use to keep track of how long it has been looping.

✔ **Condition:** A Boolean expression to be evaluated with each iteration of the loop.

✔ **Final expression:** An expression to be evaluated after each loop iteration.

Here's how our Hello, JavaScript loop works:

1. A new variable — in this case, `counter` — is initiated with the value of 0.

2. A test is done to check whether counter is less than 500.

   If it is, then the statements inside the loop are run. In this case, the `console.log` statement will print out `Hello, JavaScript!`

3. The final expression *increments* (adds 1 to) the counter variable.

4. The condition statement is evaluated again to determine whether `counter` is still less than 500.

   If so, the statements inside the loop are executed again.

5. The final expression increments the counter again.

6. Steps 2 and 3 keep running until the condition (`counter < 500`) is no longer true.

Writing and using for loops

One very useful thing about `for` loops is that you can use the counter inside the `for` loop to change the output of the statements inside the loop.

The most basic example of this technique is to use the `for` loop to count. Listing 17-1 shows an app that displays a countdown in alert statements.

Listing 17-1 **JavaScript Countdown**

```
for (var i = 10; i > 0; i--) {
  alert (i);
}
alert ("Blast Off!");
```

Follow these steps to test out this program:

1. Go to `http://jsfiddle.net` and log in if you're not already.

2. Open a new program by clicking the JSFiddle logo.

3. Type the code in Listing 17-1 into the JavaScript pane.

4. Click the Run button to run the program.

   An alert box appears with the number 10 in it. When you click OK in the alert box, a new alert with the number 9 in it appears. The alerts appear like this until the value of the counter variable (i) is no longer greater than 0. At that point, the loop will exit and a final alert will appear, containing the phrase "Blast Off!"

Counting is a great use for `for` loops, but there's an even better and more useful thing that you can do with `for` loops: looping through arrays.

Listing 17-2 shows a program that creates an array containing names of people. The `for` loop outputs the same sentence with each of the names inserted into it.

Listing 17-2   Outputting Array Values with for

```
var myFriends = ["Agatha", "Agnes", "Jermaine", "Jack"];

for (var i = 0; i < myFriends.length; i++){
  alert(myFriends[i] + " is my friend.");
}
```

To use a `for` loop to output all the values in an array, you just use the `length` property of the array to find out how many elements are in the array and you use that to perform the loop that same number of times.

Then, inside the loop, you use the counter variable (i, in this case) to output the corresponding array element.

When you know how to output array elements, you can do all sorts of cool things with `for` loops. For example, in the next section, we use a `for` loop to provide a randomized five-day weather forecast!

Random Weather Forecasting

Welcome to Anytown, USA! We have a saying here: "If you don't like the weather, wait five minutes!" And we mean it! It seems like the weather here is completely random. One day it snows, the next day it's hot and humid. There's really no predicting — which is why we've hired you.

Your job as our new meteorologist is to come up with totally random weather forecasts so that we can print them in the newspaper and talk about them on the TV.

Ready to get started? Okay, let's forecast!

The first thing we need to do is understand how to get random values in JavaScript. Move on to the next section to find out!

Using Math.random()

JavaScript has a built-in function that's used for creating random numbers. This function is called `Math.random()`.

Every time you run the `Math.random()` function, it creates a random decimal number between 0 and 1. Using this random value, you can do all sorts of things that are necessary for game programming, including adding an element of surprise to the movement of monsters or randomly selecting elements from arrays to create crazy weather forecasts.

Listing 17-3 shows a simple program that pops up a random value every time it's run. Try running the program several times (in the JavaScript console or in JSFiddle) to verify that you don't get the same value twice.

Listing 17-3   A Random Number Alert

```
alert(Math.random());
```

Figure 17-2 shows the random number that we got when we ran this statement in JSFiddle.

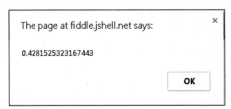

The page at fiddle.jshell.net says: ×

0.4281525323167443

                                                    OK

Figure 17-2: A random number.

What programmers usually do with these long decimal numbers, is to use operators and other functions to create the values or the range of random values that they need.

If you want a random number between 0 and 10, you can multiply the random number by 11, like this:

```
alert(Math.random() * 11);
```

If you want to remove the decimal numbers from the result, you can use the `Math.floor()` function, like this:

```
alert(Math.floor(Math.random() * 11);
```

If you want a random number between 10 and 1,000, you can multiply the random value by the result of subtracting the smallest number from the largest number and then adding the smaller number to that result, like this:

```
alert(Math.floor(Math.random() * (1000 - 100) + 100));
```

If you want to choose a random element from an array, it works the same way as picking a random number from a range starting with 0. Just multiply the random number by the length of the array.

For example, Listing 17-4 creates an array called `myFriends` and then uses `Math.random()` to choose one element from that array and alert the value of it.

Listing 17-4 **Finding a Random Friend**

```
var myFriends = ["Agatha", "Agnes", "Jermaine", "Jack"];
var randomFriend = Math.floor(Math.random() *
        myFriends.length);


alert(myFriends[randomFriend]);
```

When you run this program in JSFiddle, the result will be that an alert with a random friend name will appear, as shown in Figure 17-3.

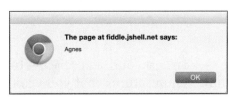

Figure 17-3: Choose a random friend.

Now that you understand how to get random data using JavaScript, let's move on to writing the app!

Writing the app

To write the random weather forecast, follow these steps.

1. Go to `http://jsfiddle.net` and log in if you're not already logged in.

2. Create a new program by clicking the JSFiddle icon.

3. Open the Fiddle Options panel on the left and enter a name for your program, such as **Random Weather**.

4. Click Save in the top menu to save your work and publish it to your Public Dashboard.

5. In the HTML pane, create a `div` element with an `id` of `5DayWeather`, like this:

   ```
   <div id="5DayWeather"></div>
   ```

6. In the JavaScript pane, start out by creating an array of the days of the week:

   ```
   var days = ["Monday","Tuesday","Wednesday","Thursday","Friday"];
   ```

7. Create a second array called weather.

   The elements in this array should be different types of weather. Feel free to put in as many different types of weather as you can think of. Here's our list:

   ```
   var weather = ["Sunny", "Partly Sunny", "Partly Cloudy",
                  "Cloudy", "Raining", "Snowing", "Thunderstorm",
                  "Foggy"];
   ```

8. Create two variables — `minTemp` and `maxTemp` — to hold the minimum and maximum temperatures that you want the random weather program to output.

   Here are our numbers (in degrees Fahrenheit):

   ```
   minTemp = 0;
   maxTemp = 100;
   ```

9. Start a new function, called `generateWeather()`.

   ```
   function generateWeather() {
   ```

10. The first line in the body of the function will start a `for` loop that will loop through each of the days of the week.

    ```
    for (var i = 0; i < days.length; i++) {
    ```

11. Declare a new variable, `weatherToday`, that will get a random element from the weather array.

    ```
    var weatherToday = weather[Math.floor(Math.random() * weather.
                length)];
    ```

12. Declare a new variable, `tempToday`, that will get a random temperature between the values of your `minTemp` and `maxTemp` variables.

```
var tempToday = Math.floor(Math.random() * (maxTemp - minTemp) +
        minTemp);
```

13. Use `innerHTML` to output the values of `weatherToday` and `tempToday` inside the `div` element by adding the following code to the JavaScript pane.

```
document.getElementById("5DayWeather").innerHTML += "<div id='" +
        days[i] + "' class='" + weatherToday +
        "'><b>Forecast for " + days[i] + ":</b><br><br>" +
        weatherToday + " and " + tempToday + " degrees.</
        div>";
```

Notice that the above code adds the name of the day of the week as an ID attribute and the type of weather as a class attribute. We'll use these later on to style the elements using CSS.

14. Close the loop and the function with closing curly brackets.

```
    }
}
```

15. Finally, insert a call to the `generateWeather` function after the variable declarations and above the function.

```
generateWeather();
```

16. Click Update and then Set as Base in the top menu to save your work.

The finished JavaScript code should look like Listing 17-5.

Listing 17-5   The Finished JavaScript Code

```
var days = ["Monday", "Tuesday", "Wednesday", "Thursday",
        "Friday"];
var weather = ["Sunny", "Partly Sunny", "Partly Cloudy",
        "Cloudy", "Raining", "Snowing", "Thunderstorm",
        "Foggy"];
```

(continued)

Listing 17-5 *(continued)*

```
var maxTemp = 100;
var minTemp = 0;


generateWeather();


function generateWeather() {
  for (var i = 0; i < days.length; i++) {
    var weatherToday = weather[Math.floor(Math.random() *
        weather.length)];
    var tempToday = Math.floor(Math.random() * (maxTemp -
        minTemp) + minTemp);


    document.getElementById("5DayWeather").innerHTML +=
        "<div id='" + days[i] + "' class='" +
        weatherToday + "'><b>Forecast for " + days[i] +
        ":</b><br><br>" + weatherToday + " and " +
        tempToday + " degrees.</div>";
  }
}
```

When you run this program (by clicking Run in the top menu of JSFiddle) the result is the five weekdays followed by a weather prediction for each, as shown in Figure 17-4.

Figure 17-4: The result of running Listing 17-5.

Inspecting the results

Now we have a basic weather forecast, but it's not very visually appealing. Fortunately, we had the foresight to add `id` and `class` attributes to each `div` in the output.

Follow these steps to inspect the output in the Result pane and see the HTML elements and their attributes that have been added by the JavaScript look:

1. Click Update or Run in the top menu bar in JSFiddle.

    The Result pane updates with a new list of forecasts.

2. Choose Chrome ➪ More Tools ➪ Developer Tools.

    The Chrome Developer Tools open.

3. Click the Elements tab in the Chrome Developer tools.

    The Elements panel, shown in Figure 17-5, appears.

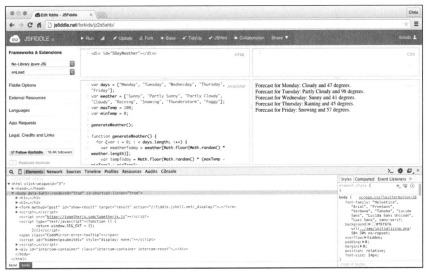

Figure 17-5: The Elements panel in the Developer Tools.

4. Click the Inspector tool (which looks like a magnifying glass) in the upper left of the Elements panel.

5. Move your mouse over the Results pane.

   Elements within the pane will become highlighted as your mouse moves over them, as shown in Figure 17-6.

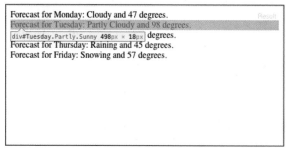

Figure 17-6: Highlighting elements in the Result pane.

6. While your mouse is hovered over one of the days of the week in the Result pane, click it.

   The Elements panel updates to highlight the code that created the element you clicked, as shown in Figure 17-7.

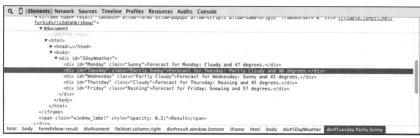

Figure 17-7: The element you clicked is highlighted.

7. Click some of the other elements in the Result pane and see how the `id` attributes, classes, and content of each element are different.

In the next section, we use the `id` and `class` attributes to apply styles to the output of the program.

Styling the app

By selecting elements by their `id` and `class` attributes, we can style each day, and customize the look of the days based on the weather predicted for that day.

Follow these steps to apply some style to the app:

1. Create a rule in the CSS pane to style each of the days the same using this code.

```
#Monday, #Tuesday, #Wednesday, #Thursday, #Friday {
    width: 18%;
    height: 200px;
    float: left;
    border: 1px solid black;
    padding: 2px;
    font-family: sans-serif;
    font-size: 12px;
}
```

This rule creates a border, a width and height, a font family, and some padding on each of the days of the week. We've also set the `float` property equal to `left` in order to make all the days be side-by-side rather than stacked.

2. Create a rule for several of the different types of weather using this code:

```
.Sunny {
    background-color: skyblue;
}
.Raining {
    background-color: lightgrey;
}
```

```
.Cloudy {
    background-color: #eee;
}
.Thunderstorm {
    background-color: #333;
    color: #fff;
}
```

When you have spaces in a `class` attribute (such as in `Partly Sunny` and `Partly Cloudy`), the two words are treated as separate class attributes. So, an element with a class value of `Partly Cloudy` will be styled using the CSS associated with `.Cloudy`, and an element with a class value of `Partly Sunny` will be styled using the CSS associated with `.Sunny`.

3. Click Update and Set as Base to save your work.

   The Result pane updates and displays your forecast in a new, more attractive format, as shown in Figure 17-8.

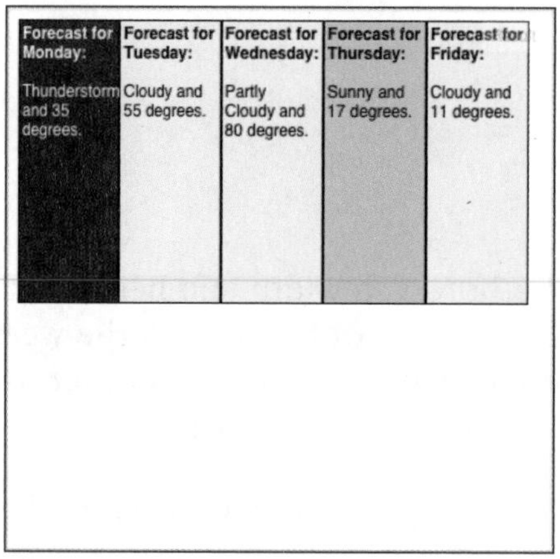

Figure 17-8: The finished Weather Forecast app.

Using While Loops

The `while` **loop will** continue to perform its loop as long as its conditions are met. The `while` loop will do the job until it's done — no questions asked!

In this chapter, we use a `while` loop to write a game that will keep buying you sandwiches until you run out of money. The object of the game is to make your lunch money last all week.

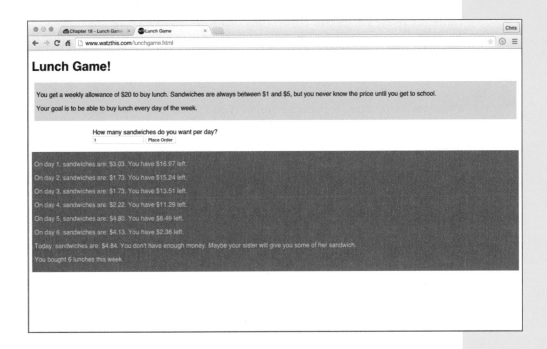

Writing a while Loop

Compared to `for` loops, `while` loops are pretty simple. They only have one part — a Boolean expression — that determines whether the loop will run and continue to run.

Here's an example of a `while` loop:

```
while (money > 0) {
    buyThings();
    saveMoney();
    payTaxes();
}
```

This loop executes the three functions — `buyThings()`, `saveMoney()`, and `payTaxes()` — as long as the value of the money variable is greater than 0.

The `for` loop has a final expression that changes the value of the counter. The `while` loop requires you to have an expression or expressions inside the loop that can change the result of its condition.

The three function calls we created inside the `while` loop are just made up names. If we were to actually write these functions, they would need to update the value of the money variable so that the loop stops at some point (but, of course, this is one loop we hope doesn't stop!).

If you don't modify the value of the variable in a `while` loop's condition, you may create what's called an infinite loop. An infinite loop won't damage your computer, but it will likely cause your web browser to freeze up and cause you to have to force it to quit — risking losing any unsaved changes. So, make sure to check your `while` loops carefully to make sure they're not infinite!

A `while` loop can do everything that a `for` loop can do, but the coding is just a bit different. Let's take a look at the three uses for `for` loops that we talk about in Chapter 17 and show how to do them with `while`.

Looping a certain number of times

Listing 18-1 shows how you can use a `while` loop to log `Hello, JavaScript!` to the console window 500 times.

Listing 18-1   Logging Hello, JavaScript

```
var i = 0;
while (i < 500) {
    console.log(i + ": Hello, JavaScript!");
    i++;
}
```

Notice that the program in Listing 18-1 contains all the same three parts that are in a `for` loop (initialization, condition, and final expression), but only the condition is inside the parentheses. The initialization (`var i = 0;`) is before the `while` loop, and the final expression (`i++`) is inside the `while` loop.

Counting with while

To create a loop that counts, you can just modify a variable inside every pass through the loop and use that variable inside other statements in the loop.

Listing 18-2 shows a countdown like the one from Chapter 17, but using a `while` loop.

Listing 18-2   Count Down with while

```
var count = 10;
while (count > 0) {
  alert(count);
  count--;
}
alert("Blast Off!");
```

Looping through an array with while

Looping through arrays with `while` is easier than it is with `for`. To loop through an array with `while`, change the condition in the loop to test whether an array element has been declared.

To test whether an element has been declared, just put the name of the array with a counter variable inside the parentheses after the `while` keyword.

For example, Listing 18-3 shows an example that loops through a list of people's names.

Listing 18-3   **Looping through a List of Names**

```
var people = ["Deborah","Carla","Mary","Suzen"];
var i = 0;
while (people[i]) {
  alert(people[i]);
  i++;
}
```

The condition between the parentheses in a `for` loop or a `while` loop is a Boolean expression, which means it evaluates to either `true` or `false`. When you use an array element, such as `people[5]` as a Boolean expression, it will be true as long as there is an element in the array at that array position.

Coding the Lunch Game

The Lunch Game is a unique combination of a game of chance and a game of math. The object of the game is to try to budget so that you have sandwiches for every day of the week.

But, here's the catch: You go to the strangest school in the world, and you don't know how much sandwiches will cost until the sandwiches are made — but you have to buy all your sandwiches for the week before the week starts!

You do know that sandwiches will always cost between $1 and $5. So, depending on your luck, you'll be able to buy somewhere between 4 and 20 sandwiches.

How much risk are you willing to take? Will someone come to your aid and give you part of their sandwich if you run out before the week ends? How many sandwiches can you eat?

All these questions, and more, will be answered in the Lunch Game.

Forking the code

To get started with writing the Lunch Game, follow these steps:

1. Go to our JSFiddle Public Dashboard at `http://jsfiddle.net/user/forkids/fiddles`.

   You see the list of all our public programs.

2. Find the program named "Chapter 18 – Lunch Game – Start," and click the title to open it.

   The starter program opens, as shown in Figure 18-1.

We've written the HTML, CSS, and most of the JavaScript for you. The only thing left for you to do is to write the `buyLunches()` function.

In the next section, we show you how to do it!

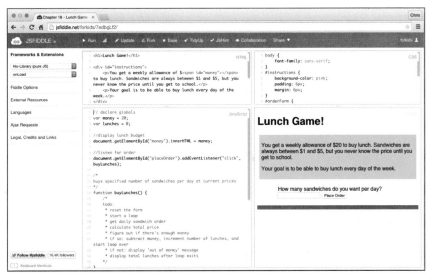

Figure 18-1: The starter program for the Lunch Game.

Writing buyLunches()

Listing 18-4 shows the starter code and comments for the buyLunches() function.

Listing 18-4   The Starting Point for buyLunches()

```
/*
buys specified number of sandwiches per day at current
        prices
*/
function buyLunches() {
    /*
    todo:
     * reset the form
     * start a loop
     * get daily sandwich order
     * calculate total price
     * figure out if there's enough money
     * if so: subtract money, increment number of lunches,
         and start loop over
     * if not: display 'out of money' message
     * display total lunches after loop exits
    */
}
```

Follow these steps to write the body of the function to match these instructions:

1. Inside the body of the buyLunches() function, make a call to the resetForm() function and initialize a variable for tracking the current day, like this:

   ```
   resetForm();
   var day = 0;
   ```

2. Create a loop that will buy sandwiches until you're out of money.

   ```
   while (money > 0) {
   ```

3. Get the current price of sandwiches by making a call to the `getSandwichPrice()` function and assigning the return value to a variable.

```
var priceToday = getSandwichPrice();
```

At this point, take a look at the `getSandwichPrice` function. Its purpose is to randomly generate a number between 1 and 5 and return that value.

4. Get the number of sandwiches that the user entered into the form field.

```
var numberOfSandwiches = document.
              getElementById("numSandwiches").value;
```

5. Calculate the total price by multiplying the number of sandwiches that you want by the current sandwich price.

```
var totalPrice = priceToday * numberOfSandwiches;
```

6. Find out whether there's enough money to buy the sandwiches.

```
if(money >= totalPrice) {
```

7. If there is enough, subtract the total price from the current money balance.

```
money = money - totalPrice;
```

Congratulations! You've successfully purchased a lunch!

8. Increment the `lunches` variable, which keeps track of how many lunches were purchased.

```
lunches++;
```

9. Output a message to tell the user the price of the sandwiches he just bought and how much money he has left.

```
document.getElementById("receipt").innerHTML += "<p>On day " +
        day + ", sandwiches are: $" + priceToday + ". You
        have $" + money.toFixed(2) + " left.</p>";
```

Notice that we've attached the `toFixed()` method to the money variable. The `toFixed()` method converts a number to a string, while keeping the number of decimals specified within the parentheses. In this case, because we're printing out a currency value, we use two decimal places.

10. Next, start the `else` clause of the `if...else` to handle cases where the amount of money left isn't enough to buy the specified number of sandwiches.

```
} else {
```

11. When the else clause runs, output a message that's special for when the user doesn't have enough money for another lunch.

```
document.getElementById("receipt").innerHTML += "<p>Today,
        sandwiches are: $" + priceToday + ". You don't have
        enough money. Maybe your sister will give you some
        of her sandwich.</p>";
```

12. Still within the `else` clause, set the value of money equal to 0 in order to prevent the loop from running again.

```
money = 0;
```

13. Finish the `if...else` statement and the `while` loop with curly brackets.

```
    }
}
```

14. When the loop completes, output the total number of lunches that the user was able to buy.

```
document.getElementById("reciept").innerHTML += "<p>You bought " +
        lunches + " lunches this week.</p>";
```

15. Close the function with a curly bracket.

```
}
```

16. Click Update and Set as Base in the top menu to save your work.

Trying it out

The finished Lunch Game is shown in Figure 18-2.

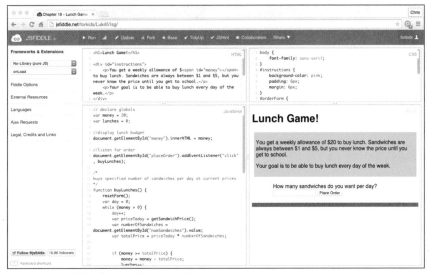

Figure 18-2: The finished Lunch Game.

If you enter a number into the text field and press the Place Order button, the program calculates how many lunches you can buy, using random sandwich prices. ***Remember:*** A lunch consists of one or more sandwiches, according to your input.

Try out the program several times by entering new numbers into the text input field and pressing the Place Order button. You see that the random numbers and the number of lunches you can buy per week vary quite a bit.

Figure 18-3 shows one possible outcome of running the program.

Figure 18-3: Running the Lunch Game.

Moving to Your Own Website

When you have a game that you're proud of and you want to share with the world on your own website, you need to move beyond the walls of JSFiddle. In this section, we show you how to do that!

Understanding web hosting

Every website has a unique address that people can use to visit it. In order to get your own address on the Internet, you need to sign up with some sort of web hosting company. JSFiddle is a web hosting company that provides a free testing area for people to make programs with JavaScript, HTML, and CSS.

JSFiddle is great, but it has its limits, such as the fact that it lets anyone copy and modify your code, and it doesn't give you the option of having your own domain name (such as www. mywebsite.com).

Most web hosting companies charge a monthly fee for uploading your web pages to the Internet. However, there are some that give out free trial accounts. In this section, we show you how to set up and use a free trial account with x10Hosting (`www.x10hosting.com`).

It's possible that x10Hosting may choose to start charging for trial accounts or change in some way before we have a chance to update this book. If this happens, you can find different free hosting options by searching the web for "free web hosting."

Getting started with x10Hosting

Follow these steps to create an account and a website at x10Hosting:

1. Open your web browser and go to `www.x10hosting.com`.

   You see the home page, featuring a button labeled Sign Up Now, as shown in Figure 18-4.

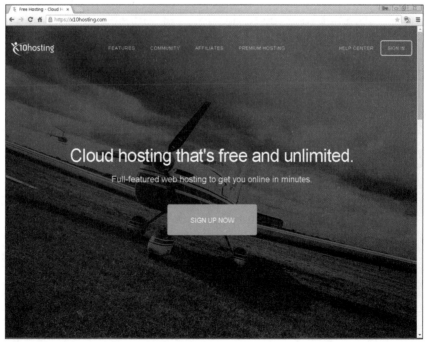

Figure 18-4: The home page of x10Hosting.

2. Click the Create My Account button.

   A form where you can enter a name for your custom web address appears.

3. Choose a name for your hosting account, as shown in Figure 18-5, and click Continue.

Try our web hosting now. It's super-easy and completely **FREE!** No strings attached.

codingJSforkids   .x10host.com   CONTINUE

Figure 18-5: Choosing a name for your account.

4. On the next screen, enter your email address and click Continue.

5. Choose a password for your account, and click Continue.

6. Click to agree to the terms of service, and click Submit to finish signing up.

   An email confirmation is sent to you.

7. Click the link in the email to confirm your account.

   If you don't get the email within a few minutes, check your spam folder.

8. When your account is confirmed, click Continue to log in.

   It may take minute for your account to be ready. If you see a message telling you to wait, take a break and then come back and click the Continue button when it becomes available.

9. Enter your name on the next page to personalize your account, and then click Continue.

10. When your domain is set up, you see a page with a help window, a link to your domain, and a link that says Open cPanel.

11. Click the link that says Open cPanel.

    Your control panel opens.

12. Click the Add Website link.

13. Give your site a name, leave the default domain selected, and leave the address path text input blank, as shown in Figure 18-6.

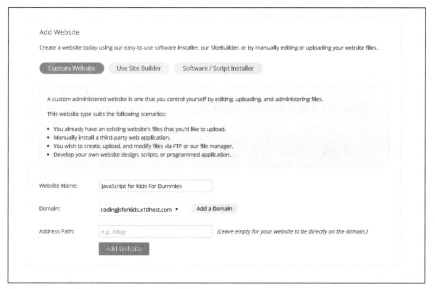

Figure 18-6: Creating a new website.

14. Click Add Website.

    Your new site is created and you see the unique website address.

TIP

Make a note of this website address. You'll be using it later!

15. Click Continue to My Websites.

16. In the control panel for your website, click the File Manager link.

    A window opens, showing you the files and directories in your web hosting account (see Figure 18-7).

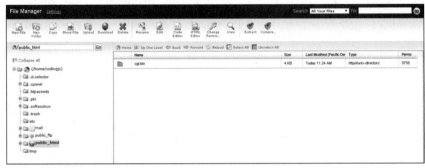

Figure 18-7: The File Manager.

17. Click New File at the top of the screen.

18. Name the new file `lunchgame.html` and click Create New File.

19. Highlight the new file by clicking it, and then click Code Editor in the top menu.

20. If this is your first time using the code editor, a window opens asking you to choose an "encoding"; click the Disable Encoding Check link.

    A blank page opens in the code editor.

21. Type the HTML from Listing 18-5 into this blank page.

Listing 18-5 **A Standard HTML Template**

```html
<!doctype html>
<html>
<head>
  <title>Lunch Game</title>
<style>
</style>
<script>
function init() {

}
</script>

</head>
<body onload="init();">

</body>
</html>
```

22. In another browser tab, go back to your Lunch Game in JSFiddle.

23. Copy everything inside the HTML pane, and paste it between the opening and closing body tags in the code editor for your `lunchgame.html` file.

24. Copy everything inside the CSS pane in JSFiddle and paste it between `<style>` and `</style>` in the `lunchgame.html` file.

25. Copy the first lines from the JavaScript pane, up to the function declaration for the `buyLunches()` function, and paste it in the function body for the `init()` function in the `lunchgame.html` file, as shown in Listing **18-6.**

Check your code carefully after you paste, to make sure that it matches Listing 18-6 exactly.

Listing 18-6   Finishing the init() Function

```
function init() {
// declare globals
var money = 20;
var lunches = 0;

//display lunch budget
document.getElementById("money").innerHTML = money;

//listen for order
document.getElementById("placeOrder").
            addEventListener("click", buyLunches);
}
```

The init() function runs as soon as the web page is loaded.

26. Paste the rest of the JavaScript from the JavaScript pane in JSFiddle below the init() function, but still between the <script> and </script> tags.

27. Click Save in the upper-right corner of the screen.

28. Click Close, just to the left of the Save button.

 If you get a message regarding the character encoding, you can just close it by clicking OK and you're returned to the File Manager.

29. Go to your website address in a new browser tab.

 You see a list of the files in your website. Currently, you should only have a folder called cgi-bin and your lunchgame.html file.

 If you don't want to see this list of web pages, you can create a new HTML file called index.html, and it will appear when you visit your website instead.

30. Click `lunchgame.html` to open the Lunch Game.

The Lunch Game appears in your browser window, as shown in Figure 18-8.

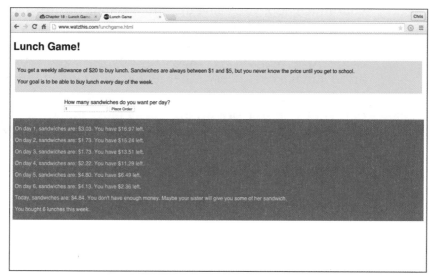

Figure 18-8: The finished Lunch Game, hosted on your own website!

Building a Lemonade Stand

While working on your random weather forecaster and your lunch app, you came up with a genius business idea: You could combine the two programs to open a lemonade stand!

As the local weather forecaster for Anytown, you should have an advantage over every other lemonade stand in the area. Here's how it works: People buy more lemonade when it's hot out. They're also more willing to pay more money to buy lemonade when it's hot out. By setting your lemonade price and deciding how much lemonade to make based on the weather, you can maximize your profit and minimize wasted lemonade.

In this chapter, you learn how to build a lemonade stand game.

Forecast for Monday:	Forecast for Tuesday:	Forecast for Wednesday:	Forecast for Thursday:	Forecast for Friday:
Partly Cloudy and 98 degrees.	Partly Sunny and 106 degrees.	Raining and 56 degrees.	Foggy and 45 degrees.	Snowing and 98 degrees.

How many glasses of lemonade do you want to make this week?

    hint: think big!

How much will you charge for a glass of lemonade this week?

    more than .5

    Open The Stand!

Playing the Game

Before we get started building the lemonade stand game, let's try it out and see how it works!

Follow these steps to open and play the game:

1. Go to our JSFiddle Public Dashboard at `http://jsfiddle.net/user/forkids/fiddles`.

2. Find the program titled "Chapter 19 – Lemonade Stand" and open it by clicking the title.

   The game will open and run. You see the Lemonade Stand game, as shown in Figure 19-1.

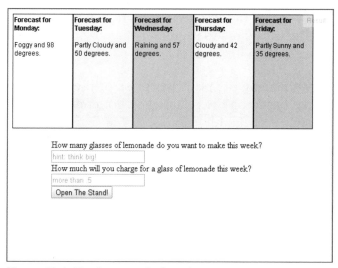

Figure 19-1: The Lemonade Stand game.

3. Take a look at the weather forecasts for the week, in the top part of the Result pane.

   These are the daily weather forecasts that the game will use to help calculate how many glasses of lemonade your stand sells.

4. Enter a number in the field labeled "How many glasses of lemonade do you want to make this week?"

   Remember that you're making lemonade for the whole week, so the number should be large enough that you don't run out of lemonade before Friday! *Hint:* Try different quantities, including some values in the hundreds.

5. Enter the price you want to charge per glass.

   Your cost (how much you pay to make it) per glass is $0.50, so make sure to price your lemonade higher than what it costs you to make it.

6. Click the Open the Stand button.

   A report of your daily and weekly sales will be displayed. Note the last line of the report, which tells you how much profit you made. Is this number greater than 0, or is it negative? If it's greater than 0, good job!

7. Try changing the price per glass or the number of glasses you make based on the results you got and click Open the Stand again.

   Do you notice any patterns in how the profit increases or decreases based on the price of lemonade? Can you figure out how to maximize the profit and minimize the number of glasses of lemonade you have left over?

8. Click Run in the top menu of JSFiddle to generate a new week's worth of weather and then try the game again.

9. Compare the number of glasses sold to the temperature each day.

   Notice that the daily temperature changes how many glasses of lemonade you sell.

Now that you've seen the lemonade stand program in action, let's back up and talk about a few math and business ideas that the game is based on.

Whether you're running a lemonade stand or just managing your own allowance and how much you spend on comic books and candy, these basic principles of economics apply.

A Lesson in Business

When you open a lemonade stand, you're running a business. As a new business owner, your primary goal is to make enough profit to be able to continue running the lemonade stand.

You may have other goals for running a lemonade stand as well, such as to spend your days outside in the sun, or to have fun talking with customers, or to learn to make the very best lemonade in the world. But if you don't make enough profit to be able to keep the lemonade stand running, you can't enjoy the other benefits of having a lemonade stand.

In order to make a profit selling lemonade, you need to understand your customers and why they buy lemonade from you. Just as you may have many different reasons for running your lemonade stand, customers may have many different reasons for buying lemonade from you and many different factors influence their decision. A few of the factors may include the weather, the price, how much money they have, where your lemonade stand is located, and how your lemonade tastes. Something as simple as buying and selling lemonade can actually be very complicated!

In order to make a game out of a lemonade stand, we need to focus on just a few of the many factors that are involved in the process.

Making a profit

Profit is what's left over from the total revenue of a business (all the money that comes in) after expenses (everything that the business spends money on).

In a lemonade stand, you may have all the following expenses: lemons, sugar, ice, cups, and stand maintenance (things like paint, repairs, and so on). You've done the math, and calculated that when you combine all your expenses, the cost for you to make a cup of lemonade is about $0.50. In order to make back your investment in the lemonade stand, you need to earn at least $0.50 for each glass of lemonade that you make.

Understanding your customers

As you know, the temperature in Anytown changes all the time, but one thing is for sure: The hotter it gets, the more lemonade people buy. But if the price of lemonade is too high, people won't buy it.

As a lemonade stand owner, your goal is to figure out how much lemonade to make and how much to charge for it in order to make the greatest profit.

Understanding the math

Here's the basic formula that our game uses to calculate how much lemonade is sold each day:

Glasses Sold = Temperature ÷ Price

For example, if the temperature is 100 degrees, and the price of lemonade is $2, the math looks like this:

Glasses Sold = 100 ÷ 2

The result is that you sold 50 glasses of lemonade.

However, if the temperature is lower, say 50 degrees, the formula looks like this:

Glasses Sold = 50 ÷ 2

The result is that you only sold 25 glasses of lemonade.

However, if you lower the price of lemonade to $1, the math looks like this:

Glasses Sold = 50 ÷ 1

The result is that you can sell 50 glasses of lemonade at the lower price when the temperature is lower.

Graphing sales, temperature, and price

Understanding the relationship among glasses sold, temperature, and price is important to master the game. Follow these steps to visualize this relationship using a 3D graph:

1. Go to `www.wolframalpha.com` in your web browser.

   You'll see the homepage of WolframAlpha, as shown in Figure 19-2.

Figure 19-2: The WolframAlpha home page.

2. In the search form, type **3D plot**.

   You see the search results with a Function to Plot field, as shown in Figure 19-3.

Figure 19-3: The Function to Plot field.

3. Below the Function to Plot field, click the Variables and Ranges link.

   Additional fields appear, as shown in Figure 19-4.

▪ function to plot:	x^2+y^2
▪ variable 1:	x
▪ lower limit 1:	-10
▪ upper limit 1:	10
▪ variable 2:	y
▪ lower limit 2:	-10
▪ upper limit 2:	10

Figure 19-4: Variables and ranges.

4. In the Function to Plot field, enter **z = x/y**.

   The letter z represents the number of glasses sold, the letter x represents the temperature, and the letter y represents the price.

5. In the Lower Limit 1 field, enter **0**.

   The Lower Limit 1 field represents the lowest value we want to graph for the variable *x*, which corresponds to the temperature value in our lemonade stand.

6. In the Upper Limit 1 field, enter **100**.

   This represents the maximum temperature value that we'll graph.

7. In the Lower Limit 2 field, enter **0**.

   This represents the lowest value for price in the lemonade stand.

   At $0 per glass, you're sure to sell a lot of lemonade, but we don't recommend this strategy in the long run if you're trying to run a business!

8. In the Upper Limit 2 field, enter **10**.

   It's unlikely that you'll want to charge anyone more than $10 for a glass of lemonade, so we'll set the upper limit to 10.

9. Click one of the orange equal sign buttons next to the input fields to graph your function.

   The results appear, and you see a graph similar to the one shown in Figure 19-5.

Notice that on the graph in Figure 19-5, the highest possible number of glasses of lemonade sold happens when the temperature is at the maximum and the price is at the minimum.

WolframAlpha can do a lot of really interesting things! Feel free to try out different values and try making different graphs.

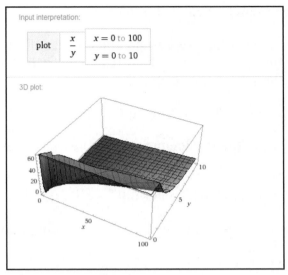

Figure 19-5: Graphing the relationship between glasses sold, temperature, and price.

Building the Game

Now that you have a better understanding of the math behind the lemonade stand, let's build the game!

We've already started building it for you, so the first step is to fork our code to make your own copy.

Forking the code

Follow these steps to make a copy of the starter app:

1. Log in to JSFiddle and go to our public dashboard at `http://jsfiddle.net/user/forkids/fiddles`.

2. Find the program named "Chapter 19 – Lemonade Stand – Start" and click its title to open it.

3. Click the Fork link in the top menu to create your own copy of the program.

4. Open the Fiddle Options in the left navigation and change the title to "(Your Name)'s Lemonade Stand."

5. Click Update and then Set as Base to save your own copy of the Lemonade Stand game.

Writing the JavaScript

Take a look at the starter program for the Lemonade Stand game. We've written enough HTML and CSS to get you started, but the JavaScript pane is completely blank.

When you run the program, the HTML shows up in the Results pane, but clicking the button doesn't do anything.

Let's walk through each thing that the Lemonade Stand needs to do and write code and comments as we go.

Creating globals

The first thing we'll do is to define some global variables that will be used in the program. We'll need the following:

✔ An array of days of the week

✔ An array of weather types

✔ Minimum and maximum temperature values

✔ The cost of making a cup of lemonade

✔ An array to hold actual daily temperatures

Before writing any code, create comments in the JavaScript window for each of these items, as shown in Listing 19-1.

Listing 19-1 Create Comments for Variables

```
// create days of week array

// define types of weather
```

(continued)

Listing 19-1 *(continued)*

```
// set min and max temperatures

// cost (to you) of a cup of lemonade

// array for storing daily temps
```

Now that we have comments, follow these steps to fill in the actual variable declarations.

1. Under the first comment (`create days of week array`), type the following:

```
var days = ["Monday", "Tuesday", "Wednesday", "Thursday",
        "Friday"];
```

2. Under the next comment (`define types of weather`), create an array of descriptions of weather.

   Here's our array as an example:

```
var weather = ["Sunny", "Partly Sunny", "Partly Cloudy",
        "Cloudy", "Raining", "Snowing", "Thunderstorm",
        "Foggy"];
```

   Feel free to add or delete any types of weather you like.

3. Under the next comment (`set min and max temperatures`), create two new variables to hold the coldest and hottest temperatures that you'd like to use in your game.

   Here's our example code:

```
var maxTemp = 100;
var minTemp = 0;
```

4. Under the next comment (`cost of a cup of lemonade`), declare a variable named `lemonadeCost` and give it a numeric value of your cost to make a cup of lemonade, in dollars.

```
var lemonadeCost = 0.5;
```

5. Create an empty array, called `dailyTemp`, to hold the daily temperature values.

   ```
   var dailyTemp = [];
   ```

6. Click Update to save your work.

7. Your JavaScript pane should now look like Listing 19-2.

Listing 19-2   The Globals Have Been Created

```
// create days of week array
var days = ["Monday", "Tuesday", "Wednesday", "Thursday",
            "Friday"];

// define types of weather
var weather = ["Sunny", "Partly Sunny", "Partly Cloudy",
            "Cloudy", "Raining", "Snowing", "Thunderstorm",
            "Foggy"];

// set min and max temps
var maxTemp = 100;
var minTemp = 0;

// cost (to you) of a cup of lemonade
var lemonadeCost = 0.5;

// array for storing daily temps
var dailyTemp = [];
```

Generating weather

The next step in writing our program is to generate the weather. Fortunately, we already have a function for generating random weather — namely, the random weather app that we wrote in Chapter 17.

We're going to make one addition to the `generateWeather` function from our random weather app created in Chapter 17. We'll store the daily weather in a global array called `dailyTemp`.

Follow these steps to write the `generateWeather` function:

1. Write a comment describing the purpose of the function.

```
/**
generates weather for the week
**/
```

2. Write the function head.

```
function generateWeather() {
```

3. Create two function variables to hold the current weather and temperature.

```
var weatherToday;
var tempToday;
```

4. Start a for loop to cycle through each day of the week.

```
for (var i = 0; i < days.length; i++) {
```

5. Get a random element from the weather array and assign it to `weatherToday`.

```
weatherToday = weather[Math.floor(Math.random() * weather.
        length)];
```

6. Get a random temperature between the values of `minTemp` and `maxTemp`.

```
tempToday = Math.floor(Math.random() * (maxTemp - minTemp) +
        minTemp);
```

7. Store the temperature in the `dailyTemp` array.

```
dailyTemp[i] = tempToday;
```

8. Output a message describing the day's weather.

```
document.getElementById("5DayWeather").innerHTML += "<div id='" +
        days[i] + "' class='" + weatherToday +
        "'><b>Forecast for " + days[i] + ":</b><br><br>" +
        weatherToday + " and " + tempToday + " degrees.</
        div>";
```

9. Close the loop and the function.

```
    }
  }
```

10. Call the function when the program loads, by typing the following below the global variable declarations.

```
generateWeather();
```

11. Click Update to save your work.

That completes the weather generation function. If you did everything correctly, a table of the week's weather should display in the Result pane now, above the input fields, as shown in Figure 19-6.

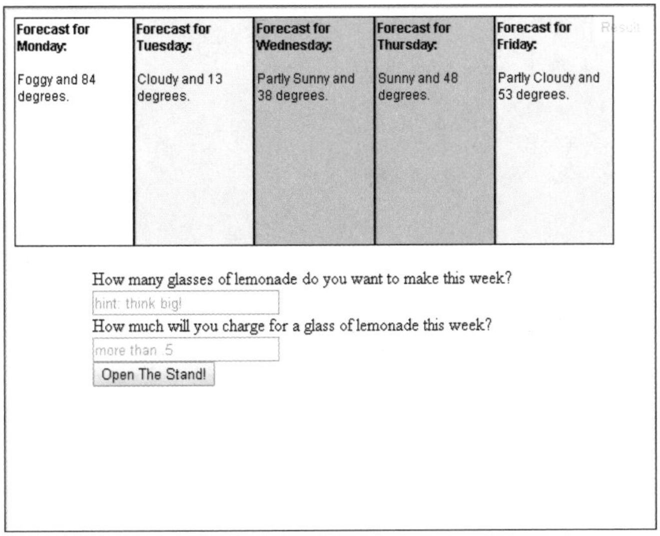

Forecast for Monday:	Forecast for Tuesday:	Forecast for Wednesday:	Forecast for Thursday:	Forecast for Friday:
Foggy and 84 degrees.	Cloudy and 13 degrees.	Partly Sunny and 38 degrees.	Sunny and 48 degrees.	Partly Cloudy and 53 degrees.

How many glasses of lemonade do you want to make this week?

hint: think big!

How much will you charge for a glass of lemonade this week?

more than .5

Open The Stand!

Figure 19-6: The Result pane, containing weather and input fields.

Compare your JavaScript with the code in Listing 19-3 and make sure that they match before moving on.

Listing 19-3   The Completed Globals and the generateWeather Function

```
// create days of week array
var days = ["Monday", "Tuesday", "Wednesday", "Thursday",
        "Friday"];

// define types of weather
var weather = ["Sunny", "Partly Sunny", "Partly Cloudy",
        "Cloudy", "Raining", "Snowing", "Thunderstorm",
        "Foggy"];

// set min and max temps
var maxTemp = 100;
var minTemp = 0;

// cost (to you) of a cup of lemonade
var lemonadeCost = 0.5;

// array for storing daily temps
var dailyTemp = [];

// make the week's weather
generateWeather();

/**
generates weather for the week
**/
function generateWeather() {
    var weatherToday;
    var tempToday;
    for (var i = 0; i < days.length; i++) {
        weatherToday = weather[Math.floor(Math.random() *
            weather.length)];
        tempToday = Math.floor(Math.random() *
            (maxTemp - minTemp) + minTemp);
        dailyTemp[i] = tempToday;
```

```
document.getElementById("5DayWeather").innerHTML
    += "<div id='" + days[i] + "' class='" +
    weatherToday + "'><b>Forecast for " + days[i]
    + ":</b><br><br>" + weatherToday + " and " +
    tempToday + " degrees.</div>";
    }
}
```

Opening the stand

The next function we'll create is the one that opens the stand and calculates the number of glasses sold for the week.

Follow these steps to write the openTheStand function.

1. Write a comment describing the function and then write the function head.

   ```
   /**
   calculates glasses of lemonade sold
   **/
   function openTheStand() {
   ```

2. Create three new variables — one to hold the daily number of glasses sold, one to hold the weekly total, and one to hold the number of glasses we have left to sell — and initialize all three with 0.

   ```
   var glassesSold = 0; // daily
   var totalGlasses = 0; // weekly
   var glassesLeft = 0; // left to sell
   ```

3. Call a function named resetForm(), which resets the report area of the program so that it can be run multiple times without restarting the game.

   ```
   // clear previous results
   resetForm();
   ```

We'll write the resetForm function after we finish openTheStand();.

4. Get the values from the form fields.

```
// get input
var numGlasses = Number(document.getElementById("numGlasses").
        value);
var glassPrice = Number(document.getElementById("glassPrice").
        value);
```

5. Create a new loop to cycle through each day of the week.

```
for (var i = 0; i < days.length; i++) {
```

6. Calculate the number of glasses sold.

```
// glasses sold depends on temp and price
glassesSold = Math.floor(dailyTemp[i] / glassPrice);
```

7. Calculate how many glasses are left.

```
// how many glasses do we have now?
glassesLeft = numGlasses - totalGlasses;
```

8. Write an `if...else` statement that checks whether you're out of lemonade.

```
// we can't sell more than we have
if (glassesSold > glassesLeft) {
    glassesSold = glassesLeft;
}
```

If `glassesSold` is greater than what we have left, just sell what we have left by setting the `glassesSold` variable equal to what's left.

9. Increase the weekly total of glasses sold.

```
// increase the weekly total
totalGlasses = glassesSold + totalGlasses;
```

10. Display the daily totals.

```
// display daily total
document.getElementById("result").innerHTML += "<p>" + days[i] +
        ", you sold " + glassesSold + " glasses of
        lemonade.</p>";
```

11. Finish the loop with a curly bracket.

    ```
    }
    ```

12. Make a call to the function that will display the weekly results, passing it three arguments: numGlasses, glassPrice, and totalGlasses.

    ```
    displayResults(numGlasses,glassPrice,totalGlasses);
    ```

13. Finish the function by typing a closing curly bracket.

    ```
    }
    ```

14. Save your work by clicking Update.

If you did everything right, your openTheStand function should match the code in Listing 19-4.

Listing 19-4   **The openTheStand Function**

```
/**
calculates glasses of lemonade sold
**/
function openTheStand() {
    var glassesSold = 0; // daily
    var totalGlasses = 0; // weekly
    var glassesLeft = 0; // left to sell

    // clear out previous results
    resetForm();

    // get input
    var numGlasses = Number(document.
        getElementById("numGlasses").value);
    var glassPrice = Number(document.
        getElementById("glassPrice").value);
```

(continued)

Listing 19-4 *(continued)*

```
for (var i = 0; i < days.length; i++) {

    // glasses sold depends on temp and price
    glassesSold = Math.floor(dailyTemp[i] /
        glassPrice);

    // how many glasses do we have now?
    glassesLeft = numGlasses - totalGlasses;

    // we can't sell more than we have
    if (glassesSold > glassesLeft) {
        glassesSold = glassesLeft;
    }

    // increase the weekly total
    totalGlasses = glassesSold + totalGlasses;

    // display daily total
    document.getElementById("result").innerHTML +=
        "<p>" + days[i] + ", you sold " + glassesSold +
        " glasses of lemonade.</p>";

}

displayResults(numGlasses, glassPrice, totalGlasses);

}
```

Resetting the program

One of the first things that the openTheStand() function does is to make a call to a function called resetForm(). This function is very simple. Its sole purpose is to clear out the content from the report area of the program so that you can run the program again without the results being added to the bottom of the previous output.

Listing 19-5 shows the complete code for resetForm(). Type this function into the JavaScript pane, underneath the openTheStand() function (at the very end of the code in the JavaScript pane).

Listing 19-5   The resetForm() Function

```
/**
resets the game so that a new order can be placed
**/
function resetForm() {
    document.getElementById("result").innerHTML = "";


}
```

After you've written the resetForm() function, click the Update link to save your work.

Displaying a report

The final function in the Lemonade Stand game is the display-Results() function. This function calculates weekly results using arguments supplied to it by the openTheStand() function and outputs a report about how you did.

Follow these steps to write displayResults().

1. Write a comment describing the function and the function header, with three parameters: weeklyInventory, glassPrice, and weeklySales.

    ```
    /**
    calculates results and displays a report
    **/
    function displayResults(weeklyInventory, glassPrice, weeklySales)
        {
    ```

2. Calculate your total revenue by multiplying the total number of glasses sold times the price that was paid for each glass.

    ```
    var revenue = weeklySales * glassPrice;
    ```

3. Calculate your expenses by multiplying the number of glasses of lemonade you made times the cost (to you) of each glass.

    ```
    var expense = weeklyInventory * lemonadeCost;
    ```

4. Calculate how many glasses are left over by subtracting the total sales from the number of glasses you made.

```
var leftOver = weeklyInventory - weeklySales;
```

5. Calculate your profit by subtracting expenses from the total revenue.

```
var profit = revenue - expense;
```

6. Write out the final report using the following four statements:

```
// print out the weekly report
document.getElementById("result").innerHTML += "<p>You sold a
          total of " + weeklySales + " glasses of lemonade
          this week.</p>";
document.getElementById("result").innerHTML += "<p>Total revenue:
          $" + revenue + ".</p>";
document.getElementById("result").innerHTML += "<p>You have " +
          leftOver + " glasses of lemonade left over.</p>";
document.getElementById("result").innerHTML += "<p>Each glass
          costs you $" + lemonadeCost + ". Your profit was $"
          + profit + ".";
```

7. Finish the function with a closing curly bracket.

```
}
```

8. Click Update to save your work.

The final function should match Listing 19-6.

Listing 19-6   The Final displayResults Function

```
/**
calculates results and displays a report
**/
function displayResults(weeklyInventory, glassPrice,
          weeklySales) {
   // calculate results
   var revenue = weeklySales * glassPrice;
   var expense = weeklyInventory * lemonadeCost;
```

```
var leftOver = weeklyInventory - weeklySales;
var profit = revenue - expense;

// print out the weekly report
document.getElementById("result").innerHTML += "<p>You
        sold a total of " + weeklySales + " glasses of
        lemonade this week.</p>";
document.getElementById("result").innerHTML +=
        "<p>Total revenue: $" + income + ".</p>";
document.getElementById("result").innerHTML += "<p>You
        have " + leftOver + " glasses of lemonade left
        over.</p>";
document.getElementById("result").innerHTML +=
        "<p>Each glass costs you $" + lemonadeCost + ".
        Your profit was $" + profit + ".";
}
```

Finishing and testing the program

If you try out the program now, you'll discover that it doesn't do anything except print out the random weather forecast.

There's one thing left that we need to do. Do you know what it is?

If you said that we need to listen for the `click` event on the button, you're exactly right. The `click` event is the switch the makes the lemonade stand work.

Follow these steps to finish the program and test it out.

1. Type the following code before the function declarations in the JavaScript pane:

   ```
   // listen for order
   document.getElementById("OpenTheStand").addEventListener("click",
           openTheStand);
   ```

2. Click Update and Set as Base to save your work.

   The final code in the JavaScript pane should match Listing 19-7.

Listing 19-7   The Lemonade Stand Program

```javascript
// create days of week array
var days = ["Monday", "Tuesday", "Wednesday", "Thursday",
        "Friday"];

// define types of weather
var weather = ["Sunny", "Partly Sunny", "Partly Cloudy",
        "Cloudy", "Raining", "Snowing", "Thunderstorm",
        "Foggy"];

// set min and max temps
var maxTemp = 110;
var minTemp = 32;

// cost (to you) of a cup of lemonade
var lemonadeCost = 0.5;

// array for storing daily temps
var dailyTemp = [];

// listen for order
document.getElementById("OpenTheStand").
        addEventListener("click", openTheStand);

// make the week's weather
generateWeather();

/**
generates weather for the week
**/
function generateWeather() {
    var weatherToday;
    var tempToday;
    for (var i = 0; i < days.length; i++) {
        weatherToday = weather[Math.floor(Math.random() *
            weather.length)];
        tempToday = Math.floor(Math.random() * (maxTemp -
            minTemp) + minTemp);
        dailyTemp[i] = tempToday;
```

```
            document.getElementById("5DayWeather").innerHTML
                += "<div id='" + days[i] + "' class='" +
                weatherToday + "'><b>Forecast for " + days[i]
                + ":</b><br><br>" + weatherToday + " and " +
                tempToday + " degrees.</div>";
        }
}

/**
calculates glasses of lemonade sold
**/
function openTheStand() {
    var glassesSold = 0; // daily
    var totalGlasses = 0; // weekly
    var glassesLeft = 0; // left to sell

    // clear previous results
    resetForm();

    // get input
    var numGlasses = Number(document.
            getElementById("numGlasses").value);
    var glassPrice = Number(document.
            getElementById("glassPrice").value);


    for (var i = 0; i < days.length; i++) {

        // glasses sold depends on temp and price
        glassesSold = Math.floor(dailyTemp[i] /
            glassPrice);

        // how many glasses do we have now?
        glassesLeft = numGlasses - totalGlasses;

        // we can't sell more than we have
        if (glassesSold > glassesLeft) {
            glassesSold = glassesLeft;
        }
```

(continued)

Listing 19-7 *(continued)*

```
        // increase the weekly total
        totalGlasses = glassesSold + totalGlasses;

        // display daily total
        document.getElementById("result").innerHTML +=
            "<p>" + days[i] + ", you sold " + glassesSold +
            " glasses of lemonade.</p>";

    }

    displayResults(numGlasses, glassPrice, totalGlasses);

}

/**
calculates results and displays a report
**/
function displayResults(weeklyInventory, glassPrice,
            weeklySales) {
    // calculate results
    var revenue = weeklySales * glassPrice;
    var expense = weeklyInventory * lemonadeCost;
    var leftOver = weeklyInventory - weeklySales;
    var profit = revenue - expense;

    // print out the weekly report
    document.getElementById("result").innerHTML += "<p>You
            sold a total of " + weeklySales + " glasses of
            lemonade this week.</p>";
    document.getElementById("result").innerHTML +=
            "<p>Total revenue: $" + revenue + ".</p>";
    document.getElementById("result").innerHTML += "<p>You
            have " + leftOver + " glasses of lemonade left
            over.</p>";
    document.getElementById("result").innerHTML +=
            "<p>Each glass costs you $" + lemonadeCost + ".
            Your profit was $" + profit + ".";
}
```

```
/**
resets the game so that a new order can be placed
**/
function resetForm() {
    document.getElementById("result").innerHTML = "";


}
```

3. Enter a value into the form field labeled "How many glasses of lemonade do you want to make for the week?"

4. Enter a value into the form field label "How much will you charge for a glass of lemonade this week?"

5. Press the Open the Stand button.

   You see how many glasses of lemonade you sold each day, followed by the weekly totals and the profit, as shown in Figure 19-7.

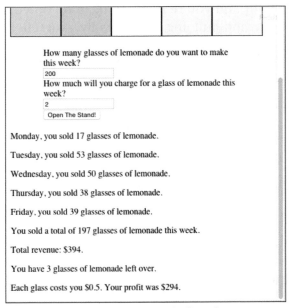

Figure 19-7: The final Lemonade Stand game.

How did you do? Did you make a profit? Can you increase your profit by changing the price or number of glasses? Does one of the methods of increasing profit seem to work better than the other? What happens when you set either the price or the glasses of lemonade to a very large number? What happens when either one is set to a very small number?

When you're ready, move on to the next section to get some ideas for improvements you may want to make to the Lemonade Game!

Improving the Lemonade Game

The Lemonade Game is interesting and demonstrates a number of important JavaScript principles. By now, however, you likely have ideas for how it could be improved to be more of a challenge, more fun, or more realistic.

If you've made it this far in the book, you have a good understanding of JavaScript and you're ready to head off on your own and start modifying and building programs by yourself. Excellent work!

Here are a few ideas to get you started with making modifications to the Lemonade Stand game:

- Allow the user to control the price and how much lemonade is made on a daily basis, rather than weekly.

- Factor the type of weather (rainy, snowy, and so on) into the calculation of how many glasses were sold, instead of just using the temperature.

- Randomize the cost (the price you pay) per glass of lemonade.

- Write more HTML and CSS to improve, or just change, the look of the game.

- Create a button that generates new random weather for a new week, instead of making the player start the game over when they want a new week of weather.

✔ Save the user's high score in a variable and let them know if they improve from game to game.

✔ Calculate the cost of lemonade based on values for the price of lemons and the price of sugar, as well as how many lemons and how much sugar it takes to make how many glasses of lemonade.

✔ Create random events in the game, such as blizzards or dogs that knock over the stand, which sometimes cause no lemonade at all to be sold on a day.

These are just a few of the hundreds of different improvements that could be made to the Lemonade Stand game. If you make an improvement that you want to share, please show it to us on Facebook, Twitter, or via email at info@watzthis.com. We're excited to see what you come up with!

Index

Symbols and Numerics

+ (addition), 150–151
&& (and operator), 239
== (equality operator), 145–148, 234
> (greater than operator), 149, 151
>= (greater than or equal to
    operator), 149–150
!= (inequality operator), 148
|| (or operator), 239
=== (strict equality operator), 147,
    234
!== (strict inequality operator),
    148–149
; (semicolon)
  in CSS declarations, 93
  to separate statements, 25, 31

A

Activity Calendar program,
    255–266
  building, 261–266
  Date object, 257–261
  forking, 256–257
  introduction to, 255
  using, 256
addEventListener method,
    111–113, 116, 163
addition (+), 150–151
addition operator, 140

addTheThing( ) function, 216, 222
addToTheList( ) function, 216,
    219–222
<a> element, 79
alert( ) command, 44–46
alert( ) function, 193
alert keyword, 25
alt attribute, 82
and operator (&&), 239
animation
  creating with JavaScript, 115–117
  Douglas the JavaScript Robot,
      104–122
    adding a second animation
        function, 118–122
    animating another element, 118
    arm sweep animation, 118–120
    changing CSS with JavaScript,
        105–106
    creating animations with
        JavaScript, 115–117
    experimenting with Douglas,
        108–109
    handling events, 111–113
    making Douglas dance, 109–111
    modifying Douglas with JavaScript,
        106–108
    writing a listener, 113–115
appendChild( ) method, 222
arguments, passing, 195
arithmetic operators, 140–143
arm sweep animation, 118–120

array methods, 177–178
  in JSFiddle, 178–179
arrays, 173–189
  changing element values, 176–177
  creating and accessing, 175–176
  definition of, 174–175
  empty, 278
  in general, 173
  getting array values, 176
  storing different data types in, 175
  variables inside, 176
askQuestion( ) function,
    280–283, 287
assignment operator, 43
asterisk (*), to multiply numbers, 20
<audio> tag, 73

B

backslash ( )
  printing a, 28
  in a string, 27
*Beginning HTML5 and CSS3 For
    Dummies,* 78
beginning tags, 73
binary codes, 9–10
bit, 10
body element, 76, 91, 94, 160, 161
Boolean data type, 41–42
branching, defined, 267
bubbles, size of, 62
Bubbles demo, 55–57, 60, 64
  sharing your fiddle, 65–66
built-in functions, 191
buyLunches( ) function, 313, 314, 323
bytes, 10

C

calculateDelivery( ) function, 245,
    247, 248
calculatePrice( ) function, 242
calling a function, 194
camelCase, 35
capitalization, 29, 30, 106
capital letters, for words in variable
    names, 34
cascading
  defined, 101
  understanding, 101
Cascading Style Sheets (CSS)
  basics of, 90–91
  changing with JavaScript,
    105–109
  Function Junction, 197–200
  Martian Rescue! game, 272–276
  resizing elements with, 98–101
  Word Replacement Game, 160
cases, switch statements, 253
central processing unit (CPU), 9
checkPosition( ) function,
    203–204
Chrome Developer Tools
class selectors, 92
Clear Console Log button, 218
clearInterval statement, 117
code
  curly brackets used for grouping
    pieces of, 30
  forking
    Activity Calendar program,
    256–257
    defined, 63

JavaScript Pizzeria, 241
Lemonade Stand game, 334–335
Lunch Game, 313
Martian Rescue! game, 271
Super-Calculator, 138–139
Wish List program, 208–209
JavaScript. *See also* Martian Rescue!
   game; Wish List program
   array methods, 177–178
   changing CSS with, 105–109
   changing HTML with, 83–87
   creating animations with, 115–117
   examples of websites that use,
      13–14
   Function Junction, 200–204
   Lemonade Stand game, 335
   overview, 12–13
   Word Replacement Game, 163–165
   text in, 29–30
coding (computer programming), 8
color names, HTML, 58–59
colors, CSS, 96–97
color swatch, hexadecimal value,
   58–59
comments
   making, 31–32
   multi-line, 32
   single-line, 32
comparison operators, 137, 145–150
compilation, defined, 10, 23
compilers, defined, 8
computer programmers, first, 8
computer programming, 8
computer programs
   defined, 8
   examples of things that can be
      done by, 9

concat( ) array method, 178, 181
concatenation, 20
concatenation/assignment operator
   (+=), 164
concatenation operator, 137, 141,
   142, 153, 164
condition statement, for loops, 296
continueStory( ) function, 284, 285,
   288–290
countdown, 297–298
CPU (central processing unit), 9
createElement( ) method, 220
CSS (Cascading Style Sheets)
   basics of, 90–91
   changing with JavaScript, 105–109
   Function Junction, 197–200
   Martian Rescue! game, 272–276
   resizing elements with, 98–101
   Word Replacement Game, 160
CSS declarations, 93
CSS pane, 55–60
   dream car, 133
CSS properties, 93–96
CSS rule, 91
CSS selectors, 91–93
curly braces ( ), creating objects, 130
curly brackets ({}), 30, 31
currentPosition variable, 203, 204
customers, Lemonade Stand game,
   330
custom functions, 191–193

D

data. *See also* input
   prompting the user for input, 42–43
data types, 38–42

data types *(continued)*
  in arrays, 175
  Boolean, 41–42
  combining two different, 41
  definition of, 38
  number, 40–41
  of operands, 126–129
  string, 38–40
dayOfWeek variable, 263
debugging, origin of term, 8
declaration block, CSS rule, 91
defining a function, 193–194
Developer Tools, Chrome, 16–18
  clearing, 20
  experimenting with, 21
  introduction to, 18
  overview, 17
  potential to be misused, 18
  running your first commands, 19
displayActivity( ) function, 262, 263
displayDate( ) function, 262
display:none, turning off elements
    with, 273–275
displayResults( ) function, 345, 346,
    350
<div> elements, 79, 157, 158, 161,
    163, 211
document, 47
document.write( ), 47, 49
Double Quotes within Single
    Quotes, 29
Douglas the JavaScript Robot,
    90–103
  animating
    adding a second animation
      function, 118–122
    animating another element, 118

arm sweep animation, 118–120
changing CSS with JavaScript,
    105–106
creating animations with
    JavaScript, 115–117
experimenting with Douglas,
    108–109
handling events, 111–113
making Douglas dance,
    109–111
modifying Douglas with JavaScript,
    106–108
writing a listener, 113–115
cascading, 101
CSS colors, 96–97
CSS declarations, 93
CSS properties, 93–96
CSS selectors, 91–93
customizing your own robot, 103
positioning elements with CSS,
    101–102
resizing elements with CSS,
    98–101
responsive design, 98
dream car (dreamCar object)
color of the car, 135
configuring, 132–135
creating, 131
CSS pane, 133
customizing, 134–135
generic car, 133–134
HTML pane, 132
JavaScript pane, 134
make and model of the car, 135
model year on the price tag,
    135
price tag, 133–135

E

elements
  adding attributes to, 81–83
  positioning with CSS, 101
  resizing with CSS, 98
element selectors, 91
<em> element, 78
empty arrays, 278
ending tags, 73
equality operator (==), 145–148, 234
escaping quotation marks, 27–29
event handler
  addEventListener method, 111–112
  defined, 86
event listeners
  Listing 13-2, 214
  Martian Rescue! game, Martian
    Rescue! game, JavaScript, 279
  Wish List program, 212–214
events
  defined, 111
  examples of, 111
  handling, 111–113
  listening for, 112
  in web browsers, 111–112
event target, 112
eye bounce, 110, 113, 115

F

Facebook
  JavaScript used by, 14, 15
  sharing your programs on, 65
FF, in hexadecimal notation, 97
FILO (First In, Last Out), 75

final expression, for loops, 297
float:left property, 161
flow charts, 268–269
font-family style, 160
font size, 94
<footer> tag, 74
Fork button, 63
forking the code
  Activity Calendar program, 256–257
  defined, 63
  JavaScript Pizzeria, 241
  Lemonade Stand game, 334–335
  Lunch Game, 313
  Martian Rescue! game, 271
  Super-Calculator, 138–139
  Wish List program, 208–209
for loops, 295–308
  parts of, 296–297
  random weather forecasting
    id and class attributes, 305–307
    Listing 17-5 The Finished
      JavaScript Code, 303–304
    Math.random( ) function,
      299–301
    styling the app, 307–308
    writing the app, 301–303
  sample, 296
  writing and using, 297–298
forward slash (/), 20
frames, in an animation, 115
function body, 194
function head, 194
Function Junction, 196–205
  CSS pane, 197–200
  HTML for, 197
  JavaScript pane, 200–204
function keyword, 193

functions
  built-in, 191
  calling, 194
  custom, 191–193
  defining, 193–194
  defining parameters, 194–195
  example of, 192
  overview, 190–191
  returning a value, 195–196
  Wish List program, 215–227
    addTheThing( ), 216, 222
    addToTheList( ), 216, 219–222
    printView( ), 217–218, 224, 226
    resetInput( ), 222–224
Function technique, 194

G

games
  Function Junction, 196–205
  Lunch Game, 312–317
  Martian Rescue!, 269–292
  Word Replacement, 153–170
generateWeather( ) function, 302
getAnswer( ) function, 283, 284, 286
getDate( ) method, 258, 259
getDay( ) method, 258, 259
getElementById, 83–87
getFullYear( ) method, 258, 259
getHours( ) method, 259
getMilliseconds( ) method, 259
getMonth( ) method, 259
getSeconds( ) method, 259
getter methods, 258–259
getTime( ) method, 259
gigabyte, 10

global variables
  Lemonade Stand game, 335
  Martian Rescue! game, 278
  Wish List program, 214–215
Google Chrome, 14–16
  Developer Tools, 16–18
  installing, 16
graphing sales, temperature, and
    price, Lemonade Stand game,
    331–333
greater than operator (>), 149, 151
greater than or equal to operator
    (>=), 149–150

H

hash symbol (#)
  for hexadecimal code, 97
  for ID selectors, 92
head element, 75
headers, 76
<header> tag, 74
hexadecimal notation, 97
  for CSS colors, 58
Hopper, Grace Murray, 8
<hr> element, 79
<h1> element, 76
<h1> through <h6> elements, 78–79
HTML (Hypertext Markup Language),
    72–88
  Bubbles demo, 60–61
  changing with JavaScript, 83–87
  definition of, 72
  elements of, 78–81
  for Function Junction, 197
  getElementById, 84

Martian Rescue! game, 272–276
tags in, 61, 72–75
text without, 72
for Wish List program, 210–212
for Word Replacement Game, 156
<html> and </html> tags, 75, 77
HTML attributes, 81–83
HTML elements, defined, 73
HTML pane
  creating your first web page, 76–77
  dream car, 132
  JSFiddle, 60

I

ID attributes, 82–83
  ID selectors and, 92–93
  selecting an element with
    getElementById and, 84
ID selectors, 92–93
if...else statements
  branching, 267
  to choose between two paths, 237
  introduction to, 236–238
  and operator (&&) in, 239
  variables without operators,
    237–238
<img> tag, 73
increment operator, 117
indentation, 31
indexOf( ) array method, 178,
    181–182
indexOf( ) method, 40
inequality operator (!=), 148
init( ) function, 323–324
initialization statement, for loops,
    296

innerHTML method, 84–87
innerHTML property, 220
input
  combining output and, 48–50
  defined, 33
  prompting the user for, 42–43
  responding to, 44–46
  storing user input, 43–44
inputToReset variable, 224
Interactive Sock Puppet, 14

J

JavaScript code
  array methods, 177–178
  changing CSS with, 105–109
  changing HTML with, 83–87
  creating animations with,
    115–117
  examples of websites that use,
    13–14
  Function Junction, 200–204
  Lemonade Stand game, 335
  Martian Rescue! game
    askQuestion( ) function, 280–283
    continueStory( ) function, 284,
      285, 288–290
    element shortcuts, 278
    empty arrays, 278
    getAnswer( ) function, 283, 284,
      286
    Listing 16-4 The Starter JavaScript
      for Martian Rescue!, 277
    theEnd( ) function, 290–291
    writing the functions, 281–284
  overview, 12–13
  Wish List program, 212–229

JavaScript code *(continued)*
  declaring global variables, 214–215
  event listeners, 212–214
  Word Replacement Game code,
    163–165
JavaScript Console (Developer Tools
    Console)
  clearing, 20
  experimenting with, 21
  introduction to, 18
  potential to be misused, 18
  running your first commands, 19
JavaScript pane, JSFiddle, 61–63
JavaScript Pizzeria, 240–251
  adding the new item to the menu,
    241–243
  delivering to other cities, 243–245
  displaying the delivery fee, 245–246
  forking the code, 241
  planning improvements, 241
  programming the birthday special,
    246–248
  running current version of the
    website, 240
join( ) array method, 178, 182–183
JSFiddle
  Activity Calendar program, 256–257
  array methods, 178–179
  creating an account, 63–65
  CSS pane, 55–60
  HTML pane, 60
  introduction to, 52–53
  JavaScript pane, 61–63
  Log In page, 63–64
  overview, 51
  playing with fiddles, 54–55
  public dashboard, 53

creating your own public
  dashboard, 67–68
running your first JSFiddle
  program, 53
saving your app, 67–68
user interface, 52
viewing fiddles, 53–54
website, 52

K

kilobyte, 10

L

<label> element, 210
languages, programming
  choosing, 11–12
  examples of, 11–12
  function of, 10
lastIndexOf( ) array method,
    183–184
Lemonade Stand game, 326–353
  building the game, 334–351
    creating globals, 335–337
    forking the code, 334–335
    writing the JavaScript, 335
  business lesson, 329
  displaying a report, 345–346
  finishing and testing the program,
    347–351
  generating weather, 337–339
  graphing sales, temperature, and
    price, 331–334
  improving, 352–353
  making a profit, 329–330

opening the stand, 341–343

playing the game, 327–329

resetting the program, 344–345

understanding the math, 330–331

understanding your customers, 330

<.>length, 38

length of a string, 38–39

less-than operator (<), 150

less-than-or-equal-to operator (<=), 150

<li> element, 76, 79, 157, 158, 161, 162

line breaks, 30–31

listener

  overview, 112

  writing a, 113–115

Listing 2-1 A JavaScript Statement, 24

Listing 2-2 A Program to Print a Message 300 Times, 26

Listing 2-5 White Space Makes Programs Easier to Read, 30

Listing 2-6 Single-Line Comments, 32

Listing 2-7 Multi-Line Comment, 32

Listing 5-1 A List, 72

Listing 5-2 A Simple HTML Document, 74

Listing 5-3 Updated Home Page, 81

Listing 5-4 Updated Home Page with id Attributes Added, 83

Listing 5-5 Final JavaScript for the HTML Homepage App, 87-88

Listing 7-1 Code Required in the JavaScript Pane to Enable the Eye Bounce, 115

Listing 7-2 Finished moveRightLeft Function, 120

Listing 7-3 JavaScript Required to Implement Both of Douglas's Dance Moves, 121

Listing 10-1 Completed Markup in the HTML Pane, 168

Listing 10-2 Completed Code in the JavaScript Pane, 168-170

Listing 12-1 Function Junction CSS, 198

Listing 12-2 JavaScript Pane with Comments Indicating What to Do, 200

Listing 13-1 HTML for the Wish List Program, 212

Listing 13-2 Event Listeners, 214

Listing 13-3 Event Listeners and Global Variables, 215

Listing 13-4 Finished addTheThing( ) Function, 216

Listing 13-5 Finished addToTheList( ) Function, 222

Listing 13-6 Finished resetInput( ) Function, 224

Listing 13-7 Finished printView( ) Function, 226

Listing 14-1 Using if. . .else, 236

Listing 14-2 Using Single-Word Operators, 238

Listing 14-3 Pizza Parlor Free Delivery Rule in JavaScript, 239

Listing 14-4 Free Delivery on Your Birthday, 239

Listing 14-5 The Completed JavaScript Pizzeria Program, 248-250

Listing 14-6 The Final HTML, 250-251

Listing 15-1 Produce Different
Results for Different Input, 254

Listing 15-2 The Starting JavaScript
for the Activity Calendar, 261-262

Listing 15-3 The Finished Program,
264-266

Listing 16-1 The Beginning of the
HTML, 272

Listing 16-2 The CSS for Martian
Rescue!, 273-274

Listing 16-3 The First storyPart div,
275-276

Listing 16-4 The Starter JavaScript
for Martian Rescue!, 277

Listing 16-5 The Beginning of the
JavaScript, 280

Listing 16-6 The Finished
askQuestion( ) Function, 282-283

Listing 16-7 The Finished
getAnswer( ) Function, 284

Listing 16-9 The theEnd( ) Function,
291

Listing 17-1 JavaScript Countdown,
297

Listing 17-2 Outputting Array Values
with for, 298

Listing 17-3 A Random Number Alert,
299-300

Listing 17-4 Finding a Random
Friend, 301

Listing 17-5 The Finished JavaScript
Code, 303-304

Listing 18-1 Logging Hello,
JavaScript, 311

Listing 18-3 Looping through a List of
Names, 312

Listing 18-4 The Starting Point for
buyLunches, 314

Listing 18-5 A Standard HTML
Template, 323

Listing 18-6 Finishing the init( )
Function, 324

Listing 19-1 Create Comments for
Variables, 335-336

Listing 19-2 The Globals Have Been
Created, 337

Listing 19-3 The Completed Globals
and the generateWeather
Function, 340-341

Listing 19-4 The openTheStand
Function, 343-344

Listing 19-5 The resetForm( )
Function, 345

Listing 19-6 The Final displayResults
Function, 346-347

Listing 19-7 The Lemonade Stand
Program, 348-351

lists
changing, 85–88
ordered, 76
unordered, 76

local variables, 214

logical operators, combining
comparisons with, 238–239

loops, 295–308
for. See for loops
while
example of, 310
introduction to, 309
Lunch Game, 312–317
writing, 310–311

Lovelace, Ada, 8

Lunch Game, 312–317
  buyLunches( ) function, 313, 314, 323
  coding, 312–317
  forking the code, 313
  trying it out, 317
  web hosting, 318–325

M

machine language
  compilation into, 10
  purpose of, 10
Martian Rescue! game, 269–292
  forking the code, 271
  HTML and CSS, 272–276
  JavaScript code
    askQuestion( ) function, 280–283
    continueStory( ) function, 284, 285, 288–290
    element shortcuts, 278
    empty arrays, 278
    getAnswer( ) function, 283, 284, 286
    Listing 16-4 The Starter JavaScript for Martian Rescue!, 277
    theEnd( ) function, 290–291
    writing the functions, 281–284
  looking at (or not looking at) the story parts, 275–276
  playing the game, 269–271
  turning off elements with display:none, 273–275
  writing the story, 269
Math.floor( ) function, 300

Math.random( ) function, 299–301
megabyte, 10
methods
  array, 177–178
  defined, 39
  getter, 258–259
minus sign, 20
modulo operation, 137, 143
moveRightLeft function, 119, 120
moveUpDown listener function, 113, 118, 119
multi-line comments, 32
myElement variable, 278
myListArea variable, 215, 222

N

name/value pair, 82
newList function, 86
newListItem variable, 220, 221
number data type, 40–41

O

objects
  creating, 130–131
  overview, 46
  working with, 130–132
<ol> and </ol> tags, 75, 79
ol element, 76
openTheStand( ) function, 341, 343–345
operands, 126
  data types of, 126–129

operands *(continued)*
  object type, 130–131
  overview, 126
  Super-Calculator, 139, 140
  variables as, 127–128
Operate button, 140–144, 146–151
operator
  addition, 140
  assignment, 43
  concatenation, 137, 141, 142, 153, 164
  increment, 117
operators, 136–152
  arithmetic, 140–143
  comparison, 137, 145–150
  defined, 136
  greater than (>), 149
  greater than or equal to (>=), 149–150
  inequality (!=), 148
  less-than (<), 150
  less-than-or-equal-to (<=), 150
  logical, combining comparisons with, 238–239
  strict equality (===), 147, 234
  strict inequality (!==), 148–149
  variables without, 237–238
ordered lists, 76
or operator (| |), 239
output
  combining input and, 48–50
  defined, 33

p element (<p> and </p> tags), 61, 91
percent, as units of measurement, 98–100
period (.), for class selectors, 92
pixels, as units of measurement, 98
placeOrder( ) function, 245, 247, 248
pop( ) array method, 178, 184–185
positioning elements with CSS, 101
price tag, for dream car, 133–135
Print dialog box, browser's, 227–228
printing, program that prints out the words "Coding is fun!" 300 times, 25–26
print( ) method, 227
printView( ) function, 217–218, 224, 226, 227
Print Your List button, 208, 210–211, 224, 227
profit, Lemonade Stand game, 329–330
program(s)
  that prints out the words "Coding is fun!" 300 times, 25–26
  things all programs have in common, 33
programming (coding), 8
programming languages
  choosing, 11–12
  examples of, 11–12
  function of, 10
prompt command, 42
property, 39
  in CSS declarations, 93
public dashboard, 53
  creating your own, 67–68
push( ) array method, 178, 185–186, 220

P

<p> and </p> tags (p element), 61, 91
parameters, 194–195
passing an argument, 195

Q

quotes (quotation marks)
  Double Quotes within Single
    Quotes, 29
  escaping, 27–29
  inside a string, 27
  single, 28–29
  types of, 28–29
  use of, 20

R

radio buttons, Super-Calculator, 139
random weather forecasting,
    299–308
  id and class attributes, 305–307
  Listing 17-5 The Finished JavaScript
    Code, 303–304
  Math.random( ) function, 299–301
  styling the app, 307–308
  writing the app, 301–303
rectangles, elements in an HTML
    document as, 98
remainder (modulo operation), 143,
    144
replaceButton variable, 163
Replace It button, 155–157, 165
reserved words, 35
resetForm( ) function, 314, 341, 344,
    345
resetInput( ) function, 222–224
resetting the program, Lemonade
    Stand game, 344–345

resizing elements with CSS, 98–101
responding to input, 44–46
responsive design, 98–99
return statement, 195
return value, 195
  defined, 19
reverse( ) array method,
    178, 186
robotPart variable, 116
rules, 25–27

S

scientific notation, 144–145
selecting an element with
    getElementById, 84
selectors
  class, 92
  CSS, 91–93
  CSS rule, 91
  element, 91
  ID, 92–93
semicolon (;)
  in CSS declarations, 93
  to separate statements, 25, 31
setDate( ) method, 260
setDay( ) method, 260
setFullYear( ) method, 260
setHours( ) method, 260
setInterval command, 116, 117, 203
setMilliseconds( ) method, 260
setMonth( ) method, 260
setSeconds( ) method, 260
setter methods, 260

setTime( ) method, 260
shift( ) array method, 178, 187
ShinyText, 13
single-line comments, 32
slice( ) array method, 178, 188
software, defined, 8
sort( ) array method, 178, 188–189
spaces, in strings, 39
spacing, 25
<span> element, 164
speaksJavaScript variable, 238
speedUp( ) function, 202
spelling, 25, 29
splice( ) array method, 178, 189
src attribute, 82
statements
  curly brackets for, 30
  defined, 24
  example of, 24–25
  indenting, 31
  semicolon (;) for marking the end
    of, 31
  semicolon used to separate, 25
  writing, 125
stopTrain( ) function, 204
storyDiv variable, 164
<.>storyPart selector, 276
strict equality operator (===),
    147, 234
strict inequality operator (!==),
    148–149
string data type, 38–40
strings
  length of, 38
  text in, 27–29
<strong> element, 79

Super-Calculator
  comparison operators, 145–150
  forking, 138
  introduction to, 137
  name of, 138
  strings and arithmetic operators,
    141–145
  using, 139–141
switches, overview, 9
switch statements, 252–266
  branching, 267
  defined, 252
  syntax for, 253
  writing, 253–255
syntax, 22–32
  comments, 31–32
  definition of, 22
  following rules, 25–27
  making a statement, 24–25
  text in code, 29–30
  text in strings, 27–29
  white space, 30–31
syntax error, defined, 20

T

tags
  beginning, 73
  ending, 73
  HTML, 61, 72
  order in which tags are opened and
    closed, 75
tempToday( ) variable, 303
text
  in code, 29–30
  in strings, 27–29

text sizes, specifying, 94
theEnd( ) function, 290–291
theStory variable, 164
TidyUp button, 165, 211
timerDelay, 62, 63
toFixed( ) method, 316
top variable, 116, 117
toString( ) array method, 178, 180–181
trainPosition variable, 203–204
trainSpeed variable, 202–203
transistors, in general, 9
Twitter, sharing your programs on, 65
type conversion, 146–147
typeface, changing, 160
typeof command, 129–130

U

<ul> element, 76, 79
unordered lists, 76
unshift( ) array method, 178, 187
updateList function, 86, 87

V

valueOf( ) array method, 180–181
values
  of array elements, 176
    changing, 176–177
  in CSS declarations, 93
variable declarations, 34

variables
  creating, 34–35
  definition of, 34
  global, 278
    Lemonade Stand game, 335
    Martian Rescue! game, 278
    Wish List program, 214–215
  inside arrays, 176
  local, 214
  naming, 34–35
  storing data in, 36–38
  without operators, 237–238
var keyword, 34
<video> tag, 73

W

weather, generating, Lemonade Stand game, 337–341
weather forecast app
  id and class attributes, 305–307
  Listing 17-5 The Finished JavaScript Code, 303–304
  Math.random( ) function, 299–301
  styling the app, 307–308
  writing the app, 301–303
weather forecasts, Lemonade Stand game, 327
weatherToday( ) variable, 302
web application (near web app), definition of, 51
web browsers
  events in, 111–112
  overview, 14–16
web hosting, 318–325

web pages
  basic structure of, 75–76
  body element, 76
  creating your first, 76–78
  as documents, 47
  head element, 75
  h1 element, 76
  li element, 76
  ol element, 76
websites, overview, 51
while loops
  example of, 310
  introduction to, 309
  Lunch Game, 312–317
  writing, 310–311
white space, 30–31
Wish List program, 206–229
  browser's Print dialog box, 227–228
  enhancing the Wish List, 228–229
  Forking the code, 208–209
  functions
    addTheThing( ), 216, 222
    addToTheList( ), 216, 219–222
    printView( ), 217–218, 224, 226
    resetInput( ), 222–224
  HTML for, 210–212
  introduction to, 207–208
  JavaScript code for, 212–229
    declaring global variables, 214–215
    event listeners, 212–214
  running with incomplete
    functions, 217

viewing the finished program,
  207–208
women programmers, 8
Word Replacement Game, 153–170
  button area, 156
  creating a story for, 154
  creating the game, 154–160
    writing the HTML, 156
  finishing the program, 166–170
  JavaScript code, 163–165
  question area, 156
  story area, 157
  styling, 160–163
words, reserved, 35
writing statements, 125

X

x10Hosting, 319–321

Y

youShould variable, 263

Z

zero-based numbering, in general, 40

About the Authors

Chris Minnick: Chris is a JavaScript superhero who is known for being able to solve any problem. He enjoys swimming, writing, and playing guitar.

Eva Holland: Eva's superpower is her ability to get things done. She is known throughout the land as the Facilitator. She enjoys dancing, writing, and dressing up for parties.

Dedication

This book is dedicated to kids from 0 to 1100100.

Authors' Acknowledgments

We'd like to give special thanks to everyone who advised us and helped with testing and suggestions, including: Camille McCue, Ivy Jackson, Beth Burkhart, Marek Belski, Stephen Tow, Carole Jelen, our readers and students, our families and friends, our social media followers, our awesome team at Wiley, and kids everywhere who do cool things and inspire us to keep learning.

Publisher's Acknowledgments

Executive Editor: Steve Hayes

Project Editor: Elizabeth Kuball

Copy Editor: Elizabeth Kuball

Technical Editor: Camille McCue

Project Coordinator: Siddique Shaik

Cover Image: © Wiley

Apple & Mac

iPad For Dummies,
6th Edition
978-1-118-72306-7

iPhone For Dummies,
7th Edition
978-1-118-69083-3

Macs All-in-One
For Dummies, 4th Edition
978-1-118-82210-4

OS X Mavericks
For Dummies
978-1-118-69188-5

Blogging & Social Media

Facebook For Dummies,
5th Edition
978-1-118-63312-0

Social Media Engagement
For Dummies
978-1-118-53019-1

WordPress For Dummies,
6th Edition
978-1-118-79161-5

Business

Stock Investing
For Dummies, 4th Edition
978-1-118-37678-2

Investing For Dummies,
6th Edition
978-0-470-90545-6

Personal Finance

Personal Finance
For Dummies, 7th Edition
978-1-118-11785-9

QuickBooks 2014
For Dummies
978-1-118-72005-9

Small Business Marketing
Kit For Dummies,
3rd Edition
978-1-118-31183-7

Careers

Job Interviews
For Dummies, 4th Edition
978-1-118-11290-8

Job Searching with Social
Media For Dummies,
2nd Edition
978-1-118-67856-5

Personal Branding
For Dummies
978-1-118-11792-7

Resumes For Dummies,
6th Edition
978-0-470-87361-8

Starting an Etsy Business
For Dummies, 2nd Edition
978-1-118-59024-9

Diet & Nutrition

Belly Fat Diet For Dummies
978-1-118-34585-6

Mediterranean Diet

Mediterranean Diet
For Dummies
978-1-118-71525-3

Nutrition For Dummies,
5th Edition
978-0-470-93231-5

Digital Photography

Digital SLR Photography
All-in-One For Dummies,
2nd Edition
978-1-118-59082-9

Digital SLR Video &
Filmmaking For Dummies
978-1-118-36598-4

Photoshop Elements 12
For Dummies
978-1-118-72714-0

Gardening

Herb Gardening
For Dummies, 2nd Edition
978-0-470-61778-6

Gardening with Free-Range
Chickens For Dummies
978-1-118-54754-0

Health

Boosting Your Immunity
For Dummies
978-1-118-40200-9

Diabetes

Diabetes For Dummies,
4th Edition
978-1-118-29447-5

Living Paleo For Dummies
978-1-118-29405-5

Big Data

Big Data For Dummies
978-1-118-50422-2

Data Visualization
For Dummies
978-1-118-50289-1

Hadoop For Dummies
978-1-118-60755-8

Language &
Foreign Language

500 Spanish Verbs
For Dummies
978-1-118-02382-2

English Grammar
For Dummies, 2nd Edition
978-0-470-54664-2

French All-in-One
For Dummies
978-1-118-22815-9

German Essentials
For Dummies
978-1-118-18422-6

Italian For Dummies,
2nd Edition
978-1-118-00465-4

Available in print and e-book formats.

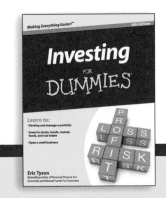
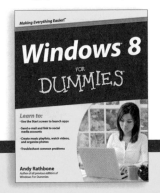

Available wherever books are sold. **For more information or to order direct visit www.dummies.com**

Math & Science

Algebra I For Dummies,
2nd Edition
978-0-470-55964-2

Anatomy and Physiology
For Dummies, 2nd Edition
978-0-470-92326-9

Astronomy For Dummies,
3rd Edition
978-1-118-37697-3

Biology For Dummies,
2nd Edition
978-0-470-59875-7

Chemistry For Dummies,
2nd Edition
978-1-118-00730-3

1001 Algebra II Practice
Problems For Dummies
978-1-118-44662-1

Microsoft Office

Excel 2013 For Dummies
978-1-118-51012-4

Office 2013 All-in-One
For Dummies
978-1-118-51636-2

PowerPoint 2013
For Dummies
978-1-118-50253-2

Word 2013 For Dummies
978-1-118-49123-2

Music

Blues Harmonica
For Dummies
978-1-118-25269-7

Guitar For Dummies,
3rd Edition
978-1-118-11554-1

iPod & iTunes
For Dummies, 10th Edition
978-1-118-50864-0

Programming

Beginning Programming
with C For Dummies
978-1-118-73763-7

Excel VBA Programming
For Dummies, 3rd Edition
978-1-118-49037-2

Java For Dummies,
6th Edition
978-1-118-40780-6

Religion & Inspiration

The Bible For Dummies
978-0-7645-5296-0

Buddhism For Dummies,
2nd Edition
978-1-118-02379-2

Catholicism For Dummies,
2nd Edition
978-1-118-07778-8

Self-Help & Relationships

Beating Sugar Addiction
For Dummies
978-1-118-54645-1

Meditation For Dummies,
3rd Edition
978-1-118-29144-3

Seniors

Laptops For Seniors
For Dummies, 3rd Edition
978-1-118-71105-7

Computers For Seniors
For Dummies, 3rd Edition
978-1-118-11553-4

iPad For Seniors
For Dummies, 6th Edition
978-1-118-72826-0

Social Security
For Dummies
978-1-118-20573-0

Smartphones & Tablets

Android Phones
For Dummies, 2nd Edition
978-1-118-72030-1

Nexus Tablets
For Dummies
978-1-118-77243-0

Samsung Galaxy S 4
For Dummies
978-1-118-64222-1

Samsung Galaxy Tabs
For Dummies
978-1-118-77294-2

Test Prep

ACT For Dummies,
5th Edition
978-1-118-01259-8

ASVAB For Dummies,
3rd Edition
978-0-470-63760-9

GRE For Dummies,
7th Edition
978-0-470-88921-3

Officer Candidate Tests
For Dummies
978-0-470-59876-4

Physician's Assistant Exam
For Dummies
978-1-118-11556-5

Series 7 Exam For Dummies
978-0-470-09932-2

Windows 8

Windows 8.1 All-in-One
For Dummies
978-1-118-82087-2

Windows 8.1 For Dummies
978-1-118-82121-3

Windows 8.1 For Dummies,
Book + DVD Bundle
978-1-118-82107-7

Available in print and e-book formats.

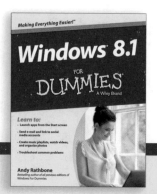

Available wherever books are sold. **For more information or to order direct visit www.dummies.com**

Take Dummies with you everywhere you go!

Whether you are excited about e-books, want more from the web, must have your mobile apps, or are swept up in social media, Dummies makes everything easier.

Leverage the Power

For Dummies is the global leader in the reference category and one of the most trusted and highly regarded brands in the world. No longer just focused on books, customers now have access to the For Dummies content they need in the format they want. Let us help you develop a solution that will fit your brand and help you connect with your customers.

Advertising & Sponsorships

Connect with an engaged audience on a powerful multimedia site, and position your message alongside expert how-to content.

Targeted ads • Video • Email marketing • Microsites • Sweepstakes sponsorship

21 Million Monthly Page Views & 13 Million Unique Visitors